UNFINISHED BLUES...

Memories of a New Orleans Music Man

Harold Battiste performing at a club on Bourbon Street, ca. 1952; *left to right:* Bob Ogden, Harold, and Dave Williams (THNOC)

UNFINISHED BLUES…

Memories of a New Orleans Music Man

by Harold R. Battiste Jr.
with Karen Celestan

PUBLISHED BY

THE HISTORIC NEW ORLEANS COLLECTION

2010

The Historic New Orleans Collection is a museum, research center, and publisher dedicated to the study and preservation of the history and culture of New Orleans and the Gulf South region. The Collection is operated by the Kemper and Leila Williams Foundation, a Louisiana nonprofit corporation.

Library of Congress Cataloging-in-Publication Data

Battiste, Harold.
    Unfinished blues— : memories of a New Orleans music man / by Harold Battiste Jr. with Karen Celestan. — 1st ed.
       p. cm.
   "Arrangements and productions": p.
  "Compositions": p.
  Includes bibliographical references and index.
   ISBN-13: 978-0-917860-55-3 (alk. paper)
   ISBN-10: 0-917860-55-1 (alk. paper)
  1. Battiste, Harold. 2. Musicians—Louisiana—New Orleans—Biography. 3. Music—Louisiana—New Orleans—20th century—History and criticism. I. Celestan, Karen. II. Title.
  ML429.B26A3 2010
  780.92—dc22
  [B]

2009051777

© 2010 The Historic New Orleans Collection
533 Royal Street
New Orleans, Lousiana 70130
www.hnoc.org

First edition. 2,500 copies
Printed by Imago

Priscilla Lawrence, Executive Director
Sarah Doerries, Editor
Jessica Dorman, Director of Publications

Book design and production by Alison Cody,
New Orleans, Louisiana

Printed and bound in Malaysia for Imago

Editorial Note: Transcriptions of Harold Battiste's letters, journal entries, and other original documents are literal, with a few exceptions made for clarity.

CONTENTS

For you . . .

Alviette Marie Antoinette Dominique

Harold Raymond III

Andrea Lynn

Marzique Kahdija

Harlis Ray

FOREWORD

When French Creole writer Alexander Dumas used the phrase "All for one, one for all" in his novel *The Three Musketeers,* he was not thinking of Black musicians in America wrestling with segregation in New Orleans. But the phrase struck a resounding chord in the soul of AFO founder Harold Battiste Jr., who initially aspired to be a jazz musician but who instead became the single most influential force in the development of late twentieth-century New Orleans jazz.

Harold Battiste had a vision so advanced that even when he articulated his hopes, some people could not grasp the concept of Black people controlling the music they created. But in the early '60s in the deep South, astounding as the concept of Black musicians owning their own intellectual and cultural creations may have been, Battiste had far more in mind: "I guess you might say my emphasis was on all. All meant owning the publishing. All meant scouting for new talent. All meant writing our own history. All meant, well, everything."

AFO succeeded beyond his wildest dreams. Within a few months AFO produced a million-selling hit record, Barbara George's "I Know." They also released the first recordings featuring seminal New Orleans musicians Ellis Marsalis, James Black, Edward Blackwell, and Alvin Batiste. Indeed, in one of those ironies that seem to characterize Black life in America, their success led to their demise. Major companies raided the AFO stable, and tempting offers to relocate to the West Coast also depleted the AFO ranks.

Some fifty years later, Harold Battiste Jr. is still a visionary. After producing both the persona and the early recordings of Dr. John, after working with Sam Cooke, after scoring a Hollywood movie, and after being one of the first Black musical directors of a nationally televised weekly music variety program, the *Sonny & Cher Show* (Battiste also produced all of the duo's gold records), Battiste returned to New Orleans ready to reactivate AFO Records, ready to cultivate a new crop of jazz artists.

Battiste became a professor of music in the University of New Orleans jazz studies program, under the leadership of Ellis Marsalis. Battiste released recordings featuring multi-reed musician Victor Goines (currently head of the Juilliard School of Music's jazz program), trumpet sensation Nicholas Payton, and legendary vocalist/educator Germaine Bazzle. Battiste also released the *Silverbook,* a compendium of AFO jazz compositions that includes sheet music, background information, and composer biographies and discographies. "My goal is to make this music and its history available to anyone and everyone who wants to know about the second fifty years of modern jazz in New Orleans," Battiste said.

Most of the books about Black music and Black musicians are not written by those who created the music. A musician making a self-reflective evaluation is rare. Given the importance of New Orleans musicians to the cultural fabric of America, *unfinished blues* is a document of historical significance.

Battiste has collected and produced the mother lode of New Orleans modern jazz. If you want to know how early Ellis Marsalis sounded, or if you want the sheet music for a James Black composition, or maybe you just want to read the bio of legendary baritone and tenor saxophonist Alvin "Red" Tyler, Battiste's AFO Foundation has the answers to your questions.

Thankfully, Harold Battiste digested the full significance of "All for one" and created an archival feast of New Orleans music that one and all can enjoy.

—*Kalamu ya Salaam*
writer, filmmaker, educator

INTRODUCTION

Insights are connections. It's just a matter of seeing the connections between things that don't appear to be connected. Each time a new connection is made, the result is a deeper or broader or better understanding. When one begins to get onto these connections, one begins to see patterns of connections, all yielding their understanding: and somewhere down the line, the connectedness of everything and everyone—the unity, balance and at-one-ness of all God's creation—becomes visible. My perspective of my story is influenced by these precepts:

New Orleans is a SOUND
A sound resulting from a long history of sounds. Original, creative, exciting, happy, sensual sounds.

New Orleans is a PLACE
A place that is alive! And lives for the music . . . for its sound. A place where the music lives in the people!

New Orleans is a PEOPLE
People who groove daily and nightly. People whose ordinary activities (walking and talking) have a groove that identifies them as New Orleanians!

I am in awe of the unique spirit conjured up by the fertile compost of cultures that exists here in New Orleans. It seems as though every culture wanted to put something in the gumbo, and—like any good gumbo mixed with happiness, stirred with joy, and cooked with love—it's got spirit.

It was that spirit which around 1900 created a musical gumbo that was so good everybody wanted some. They tell me that Buddy Bolden and his buddies served up frequent helpings of this high-spirited dish on the local scene. It wasn't long before the likes of King Oliver and Jelly Roll Morton were on the road spreading the word up north (east and west too). But you know that history. It has been fairly well documented and distributed, and that work is ongoing.

What you may not be aware of is that the spirit started working once again around 1950. The music had traversed the globe and in its travels added the offerings of many local cultures—Memphis, Chicago, Detroit, and New York . . . Paris and London, even. When it came back home it had grown into an international celebrity, but the spirit was still there, as always—original, creative, exciting, happy, spiritual!

Just as Buddy and Jelly were there in the beginning, there were young cats on the scene—in the compost—ready to receive the spirit and reignite the New Orleans flavor. I'm remembering players like the late Ed Blackwell who, along with his buddies, served up frequent helpings of the new gumbo to listeners who were not yet ready for the new taste. After all, New Orleans, with its abundance of rich sounds and flavors, was not hungry. These young players had the vision and the courage to hang tough, developing this new way to express the spirit. It would be nearly twenty years before their loving labor and dedication would bear fruit.

The jazz spirit, however, had to wait while Blackwell and his generation—men like clarinetist Alvin Batiste and pianist Ellis Marsalis—passed the torch to the children of the '60s. These young New Orleans players, with Wynton Marsalis at the vanguard, have brought acceptance, honor, and prestige to jazz such as it never had throughout history. From the halls of every major university with a jazz studies program to the halls of the United States Congress, where jazz has been designated a national treasure, the spirit has prevailed!

—Harold Battiste Jr.

prologue

Facing Eviction in L.A. (1988)

I'm sitting out in my workroom in the backyard. I've spent many hours in this space—making music, thinking good thoughts, writing some of them down. I've got a spinet piano I rented years ago with the option to buy, then I bought it. I've got a draftsman's easel for writing my scores, a desk and a couple of chairs, files and a Smith Corona electric typewriter. On the ceiling is my tribute to Sonny & Cher, where I have hung hotel keys from all over the U.S. and Europe, wherever we played.

But I'm not thinking good thoughts now. Today they're coming to take me out of my house . . . my home . . . MY home! The eviction notice came some weeks ago, and I've been going over all the stuff that's gone down since the divorce started.

I'm not leaving my home. I'm not going to surrender my life to some potbellied redneck with a piece of paper and a gun. All four of my children finished high school from this home. My family and my world woke every morning and bedded down here every night for twenty years. So where the hell do they think I'm gonna up and go now, at fifty-seven years old?

Well, I made me a sign. Actually, I made four signs, each about eighteen by twenty-four inches. Early this morning, I put them along the front edge of the garden, on the front lawn. Each sign had one word:

This has been a wonderful neighborhood with extraordinary neighbors. They will be shocked and saddened by what happens today, but someday they'll hear the whole story. . . .

Young Harold as "King of Mardi Gras" at
Booker T. Washington Elementary School,
ca. 1940 (THNOC)

1

chapter **from cradle to music**

There's an African proverb that says, "A child of the kwale bird learns how to fly." Our neighborhood was filled with people who gave me wings, and growing up there did much to shape my adulthood and my ideals concerning what I wanted and expected from my family.

Mother ran the house, cooking over a potbelly woodstove, cleaning greens and snapping beans. We had breakfast and dinner every day, except on Saturday, when we had sandwiches. We often had dinner together at the kitchen table—for sure on Sunday. And man, on Sunday! Grits, eggs scrambled with green onions, calf liver dry-fried and smothered in brown gravy, thin buttered biscuits or soft lost bread (*pain perdu,* or French toast) to dunk in hot cocoa. I'm not going to even try to talk about dinner.

Mama said the blessing, then each of us said a Bible verse. Daddy, the most peaceful spirit among us, was not a religious man, but he went along. His verse was the shortest in the Bible: John 11:35—"Jesus wept." My verse was Matthew 5:5—"Blessed are the meek: for they shall inherit the earth." I don't remember how I learned it, and I don't know if I really understood the meaning of it, but the family knew that that was *my* verse. That idea sank deeply into my character.

After cooking there was washing in a tub with a washboard and lye soap. After hanging the clothes, laden with thick starch, on the line with clothespins, we would iron with a two-iron system: work with one iron while the other was on the stove getting hot. And although the chores seemed never to stop, they always seemed to be fun. I was always trying to help with everything, and Mother would let me (except for the cooking).

Before she became my father's wife and my mother, Pearl Wilmer Booker was a teacher. She graduated from New Orleans University in 1923, a teacher-training college, or normal school, for "colored" students, located on St. Charles Avenue near Jefferson Avenue. Its history was tied to the history of Gilbert Academy, where I would later attend high school; both existed on the same St. Charles Avenue property. In 1928 NOU merged with Straight College to form Dillard University. The former NOU building on St. Charles later became the famous Gilbert Academy.

I didn't learn about mother's teaching career until I was a teenager ready for college, when she utilized her training doing substitute work now that I was out of the way. In those days, a woman was not expected to continue a career after marriage. The man was the breadwinner and the woman was the homemaker—assuming he won enough bread for her to make a home. My father was by no means a big earner, but he was a tireless worker and a frugal spender—so was my mother. By the standards of my neighborhood, which was my whole world, we were well off. Daddy had an old car and sometimes took us on long rides on Sunday evenings. We also had a two-party telephone in the house. None of my friends had those things. I never knew we were poor until we were among the first families to qualify for a house in the Magnolia Housing Project, which I was told was the first for Negroes in New Orleans.

The relationships in our household—mother, father, grandfather, grandmother, brother—were ideal. I never knew how ideal until I was well into adulthood and learned that all families were not like that. I had never seen violence in the home or among family members, not even verbal abuse. Mother's name was "Sweetheart," and Daddy's was the same. I never heard them use any other names for each other.

I Was Born (So Was Everyone!)

In the middle of the fall of 1931, my mother, Pearl Wilmer Booker Battiste (1903–1957), birthed her first and last biological child. She and my father, Harold (1900–1957), already had adopted a little boy. My father's sister, Carrie, died, leaving five children, and—as families did then—various members of the family took the children to raise. Thinking that I might be a girl, my parents-to-be took the baby boy, Alvin, whom everybody called "A."

I was born at 2108 Second Street. Our house was a shotgun double: a kind of New Orleans side-by-side duplex so called because all the rooms were in a straight line; people say that you can shoot a shotgun through the front door and it will pass through the house and out the back door. Then my parents moved in with my maternal grandparents, Wilbert and Mary Booker, who we called Mama and Papa and who lived across the street, at 2039 Second. Their house sat on the downtown/front-o'-town corner of Second and Saratoga, across the street from Fogerty's Grocery (which had formerly been Jake's) and Trapani's vegetable stand. Both owners (Fogerty and Trapani) lived in the back of their stores.

My earliest memory from childhood was of breast-feeding. In those days, breast-feeding in public was a normal thing to do, and I can vaguely remember it being done in places like the grocery and, for sure, church. I vividly recall one morning when Mother was fixing breakfast for Daddy and I decided that I

The Battiste family home at Second and Saratoga streets, ca. 1970 (THNOC)

The Eagle Tailor Shop, South Rampart Street, a Battiste family business; this photo was taken after the business had closed. (THNOC)

wanted my "ninny." I didn't cry for it, I called from the next room—I was about three years old. Mother stopped fixing Daddy's food to give me mine.

"When are you going to stop feeding that boy like that?" Daddy said, sounding angry. "If he's big enough to call you like that, he ought to be done with it!" That was the last time I was breast fed.

Grandparents

I never knew my paternal grandparents. My father's mother died before I was born, and his father, Eugene Baptiste, died in Chicago before I made five. I learned later that my family name was originally *Baptiste*, with a *p*. During a discussion among friends and acquaintances about a little class war that had erupted years before, I found out that people with the *Baptiste* name were considered to be lower-class, and so to separate and elevate themselves, some adopted the alternative spelling, *Battiste*. There must be some truth to the story, because my father's paperwork has the Baptiste name, yet I'm a Battiste.

My father was from Vacherie, Louisiana. He had come to New Orleans as a child with his father, while his mother remained in their hometown. When Eugene went north, my father was taken in by Mrs. Edith White and her husband, who had one natural son, Morris. She was a woman I would come to know as Grandma White. She operated a small dry cleaner and tailor, the Eagle Tailor Shop, at 343 South Rampart Street in the heart of Storyville, once New Orleans's storied red-light district. It became the hub of the street among the Jewish merchants. My father learned the labor—cleaning and pressing, alterations and tailoring—and Morris learned the business. Eventually my father went back to Vacherie for his brother, Courie (pronounced like *curry*), brought him back to New Orleans, and taught him the trade. I spent much of my childhood in the shop with my daddy, trying to work like the adults who worked there.

I waited on customers, tried to press pants, and learned how to prepare cuffs to be altered.

My maternal grandfather, Wilbert Booker (1881–1935), and his brothers, William and Kernan, were from Clinton, Louisiana. As young men they went to Bogalusa to work in the sawmill and, some years later, came to New Orleans, where they started selling ice, wood, and coal. By the time I came along, Papa had his "yard" well stocked and attended, and he'd established delivery routes with a mule-drawn wagon. I spent a lot of time in the yard and on the wagon, "helping" Papa.

My maternal grandmother, Mary Cooper Booker (1881–1947), was from around Baker, Louisiana. The Coopers, for the most part, settled in Baton Rouge, but Mary (known as Sister) and her two sisters, Caroline (Sis) and Sophronia (Sissy), came to New Orleans.

Mama worked as a cook for a White family in the Garden District. Dr. and Mrs. Elliot lived on Chestnut at First Street. Though it was only a few blocks' walking distance from our house, it was another economic planet. I have only a vague memory of being there once, entering through the yard into the back door and looking up ever so far at how big and tall the rooms were.

After Papa died, Mama took over running the lumberyard. I became a real help then, along with my brother, Alvin. We waited on customers and tried to chop wood and chip ice into twenty-five-pound blocks from a hundred-pound block, among other chores. Mama hired two more workers for the yard: Warren, who had worked there with Papa, and Arthur Spears, who was fresh from the country. They called her "Madame Boss." She also continued to cook for her "good" White folks. As far as I understood, they had no choice but to be good, 'cause Mama didn't take no shit from anybody—at home, in the yard, at work, or at church. I never heard Mama use profanity, or even shout—except when she "shouted" getting the Holy Ghost in church. She didn't have to raise her voice to get people's attention and respect, but there was a stern intensity that let you know how she felt.

Hijinks

I think the one time Mama went into a rage was when the priest at our neighborhood Catholic church kicked me for skating in the churchyard. I must have been about six years old when it happened, because I was big enough to have learned how to roller skate. Also, my grandfather died when I was around the same age, and this happened not long after he was gone. The incident is so memorable that I wrote about it in a journal almost thirty years later.

New Orleans, unlike many other cities in the South, did not have an "across the tracks" racial division of housing. Instead, there were many scattered pockets of Black residents throughout the city. In each of these neighborhoods—with names like "Bucktown," "Niggertown," and "Gert Town"—there was a military (the police), a merchant (who owned the corner store), and a missionary (the Catholic church and school). The local mission was St. Francis de Sales, and the chief brainwasher and ass-kicker was Father Sheridan.

Being before the days when Whites got hip to suburbia, the merchants lived with their families behind, or over, or maybe in or under, their stores. So the Trapanis lived in our neighborhood, and they had a son named Willie, who was about my age. There was another poor White family (poor White = middle-class Negro) living across the street and down the block from us, about whom I knew little except that they also had a boy around my age, a little older, named Morris Wall.

One day our unlikely threesome was out skating. As I recall, Morris and Willie were skating together in the street, but I stayed on the *banquette* (our word for *sidewalk*). I think Morris, the oldest of the three of us, had enticed Willie—who was a little stupid anyway and couldn't skate very well—to skate in the street. Morris told Willie to ask me to join them. And though Willie was trusted and liked by Black folks—partly because he was stupid but mostly because his people had the vegetable store—I wasn't about to leave the sidewalk. Mother had dared me to go in the street on those skates, and I wasn't about to get them wrapped around my head. Morris then came over to the banquette and suggested we go to the next corner and skate in the churchyard. That was the best skating pavement around, and it wasn't in the street!

St. Francis de Sales church and school occupied the northeast and southeast corners of Second and Franklin streets. The churchyard Morris was talking about was actually the front lawn of the rectory where Father Sheridan lived, or worked, or did whatever he was supposed to be doing. Inside the front gate of the wrought-iron fence on Second Street, there was a long, smooth, very skate-worthy paved walkway leading to the steps of the rectory. A few yards before it reached the steps, the walkway forked: left led to the rear of the church, straight went up the steps to the rectory, and right led to a side gate on Franklin Street.

Left, The Booker family's church, First Street M.E. (Methodist Episcopal); *right*, the rectory at St. Francis de Sales Church, ca. 1970 (THNOC)

Morris went first, I was right on his tail, and stupid Willie brought up the poor, no-skating rear. We would hit top speed just before it was time to make the sharp right leading to the side. Once out the Franklin Street gate, we'd make it back to Second Street for the high-speed sprint at the front gate. After about the third or fourth orbit, we had gotten good, and I was really pumping my little ass off. It must have been about the sixth sprint, just when I had built up to an incredible speed, when I looked up to get ready to make that critical right turn. There I saw a tall, black robe descending the rectory steps at a speed more incredible than mine. In the split-second before we were inevitably to collide, I saw a face that registered the wrath and authority of God mixed with the hate and meanness of the devil! Although panicked, I held my course and negotiated the crucial right turn that would get me out of that gate. But the Father must have had divine computers calculating my orbit and guiding his trajectory, because he managed to land his holy foot right on my tender six-year-old ass. Mama got upset when she heard about it, so mad that she wanted to shoot Father Sheridan. Yard workers had to restrain Mama; they calmed her down, preventing her from storming the rectory.

I had a babysitter named Micky when I was around four. In the early evening, she would let me walk with her around the block. One evening, some girls were jumping rope across the banquette. This was straight high jumping—not the game where they turn the rope and you have to "jump in" and do three "hots" or four "slacks"—and it looked real low from where I was way down the block, so I thought I could do it. I suddenly snatched my hand out of Micky's and took off down the block.

The girls saw me coming. As I got closer, the rope seemed to be a little higher than I'd thought, but I believed I could still make it. Wrong! I did a belly flop on the pavement and hurt everything—especially my feelings, since all the girls were laughing. When Micky picked me up and saw blood in my mouth, the world stopped. She got me back to the house where Mother and Mama—well, mostly Mama—went to work on me.

Mother was hysterical. I had hit my chin in the belly flop and nearly bit off my tongue. After Mama got the bleeding stopped, they took me to Flint-Goodridge Hospital, which, because of segregation, was one of the only hospitals that served Black people in the New Orleans area. I don't remember what they did to my tongue there, but they saved it. For years I could still see the scar.

Of course, I went on to have many more injuries over the next few years. I smashed my left thumb in the truck door, so I was rushed to Flint; multistitch gash in my head, rushed to Flint. I also had my tonsils taken out there. They knew me real well at Flint-Goodridge.

 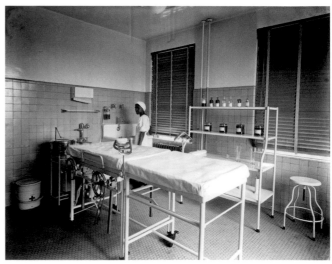

Flint-Goodridge Hospital, ca. 1932 (THE CHARLES L. FRANCK STUDIO COLLECTION AT THNOC, 1979.325)

The other side of our double on Second Street was rented to the Jacksons and the Lytles. I remember the children's names: Ben, Charles, Bernice, Katherine, and Yvonne Jackson, and Dorothy, Elaine, and Big Junior Lytle. We all played a scaled-down version of baseball called "Chicago," which could be played with six or even five players: an outfielder, first baseman, pitcher, catcher, and two batters. The infield was a single line, from home plate to first base and back to home. When a batter was out, he took the outfield position and everyone moved up.

Tom Thumb Wedding . . . Yikes!

I don't know what her position or job or ministry was at First Street M.E. (Methodist Episcopal) Church, but Sister Booker seemed to be involved in everything there. And, of course, as her fine grandson, I got way more attention than I wanted, needed, or deserved. Like in 1938, when Mama got me hooked up in a program organized to raise money for the church: a Tom Thumb wedding. These were mock ceremonies done by the children, complete with all the trimmings—costumes, rings, flower girl, ring bearer, bridesmaids, best man, preacher, organist, and of course the bride and groom. The bride was a pretty little light-skinned girl whose name I can't recall. Guess who was the groom!

Mama was a good ticket seller, so the church was full. I must have been all of seven, and I didn't feel comfortable dealing with girls, particularly in front of all those people. We had been well rehearsed on all our lines: "Do you take" . . . "I do" . . . etc. Everything went OK, considering that our mistakes were part of the entertainment. At the climax of the ceremony—"I now pronounce you man and wife, and you may now salute the bride"—I turned to the girl and she backed off! There was a tense moment, then she said, "I ain't gonna kiss him! He too Black!" No curtains to pull, no lights to dissolve, no stage to run off. Just humiliation. I believe Mama had that girl executed.

King of Mardi Gras

When I was in third or fourth grade at Booker T. Washington, located at Fourth and Magnolia streets (it became F. P. Ricard when the new Booker T. Washington High School was built in 1942), there was a contest for "King of Mardi Gras." Each class had entries, and each entry competed by selling "votes." The class winners then competed for the crown.

Between Mother's crunchy pecan brownies and Mama's persuasive salesmanship and influence at church, it was no contest for me. The queen was a girl in my class named Berweda Hatch. I vaguely remember having a parade, which stopped at my house on Second and Saratoga. I was given 7-Up in a champagne glass to use for a toast, then I tossed it to the ground. Back at school, in the decorated basement, the king and queen were supposed to take the first dance to open the ball. I don't know how Berweda felt about dancing, but I didn't know how, so I told the teacher that Berweda was too tall!

Sixty years later, Berweda and I would meet again (she's still too tall, but it's OK!).

New Home

In 1940, when I was nine, we moved to the Magnolia Housing Project on La Salle Street. There were at least forty-four apartments in the complex, each housing two or three generations (children, parents, and grandparents). Ours was a second-and-third-floor apartment; I really liked the novelty of having a view from upstairs.

We called Magnolia "the court" because the buildings formed a U on three sides of a big grassy rectangle, where we played all kinds of ball—football, baseball, kickball, and dodge ball—and with the girls we played hiding, command, and ring games. Our best sport was football. We called ourselves the "Eleven Horsemen" and we actually had what we thought was a season, which started when the real football season was ending. By that time, we had heard and seen enough football to get fired up to do our stuff. There

The Magnolia Housing Project at La Salle and Toledano streets, 1940

Small children at play, Magnolia Housing Project, from a report by the Housing Authority of New Orleans, 1942

were teams from three or four other neighborhoods to play against on our turf or theirs, but mostly ours.

None of them were as organized as we were. We each had positions. Charles Wilson was our first-string quarterback, and Eldridge Johnson was the backup quarterback. The rest of the backfield consisted of Dave "Dimp" Williams at halfback, Ernest "Bud" Eglin at tailback (running from the single wing), and "Buffalo" at fullback (running from the T formation). On the line we had Jessie, Horace, William, Cal, Othello, the Campbell brothers (Joe and Ernest), and a few names I can't remember. I played center.

Some of our games were against boys from "bad" neighborhoods, but we always won. They never started no shit because we had some older guys in our 'hood that were real "gangsters." Porky Pig, Wild Bill, Gate, and that gang had already done time, but they wanted us to stay clean. They were proud of us and protected us.

I was out playing in the court on Sunday, December 7, 1941, when we learned that "the Japs" had bombed us. I had just turned ten years old and was looking to become a Cub Scout. I was ready for my uniform and rifle. We started playing war that night. A couple of years into the war, I became a patrol leader in our troop, #127, and we collected more scrap metal and paper than anybody else.

Singing and Playing

When I was seven or eight, I started singing in the junior choir, which was great fun, because two nights a week I got to go to rehearsal. I liked to sing and it was easy for me to learn the songs. The church seemed different on a weeknight, sort of like night school but without lessons and teachers.

There was a chubby little light-skinned girl, Jeanne Armstead, that I was sweet on. She could play the piano, and that fascinated me. Another girl, Betty, came from New York to stay with her aunt, Miss Camilla, the church organist. Betty was different. Dark-skinned like me, shaped like a Coca-Cola bottle, and fast-talking. She decided to like me, and I didn't know how to get out of it—not that I wanted to get out of it, necessarily, but she was a little speedy for me.

The highlight of my junior-choir tenure was at Christmas, when the Sunday-school group did a play about the birth of Jesus. No, I didn't get to play the superstar—they used a White doll for that—but I did get to be one of the three kings bringing gifts to the Prince of Peace. As a result, I got to make my debut as a solo vocalist, singing "We Three Kings of Orient Are." The church loved it! They carried on and on about how good I sang, though I really didn't know what was so special about it.

When I was younger I showed an interest in music that no one seemed to recognize. Whenever "Midday Serenade" came on the radio, I'd get two nice bouncy forks from the kitchen and play drums. Most of the popular music of the day—all of it, really—was by White singers and bands. I knew their names and their music, but I didn't know they were White. In fact, the question never came up. Glenn Miller, Artie Shaw, Harry James, Benny Goodman, and Woody Herman were the names I heard. Rarely, if ever, did I hear about Count Basie, Duke Ellington, Lionel Hampton, Fletcher Henderson—any of the Black big bands. My mother's cedar chest (which I held on to for fifty years) was peppered with little fork holes from my drumming sessions.

Many families had a piano to entertain themselves at home, and we weren't any different. We had an upright in the front room. A song called "Penny Serenade" was popular on the radio in 1938 or 1939, and I liked it well enough to pick it out on the piano, which surprised everybody and pleased me. My musical expression, until then, had been limited to singing in the junior choir and drumming on mother's furniture. Mother—who planned a medical, not musical, future for me—took it as a warning that the piano might be a problem. When my parents were notified that we were going to get into the Magnolia Project, it was a major turning point in the family; we were "movin' on up." But mother told me she was sorry, but they wouldn't allow us to bring our piano—no pianos in the project. I wonder why?

In 1943, during my last year at F. P. Ricard Elementary School, I learned that a buddy of mine, Bud Eglin, was taking music from a teacher named Mr. Wilson, who came to the school once a week.

Harold's grammar-school graduation photo, 1944 (THNOC)

Bud had a clarinet and lived right down the driveway from me, on Sixth Street. Bud's big sister, Delores, had a boyfriend who played the saxophone, and Bud said I could come over when he brought it. I had never heard anything like that. It sounded so beautiful and wonderful! How could he do that? I learned later that her boyfriend, Sterling White, was a jazz musician. He played tunes for Delores that I had never heard, and then he would put a record on the phonograph and play along with the sax player on the record. That's when I got hooked. I knew then that I wanted to learn how to do that.

I knew that Mother was not too keen on my fascination with music, so I appealed to Daddy. He found a metal Boehm system "student" clarinet in one of the several pawnshops on Rampart Street, near the Eagle Tailor Shop. Though I didn't know it, my father must have played a little at one time, because he put it together, put my fingers over the right holes, and showed me how to get a sound. Once Mr. Wilson introduced me to the Rubank Elementary Method book, I was off to the races. I figured out all the rudiments in one week. It was all so easy . . . it made sense!

The Dew Drop Inn

After a while we were able get a downstairs apartment, I think because my grandmother was ill. Our front porch was on the main drag, La Salle Street, right across from Smith's Grocery, Uncle Dan's restaurant, and the Dew Drop Inn, all places that would have a real impact on my young life. Mr. Smith was the first Black man I had ever known who owned a real "big" grocery store, and I got my first summer job at Uncle Dan's.

I don't remember my hours, but I worked six days a week cleaning tables, stacking soft-drink cases, sweeping, and sometimes serving ice cream. Picola, the waitress, was different from any of the grown women I had ever known (except maybe my cousin Florence). She teased and embarrassed me all the time, and then when her tall, handsome boyfriend came around, they laughed at me. But I liked her. She made me feel good, and so I worked hard for my twelve dollars a week. Uncle Dan seemed to be sort of old, but with a lot of energy. He moved quickly around the kitchen cooking, and when he came out in the front once in a while, he hardly looked up but went straight to whatever he needed to do and back to the kitchen. If somebody spoke that knew him, he'd acknowledge them without slowing his pace. He had short, thinning, gray hair on his dark brown, puffy face. In fact, his whole body was puffy—not fat, but like he had played tackle or fullback when he was younger. He rarely laughed, but he was so kind and gentle you felt his smile.

Living across from the Dew Drop Inn was really something special. It was already famous, but I didn't know it at the time. Besides being the best nightclub in town, it was also a barbershop, a restaurant, and a hotel. The owner, Frank Painia, was a genius businessman. He was an uneducated country barber living in the projects who had started with a three-chair shop. I loved to go to the barber to hear the men talk and argue about things. My barber, Mr. Rip, knew how my mother wanted my hair cut: bald. There was a sign on the wall that said, IF YOU SO SMART, HOW COME YOU AIN'T RICH? That question has stayed with me all my life.

The thing that was special about the Dew Drop was the music. I could hear the music coming from there on my front porch and in my living room. It was the music of the Black stars of the day: lots of R&B, a little swing, a little jazz, a bit of jump. It was all about the rhythm, and I couldn't help but be drawn to that music because it spoke directly to my spirit. It was

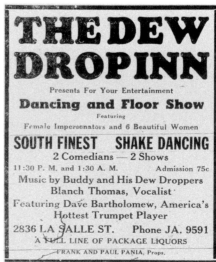

The Dew Drop Inn on La Salle Street, across from the Battistes' apartment in the Magnolia Project, was always hopping. *Opposite*: An ad from the *Louisiana Weekly*, November 10, 1945; *above, clockwise from top left:* The Dew Drop, 1953; an audience reacts to a performance by comedian Lollypop Jones, ca. 1952; Joe Jones (piano) on stage with emcee Bobby Marchand and others, 1954; PHOTOS BY RALSTON CRAWFORD (RALSTON CRAWFORD COLLECTION OF JAZZ PHOTOGRAPHY, HOGAN JAZZ ARCHIVE)

lifeblood—particular songs would just go all through me—and certainly that was also true for everyone who lived near or frequented the area. Dave Bartholomew rehearsed his band some days at the Dew Drop, and his trumpet blasted like they say Buddy Bolden's did. Stars like Ray Charles, Charles Brown, and Joe Turner would be around there all the time.

The Gilbert Academy Choice

When I entered high school in 1944, there were four options for Negroes: McDonogh No. 35, a public school with a distinguished principal and faculty; Booker T. Washington, a new public school with brand-new buildings and a large concert auditorium; Gilbert Academy, a private, Methodist school with an exceptional female principal and dedicated faculty; and Xavier Preparatory, a private, Catholic school with an established reputation in the community.

I had never heard of Gilbert Academy. I couldn't imagine going to school on St. Charles Avenue. Almost all my friends from the Magnolia Project were going to Booker T., and, as far as I was concerned, so was I. But Mother and Daddy had already decided that I was going to Gilbert. In hindsight, I know they were right. On my first day my mother, in her effort to make me look like I belonged, dressed me in knickers like Little Lord Fauntleroy. She didn't get that right. I was pointed at, laughed at, and thoroughly embarrassed.

I met two boys that first week, Clinton Moore and Bernard Beaco, who became my close friends throughout our high-school days. Dave Williams, who I already knew from Magnolia, was also in our little group—he was the halfback on our Eleven Horsemen football team. I think it was Dave who got Beaco and me to join the school band. Dave played the tenor sax. Beaco, who was small in stature, took up the flute.

Mr. T. Leroy Davis was the new band director, and I was intimidated by him from the start. He must have been a military man, because all my memories seem to be of him in uniform. Of course, his cap was always in place. When you passed him in the hall, his greeting was accompanied with a little salute. I don't remember exactly how he determined it, but he put me on third clarinet. I was the only boy at that bottom level, but it was OK because I made the band. My uniform looked just like the ones worn by Rodney Reed and Albert Joseph, the ace first-chair guys.

The band, like the school, had its share of kids from upscale families, several of whom would go on to do great things in their careers. I say "upscale," but that perception was from the mind of a kid raised in a project environment; to me, all of them seemed rich. Andrew Young, future civil rights activist and politician, was on French horn; one of our sousaphone players was Robert Collins, who became the first Black magistrate judge in New Orleans and went on to become a federal judge; Lloyd Verret, alto sax, became the first Black detective in the New Orleans Police Department.

Gilbert Academy, where Harold attended high school, ca. 1938
(DILLARD UNIVERSITY)

Playing in that band would mold my life. I had no idea back then that I would actually become a musician. My focus at the time was on playing the clarinet well enough to at least get noticed. Rodney and Albert were playing concert pieces, plus a little jazz on the sax. I could play a little jazz on my clarinet. My ear was in good shape, but my reading was not up to par. I could imitate Louis Jordan's solos, and even some Lester Young. Eddie "Cleanhead" Vinson, a jazz saxophonist who also sang the blues, had a popular record out called "Old Maid Boogie," with "Kidney Stew" on the other side. I liked those records. They sounded real hip and jazzy, the way the horns were playing with the singer. I could play it by ear on my clarinet, but I wanted to write it on music paper. I managed to get a few pages of blank paper and started counting and figuring and listening over and over until I got the whole thing, both songs, on paper.

I brought my stuff to school for Mr. Davis to look at and, hopefully, be impressed by my work. He did better than that—he got some of the good readers to play it, and after a couple of tries they sounded just like the record. Mr. Davis was quite impressed, and so were Rodney and Albert. Mr. Davis informed me that I could become an arranger—and I wondered, *What's that?* Of course I was elated, and a little surprised at all the attention I was getting. Mr. Davis sent me downtown to Werlein's, New Orleans's premier music store, to get a Glenn Miller book on arranging. The Glenn Miller book didn't work for me—it was too complicated and academic—so I continued to write by ear.

Dillard University

I was sixteen years old when I graduated from Gilbert Academy, and I had my heart and mind set on attending Southern University in Scotlandville (near Baton Rouge), the state school for Negroes. Southern was where all my friends were going, and besides, Mr. Davis was going to take over the band there, so several Gilbert band students were going too. Of course, it did not escape my thoughts that I would be away from home for the first time in my life. I could live on campus and experience life as a grown-up.

Mother had a better plan. She and Daddy thought—no, they *knew*—that I was too young to embark on that adventure. As far as they were concerned, the fact that I would stay home and attend Dillard was already settled. Mother was not comfortable with my inclination toward music: she wanted me to be a doctor, or something else "respectable." I chose music education as a major as a compromise with my mother, who had not been successful suppressing my love for music. Teaching would allow me to do something respectable.

Just like Mother and Daddy were right about Gilbert, they were right about Dillard. I had always been told that I was a smart child, but I quickly learned that I was just one among many at Dillard, where the quality of the students was especially high. And I soon realized that I was still in high-school mode—I was looking for a basketball game at lunchtime! Clinton Moore was the only guy I knew from high school

The Dillard University Band (inset) Mr. M. C. Bryant, Director.

A new year is here, but the band has neither old nor new uniforms, although the musicianship of the band is steadily improving.

On September 27, 1949, in our regular meeting, new officers were elected. They are: President, Harold Battiste; Vice President, Luther Brown; Secretary-treasurer, Norbert Harris; Librarian, Beatrice Cunningham; Reporter, Berweda Hatch; Business Manager, Alvin Meade; Personnel Manager, William Cobb; Assistant Band Directors, Willie White, Luther Brown, William Cobb.

The membership of the band has been somewhat increased this season, although three of our last year's members are not with us. As an adjunct to our regular football performances, we have four very talented majorettes; Misses Audrey Norman, Willie D. White, Claramae Slush, and Barbara Antoine. Due to the very rainy weather on October 1, 1949, we were unable to perform, but on Homecoming day we did.

Mr. Melvin Bryant, our eminent director, has plans for the coming year which each of us will strive to carry out successfully.

—Berweda Hatch

DILLARD DANCE BAND . . . First Row, left to right: Mamie Reason, William H. Cobb, Jr., Robert L. Washington, Duplain R. Gant, James C. Polite, Harold Battiste. Second Row, left to right: Janie LaRue, Donald Rhodes, Joe A. Rhinehare, Clarence Haynes, Luther Brown. Third Row, left to right: Charles Clark, Edward Brown, Melville C. Bryant (Director).

Left, Pages from the 1948 Dillard University yearbook, with a photo of Harold playing in the Dillard Dance Band; *right,* a 1949 article from the Dillard student paper, the *Courtbouillon,* written by Harold's childhood schoolmate (DILLARD UNIVERSITY)

who also went to Dillard. We became tight when we decided to start our college adventure by splitting a package of Pall Mall cigarettes. Smoking openly on campus was a privilege given to us as "college guys," and it was a big deal. It made us feel like grown men. But I eventually figured out there was more to college than cigarettes.

Our relationships with professors were formal. We called them "Mister" or "Doctor," so unless we saw their full names printed on a syllabus, we didn't even know their first names. It was a line into familiarity that we didn't cross. A few professors still stand out, though: Benjamin Quarles, dean of history; Julius Miller, physics; Mr. Morton, English; and Dr. Snowden, social science. And, of course, I remember my music professors.

A degree in music education would qualify and certify me to be a teacher. I automatically focused on the music side. Mr. Oreon Southern, the department head, was a choral person and a great organist. He didn't stay at Dillard for my full five years but was replaced by another choral person, Dr. Booker, who fascinated me because he had perfect pitch—the ability to name any note he heard. Melville Bryant was brought into the department as the instrumental music instructor. Mr. Bryant was an army warrant officer who instituted a U.S. Army Reserve Band, the 333rd, to mobilize some of the talent in the New Orleans community. The band was very successful. He brought together a lot of younger and older musicians from different parts of the city. As a private-first-class clarinetist, I met cats from back-o'-town (Gert Town), downtown (the 7th and 9th wards), front-o'-town, and Uptown. The experience gave me the best of both worlds. Mr. Bryant brought his jazz background to the 333rd just as my interest in jazz was growing. And I enjoyed broadening my knowledge of European music, which I had heard in the movies and on the radio but hadn't known anything about, especially the composers. For example, my freshman course in music appreciation taught me that the Lone Ranger theme was actually the "William

JOE JONES and his BAND..... YEAR 1946.. NEW ORLEANS, LA. MUSICAN LOCAL 496
Left to right: Joe Jones Rupert Robinson Wilbur Hogan Melvin Lastie Robert Davis Thomas Robinson Louis Barbarin Thomas Shevin Warren Skinner Clarance Thomas Louis Surgant Clarance Ford Lloyd Bellamy
Joe Jones   Age 20

Harold played in Joe Jones's band in 1949, three years after this picture was taken (TAD JONES COLLECTION, HOGAN JAZZ ARCHIVE)

Tell Overture." But I wanted to explore *our* music the same way. Some gospel music and spirituals were allowed at Dillard, but jazz and other styles of music coming from the Negro community were prohibited; that situation troubled me.

In the 333rd I met many musicians who were not in college with me, and I began to learn more about the music that was in me. Two musicians who were still in high school had a band called the Groovy Boys that played for proms and dances: Roger Dickerson on piano and Ellis Marsalis on saxophone. Roger went to McDonogh No. 35, and Ellis had been a Gilbert Academy student until it closed in 1949, when he transferred to Frances Gaudet High School. In his senior year there, whenever his bus passed Dillard, Ellis would get off and hang with me all day. When Roger and Ellis graduated they came to Dillard, where I was a senior. This is when I really started to become a part of the jazz effort. Mr. Bryant agreed to allow us to play music with a big-band feel, so I started a trio, with Ellis on bass, me on clarinet, and a new student from Texas, Cedar Walton, on piano.

My first real gig was in 1949. Joe Jones, a guy from the 7th Ward who played piano in the 333rd, had a big dance band that featured several of the cats from the army band. I was invited to rehearse with the band playing the third alto sax. I remember Dalton Rousseau and Johnnie Fernandez in the trumpet section, Julius Schexnayder on baritone sax, and Charlie Gaspard on first alto, who led the section and sounded like Johnny Hodges in Duke Ellington's band. I was thrilled to be sitting next to Charlie.

Joe got a gig for the band to play a Sunday-evening dance at the Pentagon, a club in the 7th Ward. This was to be my maiden voyage, and I was scared. Fortunately, I didn't have to take any solos, so I made it through the gig unexposed. We played a lot of Stan Kenton stock arrangements: "Artistry in Rhythm," "Artistry Jumps," "Opus in Pastels," "Peanut Vendor," and so on. We had a few originals written by local

Harold's second "real" gig was with the Johnson Brothers combo, pictured here in the *Louisiana Weekly,* May 5, 1949.

musicians who were known as arrangers, including John "Pickett" Brunious, Clyde Kerr, and Quinton Baptiste. The scores these cats wrote were to me every bit as hip as Kenton's music—and much hipper than most of our stock charts; one of Pickett's originals, "A Sultan's Dream," has stayed in all our minds over the years.

Outside, after the gig, all the cats seemed to be in little huddles, laughing and talking. Joe came over to me and put six bucks in my hand. I asked him, "What was that for?" He sort of laughed and said that was my pay for the gig. I did not understand how or why he was giving me all that money for having so much fun and feeling so good—and for just four hours! When I was working as a bus boy at Uncle Dan's restaurant, I got twelve dollars for the whole week. Years later, I learned that Joe had paid all the other cats twice as much as me for the gig!

Grooving with the Johnson Brothers

Soon I got another gig with a combo known as the Johnson Brothers. The Johnsons were two very gifted musicians from Donaldsonville, a small town about fifty miles west of New Orleans. Raymond, the older brother, played piano and sang like Charles Brown ("Merry Christmas, Baby"), and Plas, with his tenor sax, was the excitement on the front line. Their sister Gwen sang—and she was as talented as the guys (plus I had a crush on her). Their older cousin Reynold Richards played trumpet and was the group's businessman. They'd just lost their drummer, Edward Blackwell, who later would become one of the top jazz players in New York and beyond. He was replaced with a hot young drummer just out of high school, Anthony Beasley. Plas invited me to join the band playing baritone sax, to give bottom to the horns. In a lot of the popular dance music of the era, the baritone sax duplicated the bass part, like on Fats Domino's "Blueberry Hill" and "Ain't That a Shame."

I was more excited about playing with the Johnson Brothers than I was about the gig with Joe at the Pentagon. We had lots of gigs at dances and nightclubs, and I got my first uniform—a plaid tuxedo jacket. I thought I was *somebody*. More important, playing in this band gave me the opportunity to learn and analyze chord changes, progressions, and structure. There weren't any written arrangements, but the group was tight. We made up arrangements at rehearsal or on the bandstand, so, playing the baritone sax, I usually had to find the root of the harmony. But as wonderful as it was, I had to give it up. After about six months' dancing on the bandstand with that heavy baritone sax, my back started hurting and I went to the doctor. He said enough—no more!—ruling that I was too young to carry such a heavy instrument. The Johnson Brothers finally broke up when Plas got a road gig in 1951 with Charles Brown, after which he did a stint in the army.

Bus Stop Bandit

When I was a kid, I was considered fat—some kids called me "Porky Pig"—and that's how I saw myself. So as a teenager I was always shy, especially with girls. Other guys my age would brag about their conquests, but I couldn't "get some" from a girl. I just didn't have the courage. But then, while I was still a student at Gilbert Academy, I had sex with an older girl named Gloria—but our getting together only happened because she was the aggressor. It happened in the backseat of my daddy's Chevy. Whoo, yeah!

Once I had had a taste, I wanted more. Fortunately, I was sixteen, so I was driving, and the Chevy gave me "vehicular bravery." I started picking up women that I didn't know as they stood waiting for the bus. I would offer them a ride in the car, and we would end up at a motel. I thought that was the only way that I could get women.

Joe Jones heard about me picking up women for quickies and nicknamed me the "Bus Stop Bandit." On the one hand, I was embarrassed that what I was doing had gotten back to Joe, but on the flip side, it meant that I had a sexual reputation.

Soon enough, I would learn about real love.

Newlyweds Harold and Yette Battiste at a faculty reception, Beauregard Parish Training School, 1953; PHOTO BY BARRIE-SHAW STUDIO (THNOC)

chapter **2 on the road to manhood**

It's hard for me to think of marriage as just another chapter in my life story. The other parts —school, jobs—might be thought of that way, but marriage was much, much more than that. Marriage was the whole point of my life—the binding that held all the chapters together, the reason for all the other things. To participate in the creation of lives, to nurture, provide for, and protect those lives so that they might repeat the process: I thought that was everything.

I was instantly stricken when I met Alviette Marie Antoinette Dominique. It was February 1949, and I was seventeen. She was not my first girlfriend, but she was the first to light my fire so suddenly. Her full naked lips, her deep, smooth, dark-brown skin, her soft, velvet voice . . . *ummm*. She was visiting my brother's girlfriend, Beulah, who lived across the hall from Alviette's grandmother in the Magnolia Project. I was just tagging along. Beulah, probably wanting to get us out of the way, introduced me to Alviette—nicknamed Yette—with just enough sly innuendo to get something started; she knew both of us were shy. But I managed to get a phone number, and in the next few weeks we talked on the phone. She seemed to like me—a lot—which surprised and confused me. I had never felt so in love, and I found it hard to believe that she felt the same way about me.

In our courtship we experienced much of what many couples experience. There were picnics and parties, church and movies, friends and relatives, other guys in her life, other girls in mine. Of course, we didn't realize it at the time, but in the midst of all the hormonal passion and teenage fun, we were testing and adjusting our basic values regarding family, male/female roles, money, education, and other important issues. Alviette's family—mother, stepfather, older sister, and much younger brother—lived on the back-o'-town side of Claiborne Avenue, which seemed like a great distance from the Magnolia, where I met her. Before long, they got an apartment in the project—which was considered upward mobility in the 1940s. I knew from my visits to see Yette, and from conversations with her about their household, that the relationship between Miss Irma (Yette's mom) and Mr. Clarence (Yette's stepdad) was not a happy one.

Left, Harold at Camp Polk near DeRidder, LA, with the 333rd U.S. Army Reserve Band, 1952; *right*, back home in New Orleans (THNOC)

Mr. Clarence, who worked as a janitor, was not an educated man. He seemed to have developed the habits that often accompany men with low self-esteem, which were exacerbated by insensitive treatment in the home; Yette often spoke of how she disliked the way her mother treated Mr. Clarence.

In 1952 Yette graduated from Gaudet High School and I from Dillard. She enrolled at Xavier University with a scholarship. She had talked about wanting to study medicine, and Xavier was known for its pharmacy and pre-med programs. I traveled to Camp Polk that summer with the 333rd U.S. Army Reserve Band. Though we were both preoccupied by our own new, busy lives, my mind was already made up—Alviette would be my wife someday. As this notion became apparent to my mother, a bit of tension developed that I wasn't aware of at the time—she was not ready for me to settle on a mate for life. But that year apart brought Yette and me to a new level as a couple. It was our fourth year of courting with many bumps along the way, but we were committed to our future together.

A New Job: Beauregard Parish

I embarked upon this new phase of my life with what seems to me now remarkable confidence—or maybe I was too naive and dumb to realize what I was getting into. When I graduated from Dillard in May 1952, I had never lived outside of my parents' home. I had never really thought about life after college. I started applying for a job as soon as I had my certificate, and I got a call from DeRidder in midsummer. DeRidder is a small rural town in Beauregard Parish, in southwest Louisiana, about twenty miles from the Texas line and fifteen miles south of Camp Polk, where I'd just been with the 333rd. But it somehow seemed even smaller when I arrived there to live just a few weeks later, in late August.

Several families welcomed me to live with them (for a fee). I went to stay with Miss Phyllis and Uncle John at 305 Cedar Street, and that became my home away from home. I was received in the principal's office by the smiling faces of excited personnel. I met Cornelius King, principal; Mrs. Stagg, over at the grammar school; Ruthebelle Singleton, high-school vice-principal; and Churchill Paul, science teacher and football coach. I suddenly felt like one of the students, thinking to myself, *I don't belong in here with these grown folks.*

I was not prepared for the situation that was presented to me at Beauregard Parish Training School. This school didn't have a music program. They had *never* had a band. When I did my practice teaching during my final year of college, it did not include "How to Start a School Band . . . From Scratch." While setting up a strategy for getting a music program started, I was assigned a seventh-grade English class to occupy my time. This I was not ready for; I learned a lot more than I taught. But as the word got around among the students about who I was and what I had been hired to do, a buzz started. So I announced a cattle call for kids who wanted to join the band. The response was good—dozens showed up. No one had instruments, and many of them had no idea what they wanted to play. Several said they wanted to play a "band," which meant that they did not know the names of individual instruments.

I was inspired by the enthusiasm of these children—how they looked at me, eyes wide, big, open smiles. I could see into their hearts. Some of the older ones, the seniors, recognized that I was not much older than they, and they liked that.

I found a music store in nearby Beaumont, Texas, and told them about our situation. They agreed to do an exhibit at the school. Mr. King decided to make an event of it. All students—interested or just curious—and their parents were invited. The store brought a truckload of band instruments: flutes, clarinets, saxophones, trumpets, trombones, baritones, and sousaphones, and, of course, all kinds of drums and other percussion instruments. The shiny new instruments were laid out on tables in the gym, which was decorated for the occasion. A salesman talked about the various instruments, and I demonstrated each of them. Students were invited to come up and get a feel for the instruments.

The show was a big hit. The parents got involved and added their enthusiasm, energy, and money to the effort. Mr. King got the school board to get a sousaphone and a bass drum for us. We were on our way!

After the Christmas holiday, I began to make a band out of these enthusiastic, optimistic children, who had no idea of how far they had to go to reach their goal. I managed to achieve a fairly good balance for the band by carefully advising each student in the selection of an instrument. I taught individual lessons during the day, plus evenings and Saturdays. We had section sessions for the woodwinds, brass,

Harold directing the first Beauregard Parish Training School Band concert, 1953; PHOTO BY BARRIE-SHAW STUDIO (THNOC)

lower brass, and percussion. By mid-March we were beginning to sound like a band (of beginners), and we were all happy and proud.

With less than two months until the summer break, I needed to get music appropriate for end-of-year events. Finding the right music arranged for beginners was taking too long, so I wrote some myself. I had already been creating lessons for them as a customized aid to use with the Rubank Elementary Method books. I found that as I got to know individual students, I could give them music to practice that addressed their particular needs. I'd been doing that for the sections as well. So writing my own music for the spring concert and graduation made sense.

Selections for the concert were made from songs familiar to the students from school, church, or the radio: a nice mix of easy marches, a patriotic song or two, a spiritual or gospel song, and a jazzy dance tune, and for lagniappe I played a solo on my alto sax, with Miss Sadie Howard at the piano. That performance won me instant fame, and it didn't hurt Miss Howard's popularity either. After that evening, the kids wanted to make us a pair.

With such a wonderful first year, the kids and I thought it was time to get band uniforms. Looking forward to next September and football season, we wanted to be ready to hit the field and do halftime shows. Mr. King agreed to approach the school board for financial assistance. He invited me to come to the meeting with him to answer any questions the board might have. I was not surprised to find an all-White school board, but I was surprised—shocked and embarrassed—at how they addressed my principal. When it was time for us to present our request, *boy* was the first word that greeted us, and it was meant for Mr. King!

"*Boy* . . . What y'all want now?"

Mr. King, with his head hung low so as not to appear to be looking the board members in the eye, said, "Well, we have our new music teacher . . ." He explained who I was, what we were doing, what progress we had made, what we needed, and why we needed it.

Mr. Hanchey, the head man, interrupted. "Cornelius, you boys always wantin' whatever you see our children up here with . . ."

I was hurting almost to tears. I could not believe they were speaking like that to my principal with me right there! I wanted to be invisible. On the way back to school, back to our section of town, Mr. King tried to reassure me that it wasn't as bad as it seemed, that we'd be all right, but I wasn't hearing him.

Along with a few bold teachers and some involved parents, we set out to raise money in the community for the uniforms. We went public with a no-uniform parade. Some ladies made dresses for five girls to be majorettes. Several signs were made for the students to carry; since the name of the school was going to be changed to George Washington Carver High School, I made a sign that said FUTURE BAND OF CARVER HIGH. Although we were not able to raise enough for the uniforms we needed, our effort sent a strong message. I wanted the school board to know: they got a *new boy* down there. Back then you didn't do those sorts of things. But it had some effect, because the principal and I persuaded the school board to give us three instruments.

Love . . . and Marriage

Meanwhile, back home, Yette was dealing with her first year of college at Xavier, and it was not easy. The division between dark-skinned Blacks and light-skinned Blacks was a huge problem for her. Her letters never revealed the situation; instead, they focused on our love and my work. But our phone conversations revealed some of those intraracial struggles.

I planned to spend the summer of 1953 in DeRidder, working with my band of beginner musicians. I planned a trip home for the Fourth of July holiday to visit my family and, of course, to see Yette. Her aunt in Detroit had invited her to visit a few weeks later. I thought the trip would be good for her, but the

Future band of Carver High "no-uniform parade," DeRidder, 1953 (THNOC)

buzz in her family was that she might not come back—a possibility her mother wanted to prevent. Yette's mother realized that her daughter wanted to be more independent and move away from the family. She thought that a trip to Detroit would expand Yette's horizons a little too far. The two of them had been butting heads about their family life—the treatment of Mr. Clarence, sibling stuff with her sister, a host of things—and Miss Irma figured that she should try to keep Yette close to home.

June 22, 1953

Harold

I hope you had a non tiresome trip back. Please write and tell my mother something or give a good explanation for not asking her to use her water jug. You should know you are welcome to anything I have regardless to whatever it may be. Please believe me. Mother felt that you should have given her some respect in asking, but I know it's wrong for her to take the attitude she took . . . not knowing that I was going to write and tell you about it. She would have a fit if she knew, but I'm going to tell her even though she feels that I'm always trying to make hard feelings between the two of you. I much prefer being frank with a person face to face: if not, I won't say harsh words to anyone else . . . please understand me.

Harold, I'm not asking you to believe this, but I feel better telling you this once more even though I know you won't believe me and it is the truth. I received a letter from my aunt asking me to come to Detroit until school opens in September. She offered to send half the fare. I intend going so I have to write and let her know I'm coming.

I'll work about two weeks and then leave about the 2nd or 3rd week in July. Mother offered to pay Tommy's fare to make sure I'm coming back, but I'm going to try to get out of taking him. While I'm there I can decide what I'm going to do. Please grant me that favor by doing what I asked you to do. I hope I get a letter from you before I leave.

Love, Yette

June 26, 1953
305 Cedar St.
DeRidder, Louisiana

Baby!

My trip back to DeRidder was fine. I got a bit sleepy after I passed Lake Charles but I know that road well so I made it all right. Did mother tell you I called her that night about 11:30?

Yette, I would like for you to go to Detroit for school. I think it would be a wonderful experience for you . . . or for both of us. I say that because the things you learn up there you can teach me and the people you meet (and I hope you meet the right ones) you can introduce me to but, I can't see why you have to leave in July . . . or even August for that matter. Please explain that to me. Also, I think I mentioned to you that if I can, next year (1954) I'm going to get a job at home if possible. Do you think you'll be back by then? If not I can keep this job up here.

Please explain to your mother that the water jug is a life-saver to me . . . It is the only way I can get cold water at school. I didn't mean to take it but my mother got the idea and I thought it was all right. I'm very sorry I caused her to be upset.

Love, Harold

Oh yes . . . next time you write. Take your time because I can't understand what you're saying. I know my handwriting is bad but yours is getting worse than mine!!

Yette's older sister, Audry, reminded her that she was still a minor, so their mother could *make* her come home. Audry had the solution for Yette, if she really wanted to leave home for good: get married! I was surprised, unprepared, caught off guard—but when confronted with the situation, I felt compelled to act. It was going to happen anyway . . . someday. My primary task was to break the news to my mother. It was very hard to see my mother trying not to cry—I was breaking her heart. She hugged me and held me tight, like I hadn't felt since I was a little boy.

Yette and her friend Edith Chatters swung into action, getting things ready for an elopement. We had to get the marriage license at City Hall. Edith and her boyfriend, my friend and fellow musician Alvin Batiste, were our witnesses. Edith had secured a minister to do the ceremony at his home on the Westbank, across the river from New Orleans, and we had our reception there—just us! The next morning, Mrs. Battiste and I were off to DeRidder.

Real Life

My second school year at George Washington Carver High School began almost as soon as I—we!—got settled. The band was going to get uniforms after all. Now we had to get ready for football season. Things were going well with my students, and in their first uniforms they felt and looked like a proud high-school band. With the help of a few student leaders, we managed to put together a marching show for halftime and a few pep-rally tunes for the grandstands. The spring semester meant getting ready for our second annual concert, which included more challenging music than the year before. I remembered a few concert pieces arranged for younger bands from my Gilbert Academy days, and I wrote a couple of arrangements of tunes that the students and audience would recognize. I really began to feel more confident of my position among the other faculty.

My *real* life was beginning then, but I didn't realize it. Even though things were different as soon as I arrived in DeRidder with a wife, I thought I was still the same Harold. Miss Phyllis, from whom I had rented a room since I'd first come to DeRidder, suggested that I'd probably want to move now that I had a wife. I was about to say no, I felt very at home with her family, but I got a look from Yette that seemed to say I needed to talk it over with her. We found a place with Mrs. Singleton, a teacher at the school. She took Yette, who was younger than some of the students, under her wing and became a friend and surrogate parent.

Soon enough I began to get schooled about my new status. I learned that a few of the younger teachers and some of the older students were going to be "heartbroken" that I'd married. I had been warned about the broken hearts, but I was quite unprepared for the overt advances some of the senior girls made toward me. For a while I didn't even see it, but after being mugged a few times I did! Turns out, I was quite a hot item: at twenty-one years old, I was the youngest man on the faculty—and a musician from New Orleans. However, in a very short time, my marriage to Yette was accepted, and we were embraced by everyone at the school and in the community.

We had a wonderfully challenging first year of marriage. We had courted for four years, but this was a new game. This was the first time I began to feel and grasp something about my relationship with Yette, now Mrs. Battiste, that would continue to linger in the shadows of our love commitment. I realized that we weren't children anymore. Everything about my life—our lives—was different. It was all much too complex and complicated for either of us to understand then.

Yette and I enjoyed DeRidder. We took trips to the towns in the area: Lake Charles, where an old high-school bandmate of mine, Bernard Beaco, was teaching; DeQuincy, where another Gilbert buddy, Dave Williams, was a band director. Yette and I visited some of the students' homes in other little towns in the country. We were doing well in DeRidder, but the previous year's racial incidents with the school board had signaled that I would eventually have trouble in Beauregard Parish. By the end of the school year, in June 1954, my mother had found a job for me in the New Orleans school system. She wanted me back home.

Harold introduced his bride to colleagues at the Beauregard Parish Training School faculty reception, 1953. PHOTO BY BARRIE-SHAW STUDIO. (THNOC)

Back to New Orleans

I was not prepared to return home as a married man. Where would we stay? Yette and I had not talked about where we would live in New Orleans. I had never given it a thought . . . my mind had not completely clicked into married mode. I'd never thought that it needed to be thought about—until I thought about it!

Whenever I'd come home in the past, my parents' house was where I lived. So we moved in with my parents, who welcomed us with open arms. Mother seemed to be very happy—much more than Yette. Focused on my new job, I hardly noticed the tension brewing at home.

First Born

When I discovered that we had conceived and were on the way to having our first baby, I can't describe all the things I felt—happy, scared, proud, humbled. I felt as though I finally really knew what love was. Yette became more special to me, more precious and harder to understand, but it was all right. On April 6, 1955, Harold Raymond Battiste III came into the world. Because he arrived so near Easter, Mama Pearl (as Yette called my mother) called the baby her "Easter Bunny," and the name stuck.

By the end of the school year, me and Yette were ready to move out. Charles Wilson, one of my early teen buddies from the Magnolia, had just gotten married. Yette and I decided to get a place with him and his wife, Annatoe; we moved to an apartment in the Hollygrove section.

McDonogh No. 35

The other big thing on my mind was my new job. My position in the school system was as an itinerant music teacher. McDonogh No. 35 was my home school, and there were several other schools where I'd teach once or twice a week. The elementary schools I visited—Lafon, Lockett, McDonogh No. 24, McDonogh

Harold and his mother, "Mama Pearl," with newborn Harold Raymond "Bunny" Battiste III, outside her Second Street home, 1955 (THNOC)

No. 38, and McDonogh No. 6—had students who were beginners in music. One of those beginners at No. 6 was Walter Payton—who would become the father of renowned trumpeter Nicholas Payton. McDonogh No. 35 had been the first—and for many years, the only—public high school for "colored" children. It was considered to be for intellectuals, and when I started there was a new principal at the helm: Dr. Mack Spears. He fit right in with the school's established reputation, and he had a brilliant faculty in place.

Under the leadership of Edwin Hogan, No. 35 had one of the finest choral programs in the city, but the band was sad (and so was the football team!). For one thing, No. 35 didn't have a large body of students. When I got there, in 1954, it was no longer the only choice for Blacks, and since its academic standards were so high, many students chose other schools that were newer (and probably easier). Activities such as athletics and band suffered due to lack of participants. The fact that I was hired to lead the band gave me hope that more focus and support would be placed on instrumental music.

I don't remember my exact schedule, but in addition to the elementary school visits, I also went to two junior high schools: Carter G. Woodson and John W. Hoffman. Woodson was located around the corner from my parents' new home at 2418 Second Street; one of my teachers at Gilbert Academy, Miss Mercedes Tucker, was teaching there. At Hoffman I met a talented, gifted young man named Wilson Turbinton (who would later be famous as "Willie Tee") who had an alto sax and also sang. I thought he sang better than he played the sax. He played the piano too, also better than the sax.

The Gig Call

Being back in New Orleans also meant that I could once again start working as a professional musician—I needed to get reconnected to the gig call. Joe Jones, who I'd first played with in '49 at the

"The Dew Drop . . . Before the Gig"; PHOTO BY HAROLD BATTISTE JR.

Pentagon, had a combo playing clubs and dance halls in the small towns around Louisiana and Mississippi. He had the hot man, Clarence Ford, on tenor sax, so once again I'd be challenging my back by dancing with the big baritone. The gigs didn't happen often enough to interfere with my school job.

New Horizons

Sometime in 1955 I met a cat named Jimmy who hung around the Dew Drop Inn all the time. He may have been living there temporarily, as did many guys when they were on the move. Jimmy X was a Black Muslim, a member of the Nation of Islam under the leadership of the Honorable Elijah Muhammad. I had no idea what all that meant when I first heard Jimmy talking about "the Nation" and the "blue-eyed devils" and "Jakoob," but I was intrigued. Most of it seemed as far-fetched as most religious stuff, but some of what he said caught my attention: "Blacks were the original people," "White people were created by a Black scientist," etc. It didn't take long for me to match some of what he was saying with things I had experienced in my life, things I had thought about. I just didn't know that anyone else was thinking along those lines.

For about two or three weeks, I soaked up as much as Jimmy X put out. Something major was happening in the way I saw myself and, as a result, the way I saw the situation in which I was living. Jimmy disappeared, but his message stayed with me. He once asked me, "You ever looked a devil dead in the eye?" I had to think about it for a minute, but the answer was no. He said I needed to try it and see what happens.

In the early part of 1956, I was teaching a class at one of the Uptown schools on my itinerant schedule when I had a visit from the supervisor of music for the public schools, a man named Mr. René Louapre. After observing my class for about twenty to thirty minutes, he asked me to step out into the hall. "Why are you spending so much time on reading notes?" he asked. "You're wasting too much time with that . . . their parents just want to hear them play some songs."

Well, this was the time to look a devil in the eye. I locked onto his eyes. He immediately stepped back but he couldn't unlock his gaze from mine. His neck began to turn red. He looked like he wanted to say something, but I asked him, "Is this the policy at the White schools? They seem to be reading music pretty well. When do you think my students will be ready to learn how to read?" When he recovered, he told me to come before the school board downtown.

A couple of weeks later, I got a letter directing me to a meeting at the school board. Mr. Louapre was there, along with the superintendent and someone else. I was expected to defend my attitude regarding the supervisor's advice. I stood firm on my evaluation that it was not in the best interest of my students. They had already made up their minds. I was given the choice to comply with the supervisor's instructions or tender my resignation. That choice was easy. I wondered, *Am I becoming a militant?*

I started the summer of 1956 with a wife, a fourteen-month-old son, and no job. I was filled with questions: Was my teaching career finished? Should I even bother to look for another job like that? I was still in the South, and with my new knowledge of who I was—who *we* were as Black people—I thought maybe I should leave.

Los Angeles, California, May 1956
(LAMBERT/GETTY IMAGES)

chapter **3 go west**

It was June 1956, and all of us—Ed "Boogie" Blackwell, Alvin Batiste, Richard Payne, and me—had been getting together, playing the new jazz and writing tunes, and once in a while getting a paying gig. The four of us were close, and the music brought us even closer as we tried out new sounds and approaches to the music we knew. This was the genesis of our American Jazz Quintet (AJQ); when Ellis Marsalis joined our quartet we made five. The two pieces we created around this time were "Never More" and "Brownie." We were determined to be adventurous with our instruments—sometimes we succeeded and sometimes what was created wasn't worth a hill of beans—but we were just happy to be playing music.

Meantime, Ornette Coleman—who'd gotten stranded in New Orleans a few years back and stayed with one of the well-known music families, the Lasties, long enough to meet some of the cats—had sent a bus ticket to Boogie Blackwell to come out to Los Angeles. Boogie told Ellis about the bus ticket, and Ellis decided he'd like to go along—he had graduated from Dillard a year before and had not really settled on what he was going to do. When they told me about their plans, I was thinking, *There goes our drummer and piano player.* I no longer had a job—I was being thrown out of the public school system—but I had a car. So I told them, "Cash in the bus ticket, I'll drive!" Of course, I had a wife and a one-year-old son. Alviette was not very receptive to the suddenness of my no-plan, no-money adventure. Besides, I'd be leaving her and Bunny living at my parents' home. But we were young, in love, and struggling—both emotionally and financially. We needed money, but neither of us knew what we were doing or where we were going as a family. We didn't know how to have the hard conversations that couples often must engage in to solve problems; we just kind of floated along. Yette didn't want to rock the boat, and neither did I.

Road Trip

I had a new 1956 white-over-green Chevrolet 210, my second new car (my first was a 1953 green Chevrolet 210). We got some maps and figured out a way to get to Los Angeles. I can't remember Ellis doing much driving, and I know Boogie didn't, but it didn't matter, because I was thrilled just to be involved. I had never gone this far from home; hence, I never experienced the vast beauty of this country—the varieties of geography, the majesty of mountains so high they had snow at the top, rocks twice as big as my car.

We stopped in El Paso to celebrate the end of Texas. New Mexico and Arizona were hotter than New Orleans in August! When we arrived in Los Angeles via the San Bernardino Freeway, it was the midst of morning drive time. I had never seen so many lanes of cars moving so fast in my life. Then, approaching the interchange in downtown Los Angeles, we saw signs to San Pedro, Santa Monica, Hollywood, Glendale, Pasadena—and we decided to get off the freeway and ask for help.

We found Ornette's pad on St. Andrews Place just north of Santa Barbara Boulevard (now Martin Luther King Boulevard). After only about fifteen minutes of greeting and talking, Boogie unpacked his drums, set up in Ornette's living room, and we played for about two hours; after all, that's why we came here. Later that day, we rode around looking for a place to live.

Maybe it was the whole idea of being in a new city—and being in the mythical L.A.—but I decided to flirt with getting high—nothing too way out or dangerous, but just minor stuff that involved over-the-counter drugs and a little marijuana here and there. Richard Payne told me about getting a nasal inhaler from Rexall's, taking the part with the medicine that went in your nose and turning it over inside a bottle of Coca-Cola, then drinking it. Yep, it made me high. So I sat there and wrote a piece called "Ohadi," which was a take on the standard "Idaho."

But while I was out there in California fooling around, family stuff was still happening back in New Orleans.

> *July 6, 1956*
>
> *Hi, Angel*
>
> *After I wrote you yesterday, we went out to look for somewhere to stay. While looking, Ornette (Blackwell's friend) brought us by some musicians' house to see if they could tell us where to find a place. While we were there, I played the [demo] record we made at home and it sounded so good the cats thought we were from New York!*
>
> *This morning I've been looking through the papers at the homes for sale, and I think we have a wonderful chance to make it out here. By the way, we found a couple of rooms in a nice section last night. 877 E. Vernon Ave. L.A., 11 Calif. The rooms are $7.50 a week but the three of us are using 2 rooms for $15.00 . . . or, $5.00 a week for each of us. I was talking to the man who owns the place and he says there are a lot of job opportunities out here in all fields. I plan to go to the School Board today . . . if I can find it (this place is so BIG!). Rent is high but property is cheap with low down payments. When we get this car paid for, we can buy a house here easy . . . look at this sample from the newspaper.*
>
> *Pray that I get a good job so that we can make it here. Tell everybody hello for me, and kiss Bunny for me. Tell mother everything is OK so she won't have to worry too much.*
>
> *With all my love, Harold*

Yette and I wrote back and forth almost daily. On July 11 I got a letter announcing: "Harold, you can look forward to seeing us in about two weeks or less!" What? What to do? The "us" in that announcement was not just her and Bunny but included Alvin and Edith Batiste and their two children, Marcia and Alvin Jr. Did they have any idea what they were doing? Much sooner than two weeks later, I saw this old, beat-up car full of people coming down East Vernon Avenue, then slowing to a stop. That they made it to California—like the Beverly Hillbillies!—is evidence that the Creator has a master plan.

After all the celebration of their arrival and hearing the stories of their adventures along the way,

Edith got right to work getting places for the newcomers to stay. Her family ended up with a member of a large family Edith knew in L.A., the Saucers. Yette, Bunny, and I wound up in a nice home belonging to Mildred and Jessie Saucer, at 200 West Fifty-seventh Street.

Being reunited with my family, of course, meant that my time, focus, and energy were divided. A plan with a goal had not been worked out among the cats yet—we were still just looking to play and meet the players in Los Angeles. Ornette had a day job as a freight-elevator operator in a downtown department store where he could practice his ax and write tunes. Ellis, Boogie, and now Alvin were able to get together and play, but I couldn't hang with them all day. I started inquiring about job possibilities.

I located an old friend of my mother, Mrs. Annabelle Jackson, who had moved to Los Angeles years ago. Both she and her husband, Bill, worked at the post office, and they offered to put in a word for me if I wanted. I also got in touch with my third-grade teacher, Miss Glenn of New Orleans, who had become Mrs. Williams of Los Angeles. Though she was no longer teaching, she was able to advise me on the school system in L.A.

July sped by—the whole summer was moving very fast, with my life caught up in it. In August I had to report to New Orleans for the USAR Summer Camp for the 333rd Army Reserve Band. While I was in Louisiana, I also had to deal with family matters that Alviette had abruptly left behind. Her letters from California that month contained lists of things to do, and at least one apology: "Harold, darling, I hope all of this doesn't discourage you and make you nervous . . . also please forgive me for being so much trouble. I have a lot of wonderful things to tell you when you get back."

When I got back to L.A., things started to settle down. I got a night-shift gig at the terminal annex of the post office sorting sacks and stacks of mail. I endured it for five or six weeks, then one night on my lunch break I thought, I'm out here 2,000 miles from home to play music . . . why am I doing this? I walked off right then and didn't even go back to get my paycheck.

Things were beginning to take shape in our little music world. Besides practicing, writing and learning tunes, and jamming, we got a one-night-a-week gig at a Mexican joint downtown. We could play whatever we wanted because the gig didn't pay much. The other thing we did around that time was to spend a day in a little recording studio on South Broadway owned by Ted Brenson (he was actually a mailman with a hobby). We recorded demos of some of Ornette's tunes—the only title I remember was one for his lady, called "Janie." What we did that day was to mark the beginning of an unlikely and unforeseen career and future for me.

Hollywood

Because I had been a school teacher, I was chosen to find out how we could get a record contract with a label. The majors—Capitol, RCA, Columbia, Decca—all had offices in Hollywood. There were lots of smaller, independent labels that focused on certain markets like R&B, gospel, and rock and roll, but few handled jazz. Of course, at that point I didn't know that, so over the next few days I just hit the pavement in Hollywood and knocked on doors. But I never even got past the reception desk at the majors, especially when asked, "With whom do you have an appointment?"

It was, however, a fascinating learning experience—getting the feel of Hollywood, the famous streets and places—Sunset Boulevard and the Palladium, Hollywood Boulevard, Grauman's Chinese Theatre, the intersections of Sunset and Vine and Hollywood and Vine, across from the Capitol Records Tower.

At the west end of Hollywood, before it becomes Beverly Hills, I found Specialty Records, a company with a familiar face: Robert "Bumps" Blackwell, the A&R (artists and repertoire) rep for Specialty, had frequented New Orleans often, producing several hits at J&M, Cosimo Matassa's studio. All the top studio musicians in New Orleans knew Bumps, and he knew them. I was not among those cats, but many of them knew my name, and Bumps received me as though he knew me. When I presented our demo, he seemed

Art Rupe at the Venice, CA, office of Specialty Records
(MICHAEL OCHS ARCHIVES/GETTY IMAGES)

delighted, but jazz was not Specialty's thing. But he was obviously very fond of and fascinated with New Orleans. He wanted to know if there were any cats back home. He offered to hook me up with Specialty as a talent scout in the New Orleans area and arrange for studio time at Cosimo's for my jazz group.

The idea of having a native scout in New Orleans went over well with Specialty's owner, Art Rupe. He had already experienced success in New Orleans with both Lloyd Price ("Lawdy Miss Clawdy") and Little Richard ("Tutti Frutti," "Long Tall Sally," "Slippin' and Slidin'," etc.). I would be paid seventy-five dollars every two weeks.

Yette and I had begun to develop somewhat of a social life in L.A., among the few people we knew from home and some we met in California. Yette and Ornette's lady, Janie, got along especially well. When I told Yette that I might have to go back to New Orleans for Specialty and that I might have a chance to record our group, I expected resistance. Instead, she seemed to have plans of her own: she was looking for work and had some prospects, but Bunny was only eighteen months old. She wanted me to take the baby with me to New Orleans. She corresponded with her older sister, Audry, and arranged for Bunny to be taken in by their mother.

Ed Blackwell, Bunny, and me—plus an extra passenger, tenor sax player Clarence "Lukeman" Thomas—made the chilly drive back to New Orleans. The baby was very sick with a cold when we arrived, so I brought him to Miss Irma immediately. I checked back in with my parents. My dad had been in the hospital after suffering a heart attack while I was away, but he was back home. In one of his letters to me and Yette, he wrote: ". . . You are fortunate in getting work even though not permanent, you will be able to keep going until you do get something steady. You have our letter now and you know I'm home. I haven't gone to work yet. Don't know how I'm going to manage that. I don't know that I'll be able to do much anymore, but I'm thankful to God that I'm no worse off as yet."

Ed Blackwell (*left*) and Eustis Gilmet outside Mason's V.I.P. Lounge on South Claiborne Avenue (THNOC)

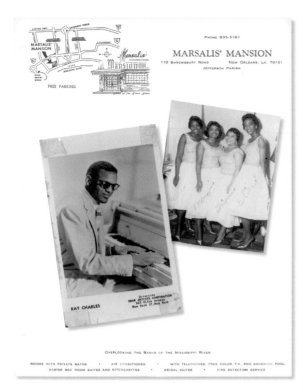

Clockwise, from left: Ray Charles and the Raeletts were among the many hot acts that stayed at the Marsalis Mansion Motel; a tour group outside the motel; young Ellis Jr. (*left*) hangs out on the grounds, which included a pool. (AMISTAD RESEARCH CENTER)

In the Studio

While I was settling back into the city, Ellis was also home, helping out at his father's hotel, Marsalis Mansion, where artists and musicians working in town often stayed. He was bragging to a group of musicians about our drummer, Boogie. The musicians were not impressed with Ellis's talk. To their surprise, Boogie himself walked up, and after they all set up and Boogie played, the band's once-skeptical drummer just gave up and left—and the band's bassist, William "Muscles" Swanson, wanted in with us. It just so happened that our bassist, Richard Payne, was not in New Orleans at the time. So Muscles learned all of our original material and made the record date in Richard's spot.

In late November 1956 we went into Cosimo's famous studio, where all of the big hits were made in New Orleans. The studio was located in the French Quarter on Governor Nicholls Street, in an old building that had rooms that were once slave quarters. None of us had been the studio players that got all the calls for recording dates in New Orleans—guys like Alvin "Red" Tyler on baritone saxophone, Lee Allen on tenor sax, and Earl Palmer on drums. Those musicians were the cream of the crop, playing with Fats Domino and Little Richard during their hit-making sessions. We were younger than those cats, and we were generally considered be-boppers who were not interested in the music they were recording. So we weren't real experienced in the studio. Everything was new and felt different—the acoustics, the way we were positioned, the microphones. It took us a while to adjust and play a couple of tunes. Once the music had been recorded and sounded good to us, once we had completed all the original compositions to our collective satisfaction, I realized that I didn't know what came next. I had never gone this far into the production of a record. In fact, the word *production* was not in use to my knowledge; we just said "make" a record.

We had gone to Cosimo's studio to make music—it turned out we made history. The music we recorded that day never saw the light of day until twenty years later. The studio kept the masters until they got paid, so I figured that Bumps—who arranged to use the studio on Specialty's account—would get the recordings. But he never did. The tracks were finally released in 1976 as part of the historic four-album boxed set *New Orleans Heritage Jazz: 1956–1966.* The original American Jazz Quintet was reissued on compact disc in 1991 as *In The Beginning.* Poet and author Kalamu ya Salaam wrote about this "beginning" in the liner notes for the CD:

> . . . So here we have it, this is literally the beginning . . . rough hewn but precise in pointing the way ahead. Confined by the prevalent three minute time length of the period, the music is unrestrained in its voicings and arrangements. This is the birth cry of modern New Orleans Jazz, a cry destined to be carried around the world by the figurative and literal sons of these musical pioneers who laid the foundations upon which subsequent generations would erect international careers. But then that is not surprising and is, in fact, a logical outcome of a musical movement whose motto is 'All For One.'

Once the recording was done, my attention needed to turn to my part of the deal: acting as a talent scout for Specialty Records. The jazz musician option was on hold pending the release of the American Jazz Quintet album. When Specialty said they wanted me to scout talent, they didn't mean jazz talent. Resigning myself to that reality, I took an optimistic view and focused on what I could learn in the job. Bumps called Art Rupe "Papa," and in a way he *was* very fatherly: he liked to teach, to explain how things worked. He often started statements to me with, "Well, you see, Bat . . ."

I had no idea of how to be a talent scout, except to remember that I was one when I heard or saw an artist I thought Bumps and Papa would like. I'd get a gig occasionally to supplement the salary I got from Specialty. They gave me no specific to-do list and didn't seem to be very concerned about my activities. Good thing, because my domestic relations were becoming stressed.

Family Trouble

My baby boy was in New Orleans being kept by my mother-in-law in the same house with my sister-in-law Audry and her two children; she didn't have a husband. I was in my parents' home, where my father was still recovering from his heart attack.

On January 5 Yette wrote me a letter revealing characteristics that surprised me—she refused to face confrontation. She had corresponded with Audry, who wanted to move out to Los Angeles. In a previous letter to me, Yette had written, ". . . it's alright with me if she [Audry] and the children want to come back out here with you . . . with the help of God, we will manage somehow." Now she wanted me to tell Audry that we did not want her to come.

I didn't know what to do. I didn't feel comfortable talking to Audry in the way Yette was asking, even though I felt that she was right in her assessment of the situation. Yette was letting me know that we couldn't be direct with Audry—we couldn't come right out and tell Audry not to come to California. Yette wanted to avoid the confrontation that was sure to come—she had already given Audry the go-ahead to come to L.A. I was truly uncomfortable, because Yette had changed her mind and wanted me to stand up to Audry but, at the same time, try to use a smooth approach to cover her change of heart. I just didn't want to get in the middle of two sisters.

Fortunately, my dealings with Specialty and Art Rupe resulted in a possible new option for us. On January 16, 1957, I wrote to Yette in L.A.:

Hi Sweetheart,

Certainly has been wonderful to receive so many letters from you and also to talk to you.

Yette, I want you to think seriously on what I tell you in this letter. The other day, after I talked to you, I called up the company. [Art Rupe] raised me from $75.00 every two weeks to $100.00 every two weeks plus 1/4 cent royalty on everything I send from here that they use. He also promised to raise my salary to $400 a month if I prove my ability to find good talent.

I've been very fortunate in life. Opportunity knocked for me as soon as I finished school. I left that job and came straight to the city and good fortune favored me again. I left that and went to California. Opportunity knocked and I took work at the post office . . . I quit. Finally, this opportunity, which is the best so far, has come. Now I begin to think . . . how long can this go on?? I've already had more good jobs than some men get in a lifetime. I thought a long time about this because I wanted to quit and come back to you. But opportunities may not continue to come my way . . . do you understand? Please consider what I'm saying and let me know what you think.

My Eternal Love, Harold

Making the move to California and all the events of the past six months had a tremendous effect on our marriage—positive and negative. Now, in the beginning of 1957, it looked as though I might be able to establish a foothold—or maybe just a toehold—in this music business. But my family situation was messed up.

Just as I was sending my January 16 letter, Yette was writing her January 17 letter, in which the things she said and the tone in which she said them let me see that we were worlds apart in our thoughts about family. I was beginning to see that Yette's upbringing was so radically different from mine. I always thought that marriage for me would follow the example I had seen in my parents' and grandparents' relationships. Yette's family was fractured and rife with problems, and that was so foreign to me. We needed to be together, but we had been raised so differently that there were a lot of philosophical ideas that didn't mesh.

Despite our struggles, by the end of January, I had managed to convince my wife to come back to New Orleans. I would get us a place of our own and begin to examine our options as a family.

You Send Me

In early May Art and Bumps wanted me to come back out to the Hollywood office—the trip would be my first plane ride. I had heard Bumps talking about how the lead solo singer with the Soul Stirrers gospel group—a cat named Sam Cooke—could be a pop star. Cooke had made an earlier recording using the name Dale instead of Sam, not wanting to offend his gospel fans by singing secular music. They kept me out West for the rest of the month. On May 21 I wrote a letter to Yette explaining that Art wanted me to stay another week. I was not aware of exactly what Bumps was up to, but I sensed that something special was brewing.

Bumps, the guitarist and arranger Rene Hall, and some other musicians were rehearsing somewhere away from the office. Specialty's office was located at 8508 Sunset Boulevard, at La Cienega. Below the street-level offices there was a sort of basement used as a practice studio. The afternoon before the session, Bumps assigned me to go into the studio and listen to Sam's original songs, looking for a B side to go with "Summertime." (All records—then on vinyl as 78s and later as 45s—had an A side, usually set as the hit, and a B side, a secondary or throwaway song, to complete the product.) Sam accompanied himself on his guitar as he went through several tunes. "You Send Me" was among them, and he sang it beautifully. The song was a simple form with common chord changes and really didn't need much arrangement.

It was the kind of piece that studio musicians could pick up without a written chart. But I thought it got a little boring when the second verse said the same as the first, so I asked him to say "You thrill me" in the second verse.

In the studio the next day, there were these White jazz background singers, the Lee Gotch (pronounced *gooch*) Singers, who Bumps had hired for the A side. When he finished recording that side and was ready to start on "You Send Me," they said they needed music to read. Bumps asked could I put something down for them. I said yes, but I was not too sure what sound to give them—gospel? R&B? pop? jazz? Since there were four of them, I decided to use four-part close harmony to get a pop/jazz sound. I don't know when Art came in the studio, but after about the fifth take he couldn't stand it any longer.

He was very upset that we had Sam sounding "White," and he seemed to blame it on those White singers. He fired them on the spot. Art had words with Bumps, and Bumps had words with Art. I stayed out of the way. Art sincerely loved Black music. He loved the sound and the spirit of it, and he had been very successful with it. He trusted his instincts. So he took over the session and tried to change the music to a more gospel/R&B feeling. But the spirit in the studio was gone for that day. No good music could happen.

In the next few days, Art and Bumps worked out a deal that gave the masters from the session to Bumps, who, in turn, made a deal with Bob Keen, who had started a new label. "You Send Me" was released on Keen Records, and Sam Cooke was born again as a pop star.

Death in the Family

Back home in New Orleans, my father was in the hospital again. When we talked, he wanted to know how things were going for me out in L.A.—he kept the conversation focused on me rather than letting me know the extent of his condition. "If you like what you're doing with those people, you stay until it's done," he said.

On June 5, 1957, at 7:15 p.m., my father died in Charity Hospital. He was fifty-six years old. Cause of death: ruptured aortic aneurysm, postoperative. Years later, as I became more aware of things that happen in hospitals where poor people are subject to students learning new procedures, I wondered— bypass surgery in 1957?

I had no way of understanding how deeply my father's death would affect me. And as I reflect on that scene from my present vantage point, I realize how little I understood of how my parents worked and sacrificed for me. I had enjoyed the assumed security of mother, father, grandmother, and grandfather, and even though Papa died when I was a child and Mama when I was in college, those losses did not leave me feeling so naked and insecure. Recognizing my mother's loss, I suddenly had to become my father.

Fortunately, there was cousin Lula from Chicago and some ladies from First Street M.E. and the Ladies Mutual Aid Society, all of whom took loving care of Mother. And of course, my brother, Alvin, and Yette were the in-house caretakers. I was both afraid and afraid to be afraid. Everything was on me: trying to get a foothold in this new work, get my little family stabilized, settle my father's business, get Mother through this hard period of grief.

Learning the Ropes

Joe Banashak was Specialty's distributor for the New Orleans region and the man I needed to know in order to learn the ropes. During late summer and early fall, with Joe's savvy and Art Rupe's clout, I began to get to know—and become known by—people in the music business: record retailers, radio-station producers and disc jockeys, club owners, singers, and songwriters. Many already knew me as a musician from the Joe Jones Band—and even all the way back to the Johnson Brothers combo.

Out in Los Angeles, Sam Cooke's record came out on Keen with "You Send Me" on the B side. But the DJs, the record stores—the *people*—made it the A side. Watching it hit was very hard for Art, not only for the money Specialty had lost. Art's ego was on the floor. He called me and confessed, "We're all in mourning out here . . . I was very closed-minded in my thinking . . ." I was brought back out to work on "sweetening" some of the Cooke tapes still in Specialty's basement. Art was always impressed with how orderly I made things down there. Art had hired a meat-truck driver/songwriter to work in the Hollywood office and help me with the task: a guy named Salvatore "Sonny" Bono.

From the start Sonny impressed me with his open and friendly manner. He was a confident charmer and deceptively smart. My being from the South and from New Orleans seemed to heighten his curiosity about me. As we began to work together and he became aware of my background—my education, my experience as a teacher, and my skills as a jazz musician, arranger, and composer—he placed me on a pedestal. He had dropped out of high school and had never even thought about music lessons.

The two of us—me and Sonny—were charged by Art with digging up the old audition tapes we did for Sam and finding enough songs to make a complete album. These tapes were done casually and quickly with only Sam's guitar for accompaniment. Ultimately there were only a few that we felt could be doctored to sound marketable: "I Don't Want to Cry," "I'll Come Running Back to You," and "I Need You Now" were among them. I wrote chord chart arrangements for rhythm sections and background voice parts similar to what I had done for "You Send Me," and Sonny hired the musicians and the Lee Gotch Singers—the same singers who had been fired from the session that started it all.

The album was released on Specialty and did fairly well—it was riding the wave set off by "You Send Me." Right after this project, Art sent me back to New Orleans to continue scouting for Specialty, and Sonny stayed in L.A. I had no earthly idea what was in store for me, certainly no clue that Sonny Bono would play such a pivotal role in the direction my career would ultimately take.

chapter **4** specialty

The previous year's adventure out West opened many new possibilities for what I could do in music. But ultimately I wound up in New Orleans again, with my wife and two-year-old son; by the fall of 1957 it had sunk in that I was back home. Balancing my activities between my two families—Yette and Bunny, my parents—and my new job left little time for my jazz goals. But that was OK; I was optimistic about my opportunities.

I had gotten the go-ahead from Art Rupe to find office space for a Specialty Records branch in New Orleans. Houston's Music Store had recently opened on North Claiborne Avenue across from the American Federation of Musicians Local 496. (At that time, the Local 496, the Musicians Protective Union, was for Black musicians; the Local 174, the Musicians Mutual Protective Union, was for White musicians. They merged in 1968.) The music store's owner, William Houston, was the president of the union, music director at L. B. Landry High School, and leader of a popular society big band. I got a front office on the second floor over his store. I had a big Specialty sign made and hung it above the sign heralding Houston's Music Store. This presence in the community, I thought, would give us an edge in the talent search. To my surprise, Houston told me that my sign helped *his* business!

As the word got out I began to get calls, mostly for information at first, but in a short while I was auditioning singers, songwriters, and groups. I developed a system that helped me evaluate artists with some degree of consistency and objectivity, and I gave written suggestions about their songs and performance. Specialty's New Orleans office became a relaxed place where musicians, most of whom were first-timers, felt comfortable. In the auditions I tried to be supportive and encouraging, particularly when an artist was struggling. I had a lot of traffic, which kept me doing more paperwork than I had anticipated. Though I'd always had a secret desire to play office—which helped me to function in an orderly way and keep track of people's stuff—I didn't have anybody to play secretary.

I recorded all the auditions, with or without accompaniment, so I could reevaluate them later. Those

Left: Musician's Union Club (AFM local 496), 1408 North Claiborne Avenue, 1967; PHOTO BY WILLIAM RUSSELL (HOGAN JAZZ ARCHIVE)

Below: Specialty Records' New Orleans office, over Houston's music store, North Claiborne Avenue, ca. 1957; PHOTO BY JAMES LAROCCA (COURTESY OF JOHN BROVEN)

I thought had promise would be sent to Los Angeles for Art and Sonny to hear. Their perception of the New Orleans beat, groove, or sound was a little behind what was actually happening and developing on the streets. Local record labels took people that we passed on, some of them among the greats, like Chris Kenner, Irma Thomas, and Allen Toussaint. After rejecting several of the tapes I sent, Art finally gave me approval to record a group called the Monitors. I had known of the lead singer, Phoenix, from his work in the opera at Xavier University. He sang high tenor (falsetto) like Bill Kenny, the famous lead singer of the Ink Spots.

notable specialty sessions

"Lights Out"
Jerry Byrne
(February 1958)
Specialty #635 was the first significant product of my relationship with a talented young guitar player named Malcolm J. Rebennack. Mac evidently had been writing and "hustling" songs quite a while before he found me at Specialty. I liked some of his tunes (he always seemed to have lots of material to offer), and I got them recorded when I could. When Mac got comfortable with Specialty and me, he brought in Jerry Byrne, the singer from his band the Spades. Jerry came off very confident—almost cocky—and up—almost hyper—in his spirit. I thought the time was right for Specialty to get in the White R&B race. Of course, the several tunes Jerry auditioned were Mac's. We settled on four for Jerry's session, with the main focus on "Lights Out." Another Specialty artist, Art Neville, contributed the romping piano solo that made this tune the most exciting cut of the session, and I played a poor imitation of Lee Allen on the tenor sax again.

"Cha Dooky-Doo"
Art Neville
(April 1958)
One day Mae Vince walked into my office with a man, a guitar, and a song. From their appearance I judged them to be Cajun swamp people or hillbillies, neither of which was Specialty's thing, but out of courtesy and curiosity I listened. The song didn't make much sense, but I really liked it, maybe due to Mae's sincerity when she sang it. When I presented the song to Art Neville, he said he could do it—being the cooperative, nice guy he is; I didn't think he would refuse. After singing it a few times, he really began to like the novel phrase Cha Dooky Doo. He gave the song his unique styling, which has kept this rendition around all these years. The session guitarist, Justin Adams, had amplifier trouble that day, an intermittent distortion. We decided to crank it up so the distortion would be constant. Years later, I read in a popular rock magazine that we introduced the fuzz-tone sound in that session.

"I Can't Stop Lovin' You,"
"Steal a Little Kiss,"
"Bad Boy"
Larry Williams
(Summer 1958)
Whenever I went into the studio with Larry Williams ("Just Because," "Bony Moronie," "Short Fat Fannie"), I had to be ready for anything. Larry was spontaneous and always overflowing with ideas. He liked the arrangement to be created in the studio by trial and error. My job was one of subtlety, controlling the flow of things happening in the studio. "I Can't Stop Lovin' You," "Steal a Little Kiss," and "Bad Boy" were all created in the studio in this way. When possible, I did the cleaning-up in postproduction. My lasting impression of Larry is one of an excited, glad-to-be-on-stage bundle of ideas—a man in charge.

(PHOTOS OF BYRNE AND WILLIAMS COURTESY OF CONCORD MUSIC GROUP, INC.; PHOTO OF NEVILLE, THNOC)

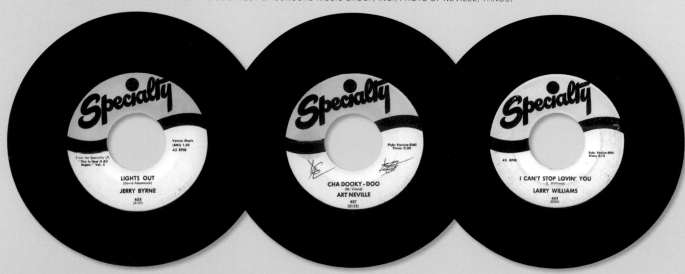

Signing and recording a group would be another first for me, and I was quite nervous dealing with the union contracts, calling the players, and renting the studio, in addition to writing the arrangements for the session and rehearsing the group. To help me get through my maiden voyage I assembled a group of experienced studio musicians, led by the guitarist and arranger Edgar Blanchard. Edgar was leader of the Gondoliers, a house band at the Dew Drop Inn. He had also already recorded as an artist for Specialty, so I felt safe with him on the set. I played my tenor sax on the session, trying my best to sound like Lee Allen, the sax man on all the hit records made in New Orleans during that time.

Lee was a gifted saxophone player with a great ear. His work quoted artists like Gene Ammons, Lester Young—jazz artists that everyone admired. Lee wasn't from New Orleans; he was from Denver or somewhere out West and had come to the city to go to Xavier. If Lee had stayed in jazz, he would have been as great as Young or Ammons, but studio work paid more than jazz gigs. Lee was more in Red Tyler's class and age group—men who were older than me. I always tried to imitate Lee but never felt like I measured up.

Lee Allen worked with us to record a timely, subject-type tune with a danceable beat, in the style of the era, called "Rock 'n' Roll Fever," and for the B side a doo-wop ballad, "Closer to Heaven," which showcased Phoenix's voice. The '50s style of music was focused on fun, stuff to play at parties or listen to on the radio as you drove around. Novelty songs like "You Talk Too Much" or "Check Mr. Popeye" (Eddie Bo's hit that sparked a popular local dance called the "Popeye") were the hip thing to do. Cats were pulling together small combos—guitar, bass, saxophone, piano, drums, and a vocalist, with some artists playing an instrument and singing—to create music that people wanted to hear. A lot of popular songs and local hits were made on the fly. Musicians would get together in folks' garages and start woodshedding (practicing), and songs were created that way. Also, some of the best music was done in the clubs, cats finding a spark in a moment and then just rolling with it. That was the beauty of the work, the spontaneous creativity that no one could see coming; it just happened and there it was: a hot sound that was pure joy.

Personal Struggles

In the midst of all this exciting work in the business, my foundation—my family—was still on shaky ground. There had been no resolution of issues with my father's business since his death, mostly because of my preoccupation with my job. Mother's health had also begun to decline rapidly. Although she had been a diabetic for as long as I could remember—as had her mother—her physical health wasn't the real problem. She had given up. She had actually said, before Daddy was even in the ground, "There's nothing left for me here . . ." I could not understand that at the time. I was here; her grandson—her Bunny—was here; the family, the church, the neighbors—all of us were here. But her Sweetheart was not, and no one else could ever take his place. She went into Flint-Goodridge Hospital on November 10, 1957, and three days later she left us.

At Mount Olivet Cemetery, my brother, Alvin, carried on "sompin' awful," as the old church folks used to say: crying and shouting, blocking them from lowering the casket, threatening to jump into the grave. In contrast, I was embarrassed because I could not cry. I carried guilty feelings about that for a long time. Years later, as I began to recognize my father in me—his ways, his manner, his expressions—I realized that he would not have cried either.

After Mother's death, I could no longer avoid dealing with my parents' estate. By 1951 they'd realized the goal of the projects—to give low-income families an opportunity to save and work toward home ownership—and purchased the shotgun double at 2418 Second Street, along with Daddy's sister, my Aunt Rita. The troublesome legal stuff had to do with the inheritance. My brother, Alvin, was really my father's nephew. There was never a legal adoption, and until Alvin went into the army in 1950, neither he nor any of the family even knew his legal name—we found out later that his given name was Albert Fall—so that's what we started calling him. My parents' half of the house was awarded to me as the legal heir. Since Albert had been raised in the family as my brother, I felt we should split the inheritance. But there were issues. Albert had developed a drinking problem. He was still living with our parents while working as a waiter at the Roosevelt Hotel. His weekly paycheck and tips went straight to the Dew Drop Inn and other bars until he was drunk, or broke, or both. By contrast, I was just beginning to build a family. Aunt Rita wanted to buy my half of the house, which would allow me the possibility of buying a home for my family. If I split my half with Albert, I would be left with less than the amount needed for a down payment. Although the choice was very difficult, I chose to act in the best interest of my young family. Albert was hurt and angry—understandably. He left the house, left the neighborhood, and moved way downtown to separate himself from the family that he felt had thrown him away. But he expressed none of this to me at the time; for years he carried bad feelings about me that he never shared.

Eventually, as things unfolded in his life that allowed the good person he had always been to surface, good things began to happen for him. He was "rescued" by a woman he'd dated years earlier. When he suffered a heart attack, she visited him in the hospital. She helped him clean up his life. Albert and Dorothy married, had a daughter, Lark, and he eventually became a deacon in the Baptist Church. He found a job as a courier for Judge Israel Augustine, and over the course of twenty years of service, he established himself as a respected and sought-after employee.

Home Sweet Home

By the spring of 1958, Art Rupe had become adjusted to the two youngsters—Sonny Bono and I—bringing new ideas to Specialty. I was beginning to feel comfortable and somewhat confident in my role—dealing with the music, production, and talent. My interactions with aspiring artists were especially fulfilling; I enjoyed helping and encouraging people with music. In many ways it was similar to my teaching experiences in DeRidder. But I was also becoming more familiar with the workings of the business side, and where the various people fit into the picture. For example, Joe Banashak of A-1 Distributors and Joe Ruffino of Ric Records were like second-level record guys—distributors. Banashak continued to be the key man for Specialty in New Orleans. (I got the impression that Specialty had some sort of financial stake in A-1.) Still, Sonny was more interested and involved than I in the business side of the industry—phone conferences with distributors, setting up payola deals with DJs, etc. In May I was brought back to Hollywood to work with Sonny at the home office and in the studio. A letter I wrote to Yette when I arrived hints at what was on my mind:

> *May 4, 1958*
>
> *Hello Honey*
>
> *I arrived safely at 8:05 on schedule after a very bumpy trip. While over Texas, the wind was very rough causing the plane to drop and rise something like 100 feet at a time. Sonny Bono and his wife, Donna, were waiting for me at the airport to bring me to their house, in their Ford convertible. We stopped and she bought a Porterhouse steak to fry for me at a Kory's, right around the corner from their house. By the way, they live in Gardina, out near the Vermont drive-in (Vermont and 140th). Sonny lives in a cozy little stucco with a wall-to-wall carpeted living and dining area, and two bedrooms (one of which she is fixing up for the baby she expects in about 3 weeks), a kitchen, bath and utility room, nice yard and two-car garage.*
>
> *After I ate the big steak, with spinach and cottage cheese (phew), we watched TV till about 1:30 a.m., then went to bed. As I write this, it is 2:30 Sunday morning and I plan to go to the studio and write some arrangements today. And also to check in to where I'll be staying. As soon as I do, I'll send you a card giving you the address. Well, so long Angel and be sweet.*
>
> *With love, Harold*

Oh yeah . . . I saw a sign up for a 3 bedroom house with a garage for $11,000.00 . . . also a three unit apartment for only $1,500.00 down and it brings an income of $155.00 a month.

During this trip, I carefully began to introduce Art to my family situation, letting him know of my goal of buying a house. I needed to learn as much as I could about financial dealings and also what help I could expect from Specialty. Art was known as a tough business negotiator with tight purse strings. His reputation generated comments like this one: "Man, he'll bargain you down to a one-cent royalty, but you can bet he'll pay you that penny!" I saw a side of him that seemed philosophical, with a soft spot for family values. Two young cats like Sonny and me, hustling, trying to get our families started, seemed just what he was looking for.

I found a house Uptown, in the Carrollton section of New Orleans, which seemed like a dream beyond my dreams. I had never been through that neighborhood before; I had assumed it was White, and it was mostly, but the FOR SALE sign was there, so I called. The issue of my race never seemed to surface, although it was in my mind. I went through all the legal hoops presented by the Rateau Real Estate Company, plus I got Specialty Records to send a letter verifying my employment to the National Mortgage Company. We qualified!

Preparing to move into our own house—the American dream! Yette, normally quite cool and restrained, was openly happy planning for the move. We hadn't thought about it, but our friends pointed out that we were the first among our group to take this step. I felt—maybe for the first time—like a real man, like the head of a household. Still, somehow I did not make the connection between buying a house and becoming a property owner. My attention was on the building, all the good feelings of family in our own home, with no thought to the land. It would be years before I began to understand the relationship between land ownership and wealth. I eventually learned that the ground itself—the land—that is what's real— the

Harold and Yette's first house, on Hickory Street in New Orleans; PHOTO BY ALISON CODY, 2009

real in *real estate*. The money or wealth that was attached to it wasn't real. It's an asset on paper that someone could use to demonstrate that they were worthy of financial respect. True wealth is in the land and the ownership of that land.

The former owner left the property in good shape. We were impressed with the hardwood floors and the high ceilings. The living room and two bedrooms seemed larger than the rooms any place I'd ever lived before. The kitchen and dining room were equally as large, with a second porch and entrance. There was a driveway along the side of the house all the way to the large backyard, where there was a two-car garage and a huge pecan tree. Yette used her exquisite decorating talents to develop color schemes for each room, and I drew floor plans with scale measurements of windows, doors, closets, etc. We went about shopping for everything from curtains to appliances. This was truly a very exciting time for us.

Our second child, Andrea Lynn, arrived in February 1959 to make the dream complete. A job, a home, a car, and two children—a boy and a girl—what more could we want? But the bubble had to burst. In March, when Andrea was only a month old, I was brought back out to the Hollywood office. I returned home in time for Bunny's birthday in April, and we had the whole summer to enjoy the house as a family.

My work for Specialty seemed less stressful during that time. I did more promoting and marketing than auditions. Art wanted me to write daily reports of my activities, which for the most part I did, but my attention was drawn to my family. I did do some recording sessions with Buddy Ace and Roy Montrell, which were small sellers. Around the time that I was introduced to these two cats, I began hearing a term— *the Chitlin' Circuit*. These musicians were rolling around the South and playing a lot of the small-town clubs that served Black folks looking for a good time on the weekends. This was like bread and butter for Ace, Montrell, Bobby "Blue" Bland, and a whole lot of other guys who made their living traveling from town to town, playing and learning.

Buddy Ace was an R&B singer in the growly, juke-joint style of Bland, and was known as the "Silver Fox of the Blues." He came out of Texas and was managed by Don Robey, owner of Duke Records, who was Houston's version of Frank Painia of New Orleans's Dew Drop Inn. Art Rupe had heard about Ace and turned him over to me because he wasn't interested in his style. Too raw, I guess. Art didn't think too much of Ace but actually thought that he was too good to throw away.

Roy Montrell was a good guitar player with jazz leanings. He was a smart guy but got hooked on drugs. He worked with me later on at All For One Records, but the drug hook was too strong. Unfortunately, Roy introduced Nat Perrilliat and Mac Rebennack (Dr. John) to heroin. I was too afraid to try anything other than a little weed, so I escaped that madness.

At the end of the summer of '59, Specialty brought me back to Hollywood—and this time they kept me there too long. Yette was alone in the new house with a new baby and a toddler. She had all the responsibilities of household management. Art kept stringing me along, saying, "Just one more week, Bat," or, "Just a few more days." I wrote several "Hi, Angel" letters to Yette, hoping to keep her spirits up and to help her understand the future potential of the work I was doing. I got a reply from her about a month later that left me with my first fear for our relationship. The body of her letter was very businesslike, but there was a postscript:

Please forgive me Harold if my letter doesn't seem warm, but I told you I don't know what it would take to make you believe that I don't have that feeling of affection any more. I lost that . . . the fact of needing you. I've needed you so much that I don't really need you any more. That's the truth. You know I [tell?] you I love you and always will for whatever may happen. It's just like when a person been in the habit of doing some one certain thing a lot and they fall into a habit. But once that habit is broken and all the things are taken away, the cure is on and that's how I feel. Now I'm not fixing to fall into it again for fear the same thing's going to happen to me. So I'm preparing you before you get home as what to expect and not to.

"I don't have that feeling . . ." That line struck me real hard, deeper than I could handle at the time. I buried it. I just put it away somewhere and continued working for the security of our little family. Still in L.A. as November came, I decided to get more assertive in my dealings with Art. I needed money, more than he was paying me, and I knew that Sonny was getting more than I was. I wrote out a script of a negotiation between him and me, in which I characterized us in our ethnic stereotypes:

November 13, 1959

NEGOTIATIONS: (Script given to employer Art Rupe by Battiste)

I understand now that it is just an accepted policy in business to bargain when it comes to money or deals. As I recollect our past together, whenever the money problem came up between us, you were naturally thinking in terms of bargaining. However, my not being a bargaining man, I'm at a disadvantage in getting what I need because I always quote what should be my last figure first. Then, the other party, thinking this figure is my beginning figure, quotes his first figure which is much less than what he thinks I really want. Starting like this, I never get what I need because I start out WRONG (being honest).

In order to prevent this scene, and in case you don't have time to talk, I've written out our little dishonest conversation which has a happy ending because it finally reaches an honest figure (which I should start out with in the first place . . . but don't.)

BAT: Art, I've figured out what I need to borrow from you to settle my home problems and re-establish my family in Los Angeles. I need a $1,350 loan and $200 expense. (beginning quote— not really what I need)

ART: Hmmm . . . Gee, Bat, that's a hell of a lot of money . . . frankly I don't see how I can loan you that much. When you said you needed loot I thought you meant 4 or 5 bills. [Four or five hundred dollars.]

BAT: Well, Art, the whole point of borrowing bread is to get enough at once to do me some good so I can secure myself at home and sustain my family a couple of months when we come back here. I don't know . . . Maybe we could make it with less . . .

ART: How much less?

BAT: Aw, I guess about $1,100 . . . (intermediate quote, getting close) . . . but I see how . . .

ART: Well, Bat, I'll let you borrow $700. See if you can make it with that, and if you can't then maybe I can come to the rescue . . .

BAT: But man, that ain't gonna make it. I just got to have at least $1,000. (honest quote at last)

ART: Hmmm . . . of course, Bat, you know you owe us $150 already.

BAT: Yes, I know.

ART: And you haven't started paying us that back yet. Now, how are you going to pay back $1,000?

BAT: You see, that's it. The $150 was just a one item shot that took care of one thing but didn't touch the whole living scene so that I could have some breathing room in my paycheck. But the grand would be enough at once to allow me to miss a few bucks a month out of my check.

ART: I see. Well, we'll include the $150 loan in your $1,000 loan and I'll ask Janet to make you a check for $850 . . .

BAT: Huh? Eight fif—?

ART: Sure, do you need it now? Or when do you want it?

BAT: Well . . . uh . . . I'd rather you mail that to me when I get home and just give me the $200 expense for traveling now.

He called all of us to a meeting: Dorothy (his secretary), Sonny, Van Meter, and me. Van was hired by Art after me and Sonny were already on board. He was in promotions—a PR man from Philly. I didn't have a lot of contact with him.

At that meeting they saw a side of me that even I rarely see. It may have been because I knew I was not getting a respectable deal for what I brought to the company, or maybe it was the letter from Yette; I don't remember. But I concluded the meeting by threatening to quit. Art responded by saying that he would get out of the business if I left. We all knew that his response was mostly drama. He did, however, make some concessions and "loaned" me some money.

I had fairly optimistic news to bring home about our financial situation, which I thought would help me deal with Yette's feelings about us. Things didn't get any worse, but they didn't get much better, either.

Alvin and Edith Batiste, our closest friends, moved into our neighborhood, just around the corner. They had been our marriage witnesses, and we had been theirs. Alvin and I had known each other since before he went to high school. He used to come by my house with his clarinet when I lived across from the Dew Drop Inn. I was about two years ahead of him, but Alvin was serious about the clarinet, and in a short time he surpassed me. He met Edith Chatters in the Booker T. Washington High School band; she also played the clarinet. Both families had two children, a boy and a girl, and there was much back and forth between our houses. Their presence in our lives at that time was a blessing, and I think we were a blessing to them too.

Harold X

Emery Thompson, a large cat that everyone called "Big Fat Emery," was New Orleans's answer to Fats Navarro. He was a superior trumpet player and had a lot of respect in our musical circle; everybody that knew us knew him. Emery got into the drug scene but continued to play music like a master. He was recruited by the Nation of Islam, and his involvement with the Nation helped him kick his drug habit. But they convinced Emery, who had changed his name to Umar Sharif, to stop playing because of concerns that he might fall back into the drug life.

Sharif convinced me to join the Nation. He was deeply in line with everything the group stood for. After several discussions I agreed to join and wrote a letter to officials in Chicago to be admitted and get my X. The protocol was to send a handwritten letter requesting admission. The Nation was strict and specific; they sent my letter back twice because it wasn't up to their standards for neatness and spelling. I made the necessary corrections, sent the proper letter, and received admittance.

Now I was Harold X, but I never changed my name in legal form or asked to be addressed in that manner. I realized that I wasn't going to adhere to the Nation's tenet of street proselytizing or regarding White people as "devils." I respected the Nation's ideals as they related to uplifting the Black race, but that's as far as things went with me.

So Long Specialty, Hello AFO

I didn't see it coming, but Art Rupe was gearing up to shut down Specialty. He had talked about how he hated the way the record business was going—payola scandals and all. He was angry that we had to have our product judged by disc jockeys before we could get airplay. The way he saw it, "DJs are radio announcers, not musicians; they should have to pay *us* for giving them music to play!" In December he asked me to close the Specialty office in New Orleans and work out of my house.

REPORTS

12-18-59

In the past three weeks, the traffic at my home-office has almost come up to that which I had at the office-office.

I've got three (maybe four) sessions on the planning board. One to be done immediately with Neville, and the others to be possibly split between Issacher, The Cousins, Angel Face (not signed yet) and Alberta Hall, if she comes through with some tough material. I understand Alberta has been with Specialty before and had a record out in the 50's or 60's. If so, I'd like to have a copy and the sales figs in her strongest area, no matter how small.

Battiste

I continued to work as though I could rescue Specialty and somehow turn things around. Sonny seemed a little less optimistic. I think he was in on some things that I didn't know about. In the middle of March, I received a letter that has been referred to as "the Bomb" ever since. In short, I got fired. Of course, it was worded in a way that sounded like something else, almost as though I was getting a better deal—I got "restructured." A series of letters ensued that characterized what was happening at the time.

3-18-60

Dear Bat:

To follow up yesterday's bomb, I would like to discuss our attitude on the artists you contacted on our behalf.

1. Those we have already signed, please advise them that we will consider any songs they have for another session. This includes Angel Face, Issacher, Neville, and The Cousins.

2. The "Blenders" sound exciting. Please sign this group on our behalf for a session—and send us their audition.

As I pointed out to you yesterday, we may make you a producer's price to handle individual sessions of the above talent. On any talent, other than the above, we would make you an even better deal.

This arrangement will give you flexibility to work for anybody you choose; and, if you're lucky on the new stuff, it can give you a nice return.

Regards, SPECIALTY RECORDS, INC.

3-22-60

Bat,

I hope Papa [Art Rupe] didn't catch you completely off guard with his letter. Van Meter got it too. This guy gets more stupid with time. I'll probably get it too. I hope to be set up and swinging (long) before I do. The only reason I'm still here is to listen to talent and keep all the pills off his back. I don't give a damn though, cause I sit around all day and work at night.

It was good talking to you on the phone. I didn't get a chance to explain all that I wanted to, so that's why I'm writing. I don't know what he proposed to you about masters, but believe me, you'll never make any money with this nut. In the first place, if you cut a good record, it wouldn't sell, and then you'll have a hell of a time cutting a good record if he has anything to do with it. This Co. is going no place but down and its going fast. He is not really interested in records. He's too damn busy. I wish you were here so you could see what I'm trying to tell you. He's a very deadly cat, as you know by now. I could go on for three days telling you how stupid he is, but since you have been out here and made the scene I know you understand. But, I don't understand why you would consider doing any more business with him. You'll only get screwed! And you know that's true. I wanta say one more thing about him, just to show how big hearted he is. When I got sick and had to [go] to the hospital, I was out for two weeks. After putting in so many hours here, (like an ass), I thought sure he'd pay, but he didn't. So, that was it man! From then on, I've been working for Sonny Bono.

Bat, as I told you over the phone, I think we could make a great team. I have really been hustling, and have a lot of good deals set up for us. The thing that I'm most excited about is that Sound [Enterprises] wants to go into the record business with me. This means free studio time and office. I think I can work something out with the musicians. Then I'll have the whole setup for nothing. I have a couple of people who will put up money for sessions if I don't get free musicians. As you know, talent is no problem, so all I need now is some luck and some good sessions.

I have been working with H. B. [Barnum]. We just finished a session the other night. Rene' Hall wants to go in with me, too. I also had a talk with Jimmy [Haskell]. The only reason I'm mentioning these names is to show that I'm not the only one who thinks it's a good deal. None of these guys have the talent that you do. I would like very much to work with you. I think we could make it. The only thing is that I want to get rolling soon, so I have to know what you're going to do.

This is just my opinion, but I think you're just wasting your time and your wonderful talent down there. Now is the time for you to set some kind of goal. You're still young and not too involved to make a good fresh start in life. I have all the faith in the world in you.

I have a lot of plans for us, Bat, but I won't go into that, though, cause I'd never finish this letter. So now I'll expect to hear from you very soon. Think over everything I said carefully. If you decide to make it out here man, hurry up. We have a future to build.

P.S. Be sure you send your letter to my home. Everybody and their dog reads mail from you.

Sonny

4-14-60

Dear Bat,

I've been waiting for your master. What happened? If you can get it out here, I'll see what I can do with it. I have a few companies I can place it with.

I wish you would keep me posted on what you're doing. When I talked to you on the phone, it sounded like things were pretty rough. I hope not. From now on, if you want to reach me, I'll be at Sound Enterprises or home. So, if you have any masters or songs you want to send me, mail them to Sound Enterprises, c/o Sonny Bono, 5539 Sunset Boulevard, Hollywood 28, California.

I cut a session the other night, and it came out great (at least I thought so). It was a biggie—15 pieces and union. I got three good releases out of it. I'm going to release them myself. I'm not going to sell the masters—I come out too short that way.

As long as you're going to stay in New Orleans, I would like to have you represent these releases as promo and salesman. You know if anything happens, I'll give you a taste. So, please write me as soon as you can and let me know if you are able to do this. Please write me soon, though, as you have tendencies to be a hang-up about writing. I'm going to write Joe, too, and see if he wants to distribute for me.

By the time you get this letter, I'll have pressings, so I'll just send them to you. When you do write, let me know how many records you want. For now, I'll send you 25.

If you need any help from out here, let me know and I'll do whatever I can.

I'm going to make it now. Be sure and let me know what you think of the sides.

Sonny

4-18-60

Hey Man [Sonny]:

I was delayed in sending the master because there was a bad distortion in the guitar amp on one of the sides. I wasn't at the session when the cats cut and I've been trying to see if we could do anything to clean the thing up. I couldn't. However, the "A" side came out good. It's called "Lover of Love." The artist is Lee Dorsey. Get whatever you think is the best deal and you're in for half of my share.

I'm going to buckle down to this typewriter and keep you hip to what's happening on my end. Right now, I'm gigging with a band which I hope will get me to L.A. These cats are all swinging, funky, versatile cats and I know they have a good chance of copping some boss gigs once we get out there.

Sounds like you cut a real boss session. I'll do my best to see that you get a fair shake in this area. If I need more than the 25 copies, I'll write. Of course, as soon as I receive them, I'll let you know what I think.

Tell everybody "hey man" for me.

Later, Battiste

Sonny had a lot of ideas, but I had ideas of my own. On my last train trip home to New Orleans from California, I had begun to formulate the concept of a musicians' cooperative to start a record company. When the train stopped in El Paso, Texas, who should board but Earl King, a New Orleans blues singer and composer who recorded the hit "Trick Bag." He became the first person to hear my idea.

chapter **5** **all for one**

For some time, I had been thinking about the economic state of Black people in America and, more specifically, Black people in New Orleans. I'd been listening to speeches from the Honorable Elijah Muhammad, messages that often spoke to the need for our people to create wealth through ownership. It seemed that every ethnic group was identified with a product or service that they owned and controlled, and it seemed that the product generally attributed to us was music: jazz, blues, R&B, gospel. We should be working toward collective ownership and control of the American music industry. In the three years I'd worked for Specialty Records, I'd become familiar with how the music business worked. I thought, *This ain't as complicated as I thought. We can do this!*

The Rationale for a Cooperative
November 19, 1959
Musicians' Cooperative Records, Inc.

This concept is founded on the principle that today's record industry is realizing tremendous success, largely due to the participation of MUSICIANS. To date, musicians have performed millions of dollars worth of music on records, but have they shared in the profits that they have contributed their talents to earning? NO! Because they have performed as laborers, thus earning a salary (a very good one by the way), and thereby eliminating any possibility of becoming eligible to share in the profits of the very lucrative Record Industry.

Let's examine a hypothetical case: Musician X, a resident of this city (New Orleans) is used on record dates, averaging 1 per week for 1 year at $48.50 per date. His gross income for the year is $2,522. Averaging 3 sides per session, then, Musician X has played on 159 sides that year (or 78 records). Obviously, Musician X is in demand because he has contributed to many hit records. Now let's say that just 1 of the 78 records on which he played sold not 1 million but 500,000 copies; had Musician X not been working for a set salary but instead 2 percent royalty, he would earn from that 1 out of 78 $10,000!

With the plan I had in mind, I would need Melvin Lastie, the union rep for the local 496. This was strictly business, part of my strategy to get proper pay and recognition for peer musicians. Melvin was from the 9th Ward, and I was from Uptown; we lived in two different worlds. Friendship would come later, but right now, we were all business. Melvin's job was to police the recording studios to make sure the musicians were all in good standing with the union, and that the recording sessions were in compliance with union rules. Melvin and I started by identifying the studio musicians with the best track records in town. We needed a foundation of basic instrumentation for the company. We approached each musician individually and laid out the plan. John Boudreaux would play drums; Peter "Chuck" Badie, bass; Allen Toussaint, piano; Roy Montrell, guitar; Alvin "Red" Tyler, saxophone; with Melvin on cornet. I was elated and surprised that this dream team of studio players—a first-call cache of musicians who were known for their experience, professionalism, and ability to make hits happen—were anxious to be a part of our experiment.

Melvin and I took the lead in finding out how to get started. We would need legal and financial advice: we needed to be incorporated and licensed by the city, the state, or somebody, and we needed money! This was all new and strange territory for both of us, but it was comforting to discover that we were not alone in our ignorance. As we made inquiries at City Hall to the various agencies, they seemed not to understand what a record company was or did. They kept trying to make it into a retail record store. We also learned that there wasn't a Black attorney in town familiar with the music business. We convinced some Black attorneys at a young law firm on Claiborne Avenue that we would provide an opportunity for one of them to learn with us. On May 29, 1961, at twelve o'clock noon, the state of Louisiana acknowledged the legal birth of AFO Records, Inc.

In the meantime, the team was ready to start making music. Because things had changed at Specialty in the spring of 1960, I was now free to function as an independent producer. The term *producer* was new to me in the record business. As an A&R man I was paid a salary, but as a producer I was on my own. I made a deal to do some A&R work for Ric Records, a local company, and with that deal came the use of their studio. Ric was located in the 300 block of Baronne Street, in New Orleans's Central Business District. There were several record distributors in the block; Ric was upstairs from All South Distributors. Ric had established itself with some of the city's best artists—Johnny Adams, Irma Thomas, Eddie Bo, Tommy Ridgley, and Martha Carter among them.

We began to gather at Ric's studio late at night, after everybody else had finished their gigs, so that we could get familiar with the room and the equipment. One night we were waiting on a bass player, Richard Payne, till after 2:00 a.m. The phone rang and Richard was on the line, calling from a phone booth on the corner to warn us that the place was surrounded by the police, guns and rifles out and ready for business. After a few minutes of fear and panic, I decided to go down and surrender, complete with a white flag, and calmly explain why we were there at that hour. They listened, and I invited them to come up and check out (search) the studio and office. One of them spotted a photo of me in a magazine article on the wall, and that sort of cooled things out. They even stayed to hear us play. We actually got them to listen to some of our music!

"You Talk Too Much"
Around this time I had started playing with Joe Jones again. Me, Joe, and a lot of young cats had just joined the union and were looking to play wherever we could. Joe had gigs every weekend out in small towns in Louisiana and Mississippi, mostly for White dances and clubs. Joe played fair piano and sang enough to do a Fats Domino repertoire. He'd gotten a song from another piano player, Reggie Hall, that we played on these gigs. The response from the people persuaded us that the song had potential.

Joe Jones, a convincing salesman, got Ric Records' owner, Joe Ruffino, to let us record the song in

Joe Jones's tour wagon outside the Ajapo Hotel in Houston, TX, 1950s (THNOC)

his studio. It was an easy session because we'd been developing the arrangement on the gigs. George Davis played bass and Leo Morris was the drummer, with Jones rounding out the rhythm section on piano. I played the tenor sax, Teddy Riley was on trumpet, and there was a third horn man I can't recall. That's how we recorded "You Talk Too Much."

When the song was released, Joe and I felt strongly that it could go all the way to the top, but we knew Ric Records never promoted nationally. Joe got Ruffino to give him three hundred dollars for the two of us to do a promotion trip. We headed east to Atlanta in Jones's station wagon, then back to Memphis and up to St. Louis. We stopped in every little town where we saw an antenna, no matter the station's format—blues, pop, country, talk, news, whatever, we left a copy of the record—and more often than not we got it played!

We got some great publicity when we landed in Chicago. Before we'd left New Orleans, I had suggested that we send a copy to Fidel Castro, who was making marathon speeches on television. I thought the name of the song alone would get a reaction. We received an official letter from Castro's staff thanking us for the record and for our support (they didn't get the joke!). We hit Johnson Publications in Chicago with our letter from Castro and got a plug—with a picture—in *JET*, a weekly magazine affiliated with *Ebony* magazine.

Our next stop was Detroit, where the record was already getting played. We hit the stations and met the DJs, some who knew us. As we were leaving, we had car trouble. The repairs left us with barely enough cash to get to New York, but we made it. When we arrived in the city we headed to Harlem. Between us, we had a bankroll of twenty-nine cents! Joe spotted a leftover newspaper with an ad for an appearance by Lloyd Price at Coney Island—we were saved! I'd known Lloyd back in the day, even toured with him for a couple of weeks in 1959. We got a penny from a security guard in the subway station so we could get two fifteen-cent tokens to take the train out to the show. By now "You Talk Too Much" was on the *Billboard* and *Cash Box* charts, and Lloyd and his manager, Harold Logan, knew about it. When we told them what we were up to, they wanted to help us out. They put us up in an apartment on Riverside Drive (across the hall from basketball giant Wilt Chamberlain!). Now, this was my first time in New York, and I was appropriately awestruck. It's big! I don't know if it was bigger than Los Angeles, but it sure was taller!

By this time Joe Ruffino had joined us in New York. We went to meet Lloyd's record-label people at Roulette. So we met these executive guys with tough-sounding names and faces to match, but they treated us real nice. They wined and dined us at one of their spots, a club called the Roundtable. I began to relax and enjoy things, but Joe Jones didn't seem as confident as he usually was. There was some talk about "You Talk Too Much" and Ric Records, but the conversation was not clear to me. It would become clear the next day, when I learned that Ruffino had already been to New York to meet with the Roulette people. That meeting had resulted in "You Talk Too Much" becoming a Roulette record. Joe knew this, but he hadn't told anyone that he'd previously recorded the song for Roulette.

Things got different from that point. Me and Joe were moved to the Alvin Hotel downtown. He had a mysterious visit from Sylvia (of the Mickey and Sylvia duo, who hit with "Love Is Strange"), with offers from Roulette. Joe began to get nervous and started talking about checking out of the hotel incognito. Fortunately, with all its complications, things turned out well. "You Talk Too Much" went on to become a big hit, and Joe Jones's signature song.

In the meantime, Lloyd Price and his manager, Harold Logan, were planning to put Joe and me in an upcoming tour. Lloyd toured with his own fourteen-piece band. He didn't know much about me, but Joe convinced him and Logan that I was the musical director they needed for the tour. The show's line-up was Lloyd, Joe Jones, the Shirelles, and Delores Ware. Lloyd was now—once again—on top. Since his first hit on Specialty, "Lawdy Miss Clawdy," he had done a stint in the army, after which he did "Just Because" for another label. That hit brought a cover recording from Specialty Records (Lloyd's former label) for Larry Williams. With the hit "Personality," Lloyd became a crossover artist, moving out of the R&B niche into the pop world, and, with his manager, he became more involved in the business side of entertainment.

The Test

Lloyd and his manager had planned a recording session for Delores Ware. They had one song for her to do, "It's Strange," and needed another. I submitted "Falling in Love," which I had written for Blanche Thomas when I was at Specialty. Joe Jones had touted me as a great arranger, so they asked me to do the charts for the session—and they needed them by the next day! I told Joe that I needed a real funky drummer for the tune. Joe called New Orleans for Leo Morris (later known as Idris Muhammad) and flew him up to New York. I was up all night writing in a hotel room, with no piano to do a check on.

Imagine: it's my first time in New York, and I'm going into a New York recording studio to face New York musicians with my unchecked charts for strings—violins, violas, and cellos. Lloyd and Logan in the booth. I was scared, but I was cool. After the first run-through of "Falling in Love," I relaxed. The musicians, particularly the string players, loved what I'd written. I got the approval I needed.

"It's Strange" called out our imported funk drummer, Leo. No one present at the session had ever heard anything like him. Singer Jackie Wilson's manager was in the booth with Lloyd and Harold Logan, and he begged to buy that track for Jackie. He couldn't believe strings could be that funky—he didn't realize that it was Leo making them feel like that. Thanks to Joe for being cheeky and bold enough to send for our drummer from New Orleans, I passed the New York test.

Juggy Comes to Town

Early in 1961 Melvin Lastie and I actually started auditioning and recording demos of potential AFO artists. We were delving deeper into the business side—manufacturing, distribution, marketing, and promotion—and this was brand new territory for us. I got a phone call from Los Angeles from a guy named Juggy Murray, who said he was looking for someone to be an A&R man for his record company in New York. He had been given my name, with high recommendations, by Sonny Bono. I thanked Mr. Murray for considering me for the position but told him that I was involved in a project I could not leave. He was curious, so I explained what we were doing. He got very excited: "Hold everything, I'm coming down there! Don't sign anything!" Then we were excited too.

Juggy spotted us at the airport. He could tell that we were looking for someone we didn't know. We didn't pick him out of the crowd—we certainly hadn't thought he would be a Black man! That was a comforting surprise. Over the next two or three days, Juggy worked out a deal for us to produce masters of artists we discovered, and he would finance the production and distribute the records on our label nationally. This was the solution to our problem regarding manufacturing, distribution, marketing, and promotion.

Recording at Cosimo's Studio

During April and May we got serious about deciding who we wanted to record to launch our company. Melvin's nephew Jessie Hill had a big hit record, "Ooh Poo Pah Doo," on the Minit label, and he wanted to record for our company. But Jessie could not break his contract with Minit, so he started scouting talent for us instead of recording. One day he came by with a singer named Barbara, and a guitar player named Prince to accompany her. Prince, whose real name was Lawrence Nelson, was the brother of Walter "Papoose" Nelson, a guitarist in Fats Domino's band. Prince had a song for Barbara to do called "You Put the Hurt on Me." When Barbara had trouble with the rhythm, he sang it to help her get the feel. He sounded so good, we decided to record him on that song and get something else for Barbara. She had the words to several songs written in a tablet, and I found chords on the piano that fit her words. The chords to the old gospel tune "Just a Closer Walk with Thee" fit perfectly with a song she called "I Know (You Don't Love Me No More)." In June 1961 we went into Cosimo Matassa's studio and recorded Prince La La and Barbara George.

Clockwise from left: AFO artists the Blenders, who had one hit with AFO, "The Graveyard." AFO used them as a test to see if Juggy Murray would actually pay (THNOC); Barbara George (AMISTAD RESEARCH CENTER); Prince La La (THNOC); ALL PHOTOS BY PORTER NEWS SERVICE.

Cosimo's, on Governor Nicholls Street, seemed always to be in some state of development. At one point, the air conditioning consisted of a big fan blowing over blocks of ice, then through a large plastic tube into the studio. But the hits kept coming out of that place! Cosimo was much more than a brilliant recording engineer—he loved the music and the people who created it. His contribution was to capture as much of the music's spirit as possible.

The musicians for the session included Nat Perrilliat on tenor sax, Chuck Badie on bass, John Boudreaux on drums, and Benny Spellman and two ladies as background singers. Due to contractual commitments to Minit, Allen Toussaint had to discontinue his affiliation with AFO; consequently, I took over on the piano. Red Tyler, who had the most studio experience and was a stellar ax man, got things started by coming up with a riff for the opening of "You Put the Hurt on Me." La La's performance in the vocal booth was outstanding. He exceeded all our expectations and invoked the spirit that made magic in the studio that day. We did a split session, two songs on each artist. Barbara's tunes were easy, partly because the feeling in the studio was right, but also because I had rehearsed it with her for a couple of days. Even though it was her first time in the studio, our rehearsals had made her a little more comfortable in the new setting. Most pop and R&B records had guitar or sax solos, but I had written a solo for Melvin to play on his cornet on "I Know." It turned out that the cornet solo was as big a hit as the song.

Hildebrand's Prediction

While awaiting the process of getting the records ready for release, we went about the business of getting ready for business. I enrolled in the Hamilton Institute of Business to take a correspondence course. We were operating out of my home, so our first letterhead and business cards had my address. With the help of our attorney, Freddie Warren, we had applied to the state to be incorporated as All For One Records, Inc. It was Melvin who thought to call it All For One. I didn't think it sounded like a good name for a record company, but when it was shortened to AFO Records, I was cool.

The word was getting out about us, and a buzz was beginning to happen. We went to meet with one of the local distributors to get some insight on how we were going to deal at this level. We went to see Henry Hildebrand, whose All South Distributors was on the ground floor of Ric Records' building. At the end of our meeting, Mr. Hildebrand, holding our black AFO business card, thought for a minute, then spoke: "Man, if you guys get a hit, y'all gonna get *all* the Black artists on AFO!"

WYLD

Larry McKinley, Bob Hudson, Groovy Gus—all the DJs must have gotten the word and been waiting for AFO's debut release. It was an unforgettable, indescribable, exhilarating moment for me when I heard Prince La La's voice for the first time on WYLD, a New Orleans R&B radio station, singing "You Put the Hurt on Me." I was alone in my car, listening to the radio, and it was our artist, our song, our music, our label, and it was on the radio, and everybody was hearing it!

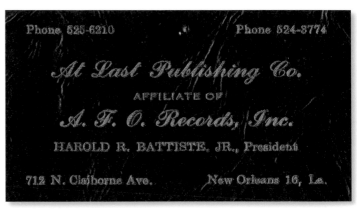

Meanwhile, a Black label owner from New York, Bobby Robinson, had sent a representative to New Orleans to record an up-and-coming body-and-fender man named Lee Dorsey, who also sang. Allen Toussaint was the intended producer for the project, but due to his contractual commitments to Minit Records, he suggested they get me. I had arranged Dorsey's first recordings, "Lottie Mo" and "Lover of Love." Allen had coached Lee for this session, so arranging and producing "Ya Ya" and "Do-Re-Mi" was simple for me.

Robinson released "Ya Ya" about two months before AFO's second release, Barbara George's "I Know," and it went to the top of the charts before our record did. Melvin and I and all the AFO team were overjoyed that in six short months we had three successful productions on the charts. We believed our destiny was to tap the wellspring of talent in New Orleans and supply the brothers up North with a string of hits.

Celebration—Too Soon?

In October 1961 we moved into offices at 712 North Claiborne Avenue, at the corner of Orleans Avenue. The area had several bars, clubs, restaurants, and various other business establishments. AFO was upstairs, above a clothing store that had just been vacated. That location proved handy for selling our records, too: we sold our music at gigs, especially at the Joy Tavern, so it was a logical thing to open a record store on an informal basis. It was almost an afterthought. We didn't even go through the process of registering the shop with the city.

AFO's office was located at the corner of Orleans and North Claiborne avenues; PHOTO BY ALISON CODY, 2009.

AFO party for music industry players at Vernon's Supper Club, 1961. *Left to right:* Henry Hildebrand, [?] Schafer, Cannonball Adderley, George Trueheart, Nat Adderley, Harold Battiste, Mel Lastie, Hoss Allen, Peter Badie, Cosimo Matassa, Alvin Tyler; PHOTO BY PORTER NEWS SERVICE (THNOC)

As we settled in to establish policies that would govern how we did business, I began to come down from the fantasy part of the dream and face all the hard realities regarding what I had gotten these cats into: artist and songwriter contracts, talent auditions, public relations and promotion, and a whole world of things that playing the piano and writing arrangements didn't help. We were a group of musicians trying to be businessmen—seriously!

The AFO executives decided to throw a bash for all the people who supported us and did so much to get us off to a great start. It was a wonderful night at Vernon's Supper Club, the hippest spot in the 'hood, where jazz sets were frequent and top-shelf. The room was filled with personalities from every part of the music scene in New Orleans, but the spotlight was on the DJs from radio station WYLD, since they were first to air our music.

We were really hot. In early 1962 the Adderley Brothers, a jazz duo out of Florida made up of brothers Julian "Cannonball" and Nat Adderley, came to New Orleans with Orrin Keepnews of Riverside Records to record with some of our players in Cosimo's studio. Cannonball, an alto saxophonist who was a part of Miles Davis's combo and would go on to reach jazz/R&B fame with the hit "Mercy, Mercy, Mercy," and Nat, a jazz cornet player in the hard bop realm, were true stars in our world. They were the shit! Their music reputation was impeccable, and they had fallen in love with the music and the people in New Orleans. Cannonball, a former schoolteacher, was a very conscious thinker and was on a path similar to ours. He admired what we had started and wanted to find ways for us to help each other.

We were on top of the world, but we may have been celebrating too soon.

Left to right: Mel Lastie, Alvin Tyler, Cannonball Adderley, Roy Montrell, Harold Battiste, Peter Badie, and Nat Adderley, 1962; PHOTO BY PORTER NEWS SERVICE (THNOC)

Mel Lastie, Harold Battiste, and Juggy Murray with Barbara George's gold record on AFO, "I Know (You Don't Love Me No More)" (THNOC)

Barbara Drops a Bomb

"I Know" had reached the top of the R&B charts in November 1961, and it was number three on the pop charts. Juggy got Barbara with a booking agency in New York and we prepared her for the road. She was only nineteen and had not seen much outside New Orleans. She was truly a diamond in the rough—*raw* rough. Melvin and I went with her on the first show at the Regal Theater in Chicago, and we hired her cousin to stay with her on the tour. We knew she would be OK when she got to the Apollo in New York because Juggy would take care of her.

In early March 1962 we got a call at our office from Barbara's mother, who said that Barbara wanted to buy her contract from AFO. I thought her mother must have misunderstood something about our agreement with Barbara, but she hadn't. We went to her house in the Desire Project to figure out what was going on. After talking through the situation with the guys, it was decided that me and Melvin better go to New York. For anyone out there who believes the myth about the so-called glamour of the music industry: the day we had in New York would kill it. It was hard, often tedious work, even though I got tremendous satisfaction (and sometimes heartache) from it.

Tuesday, 3-27-1962
Upon our arrival, met Jug at airport accidentally. He said he suspected we were coming. The scene was cold. It was obvious that a very close relation between Barbara and Jug had come about.

Wednesday, 3-28-1962
9:00 a.m. We called Allen Arrow [Juggy's lawyer]. He was not in. He was expected in a half an hour. We went to his office. We discussed the evaluation of Barbara's worth. Arrow played the middle-of-the-road part and he attempted to put Jug in an "innocent bystander" role. Also, he suggested that

Barbara pay in $7,500 plus a royalty, then we gave him our estimate of $42,000 plus royalty. Arrow said that we should meet with Jug the next day and in the meantime, he would see if he could get more money from her through Jug.

11:00 a.m. I called the Shaw Agency and talked with Dick Boone.

11:30 a.m. We went to Cash Box and talked with reporter Jerry Shifrin. He knew something was wrong with Jug and Barbara.

Noon. Went to Billboard and saw reporter Hal Rand. Hal said Jug was mad at him, also that Jug had listed Barbara in an ad as being managed by Coed Mustang? Tracked down James Arnold at Shaw. Talked with Dick Boone and Arnold. Arnold had been fired by Barbara. He was very sore because he thought he had a bright future with her and Jug. He disclosed quite a bit of incidentals which verified many of our suspicions, in effect, he said the two of them—Barbara and Juggy—were going together. We went back upstairs to make an appointment with Cannonball and also to see Jug and make sure he was aware of our meeting with Arrow. We saw Ball, but could not contact Jug nor Barbara. We saw Jug for a minute after last show about the appointment. Juggy and Barbara were leaving the theater hurriedly. Through a conversation with Leo Morris, we discovered that a friend of his was also leaving the theater in order to play drums on a recording date behind Barbara.

Thursday, 3-29-62

10:30 a.m. We had an appointment at Arrow's office with Jug and Barbara. The discussion began by Arrow making it clear that Barbara was buying her contracts from AFO and Jug was only loaning her the money. Of course, Jug insisted that he didn't want anything for his part of the contract. Barbara's opening offer was $7,500 and a 1 percent royalty on future records. Our opening offer was $46,000 straight. Barbara's second offer, after debate, was $15,000 and a penny. We countered with $25,000 with a penny after she earned the $25,000 back on future records. They went into a conference while Melvin and I were asked to stay out. They called us back in and offered $20,000 with $12,000 advance and $7,500 balance. We didn't budge from our $25,000. We debated. Jug "cried broke." He came in for the $25,000 with a $15,000 advance and $10,000 balance and one cent after the $15,000. Papers to be drawn up and signed tonight upon receipt of certified check for $25,000.

11:30 a.m. We went to BMI to check on whether our songs had been submitted and cleared through our whole file. Results are shown on my list. Ma suggested that on our 50% deals we submit our songs ourselves for our 50% and also that we return tonight to issue license on our 50%. We applied for an advance against "I Know."

1:30 p.m. We went to see Gilbert Rogers at the A.F.M. We waited awhile. When he didn't return from lunch, we set up an appointment for Friday morning. From there, we went to Passintino [a store that sold forms, copyrights, contracts and other such items for musicians] to pick up some forms and see about getting new contracts for artists.

3:30 p.m. We headed upstairs to catch the show. Barbara was on at the Apollo. Her act, in my opinion, had not improved at all since her Chicago date. Back stage while waiting to see Jug and Arrow, Leo pointed out Barbara's new Cadillac. He also told us the results of last night's secret session. He said they only got two tracks, Barbara had gone to sleep in the studio, while Jug was arguing with the musicians about what he wanted. The arranger walked out, telling Jug he didn't want his money. They went 1½ hours overtime, and all the musicians' noses were open.

10:00 p.m. Jug and Arrow came backstage to close our deal. We went to Barbara's dressing room to sign the papers and received the certified check.

AFO After Juggy— The Dream Is Gone

Although there was some jubilation in the fact that we got paid, the money—which seemed like a lot to us—was not enough to compensate in any way for our loss. We'd been very close to Barbara. My efforts at AFO were grounded in an idea that would later be called the Nguzu Saba, the Seven Principles of Kwanzaa: Umoja (unity), Kujichagulia (self-determination), Ujima (collective work and responsibility), Ujamaa (cooperative economics), Nia (purpose), Kuumba (creativity), and Imani (faith). I had entrusted my dream to a man who had a Black face on face value alone. That experience in no way dimmed my vision of my people nor the principles upon which my hopes were founded. It did, however, teach me the fallacy in judging a book by its cover.

Where would we go from here? What could or should we do next? We would need to establish our own independent identity.

New Artists

The trouble and trauma of the events with Barbara and Juggy took some effort to overcome. I knew that I did not really want to turn into a strict business person, certainly not in the record business. None of us at AFO had the temperament or personality for the rough edges of this game. So we turned our attention to what we enjoyed and did fairly well: making music!

Henry Hildebrand had predicted that, with any success, all the Black artists would flock to AFO. Several did: Tami Lynn, Eddie Bo, the Tick Tocks, Willie Tee, Wallace Johnson, Pistol, Charles Carlson, Robbie Lee, the Turquinettes, the Woods Brothers, James Booker, Drits & Dravy (Mac & Ronnie), and Shirley Raymond; and on the jazz side Johnny Adams, the Ellis Marsalis Quartet, and the American Jazz Quintet. AFO had possibly the broadest variety of artists among all the record companies in New Orleans. From blues to jazz to funk to pop, kids to adult, male and female, Black and White. We spent a lot of time in every phase of production: selecting material, rehearsing, writing arrangements, hiring musicians, and finally recording in Cosimo's studio.

The Woods Brothers, ca. 1962; PHOTO BY PORTER NEWS SERVICE (AMISTAD RESEARCH CENTER)

All of our records were great, but none of them was a hit. Some were never even released. Among those that were, Willie Tee's "Always Accused" got the most airplay. Willie (Wilson Turbinton) was a gifted young piano player/singer/songwriter whom I had known since he was in junior high. Red Tyler felt that Turbinton was not a good name for an artist, so he dubbed him Willie Tee, and the name stuck for forty years!

In 1962 AFO decided to start a subsidiary label. This was a common practice among record companies, in order to prevent the appearance of saturating the market with your label. We called it At Last Records. Our first song on that imprint, "What a Wedding Day" (At Last Records #1001), was done at Cosimo's studio in 1962. This great song by the very soulful Shirley Raymond suffered because of our losing our distribution deal with Juggy.

"To You My Love" (At Last Records #1002) was made to show off the four remarkable young Woods Brothers, trained by their postman father to do barbershop harmony. I arranged this beautiful

Germaine Bazzle song using modern close harmony, and they nailed it. After seeing the Osmonds do something similar, I made several unsuccessful attempts to get the Woods Brothers on the Andy Williams TV show.

I had produced a couple of recordings by Eddie Bo for Ric Records before AFO got started. He decided to come to us. Edwin Bocage was a seasoned musician/pianist/singer/songwriter from a famous New Orleans musical family. He penned great dance/novelty tunes, like "Slippin' and Slidin' " and "Check Mr. Popeye." He also brought us "Tee Na Na," which was the epitome of New Orleans second-line music.

In addition to recording all the artists AFO had signed, we formed a band, the AFO Executives with Tami Lynn, and started doing shows and concerts. Our main gig was at the Joy Tavern in Gert Town. Although our first fans were an adult crowd, the students at Xavier University found us, and word got around. We quickly became the hottest group in New Orleans and beyond. We would eventually take this band into Cosimo's studio and record a compendium of our most requested numbers, like "The Big BN" (the theme song of our current AFO Foundation website) and "Old Wyne."

In the meantime, Ellis Marsalis had gotten a gig at the Playboy Club in the French Quarter. This gig was a platform for him to mold the hippest jazz group in New Orleans. He and Nat Perrilliat had been working together since the American Jazz Quintet days, when Nat replaced me in that band. Ellis sent for drummer James Black, who was one semester from graduation at Southern University in Baton Rouge. In an interview a decade later, included in *New Orleans Heritage Jazz: 1956–1966*, James admitted, "That's right . . . I quit school like a fucking fool in my senior year to make a fucking gig and it didn't last but six months. It seemed like the right decision at the time. I said to myself, 'This little shit they teaching me in school, I already know that shit . . . and all them other things in the other departments, I already know all of that bull, so what am I doin' here?' That was the rationale of a twenty-year-old Black mind at the time. I was, in a way, penalized because I didn't want to waste any time. I already knew that shit, so why in the fuck should I wait just for that piece of paper? Of course, now I'd rather have it and don't need it than to need it and don't have it!"

As 1963 rolled in I knew I wanted to record some of the cats who were playing jazz, who would never be widely known and might soon lose that thing they had. I didn't care if those records never sold, but I thought they should be recorded for posterity. I wanted to finish what I had started in 1956 when I had negotiated with Specialty to let me record a jazz album. They never released it, but at least I knew that the original American Jazz Quintet was on record somewhere. AFO would also document the innovative and spirited work of the Ellis Marsalis Quartet. The liner notes from *Monkey Puzzle* tell the tale:

> . . . The Ellis Marsalis Quartet offers a convincing argument that the "Spark" (original New Orleans Spirit) was still at home. In its present form, this group is the result of seven years evolutionary progress with Ellis being the one consistent factor holding the thoughts and conceptions of the group together. During these years, the personnel has changed completely except for Ellis. As the American Jazz Quintet (its original name), the group consisted of three rhythm instruments, tenor sax and clarinet. Drummer Ed Blackwell left to heed the call of big city jazz joining with the controversial Ornette Coleman Quartet. I understand that he has also done a recording with John Coltrane. One by one, each of the original cats were replaced, and in my opinion, for the better.

> . . . Ellis and his group were tired of playing gigs at joints and clubs where the proprietor placed all kinds of restrictions on what they could or could not play. So Ellis got a stake from his father, who owns the beautiful Marsalis Mansion Motel, and opened the hippest club on the New Orleans scene . . . the Music Haven!

> — written by Harold Battiste in collaboration with writer Gilbert Chase and disc jockeys Larry McKinley and George Trueheart

Recording live was rare in 1963, and practically unheard of in New Orleans, but we thought it was the way to go—so we went! Cosimo was game: he brought all the stuff he needed out to the Music Haven and recorded five nights of great music. The cats were killing! The next Monday we went to Cos's studio to relive those nights at the Haven—but we couldn't quite make it. The problem was that Cos told us he couldn't find Nat's track on the tape. It was lost—there wasn't any tenor sax in the music, which was crucial to the overall sound. We had to abandon the live idea for the moment and redo the tunes in the studio. The Creator must have been on the job, because in addition to the superb performances from the guys, the sound Cosimo got in the studio was blessed.

Marzique Arrives!

I was even more blessed at home: our third child, our second daughter, arrived on May 6, 1963. Our first daughter, Andrea, had the privilege to name her: Marzique Kahdija. After all the stuff I had put Yette and my family through while focusing on AFO the last three years—my lack of attention and not being fully present emotionally—Marzique's entrance into our lives brought my attention back to the foundation of my inspiration and motivation.

THE MOTHER (to Yette for Marzique Kahdija, May 6, 1963)

*"Le Sacre Du Printemps" . . . The Rite of Spring
the fertility of the earth . . . the blessing of Motherhood
what more appropriate music could serve as background
to my expressions of gratitude and thanksgiving
that you are the Mother of my family.*

*I speak to you, and greet you as
Alviette, the Mother
especially at this time when Mothers all over
are being honored.
To me, you hold the highest position among all women.
Yes, for the past ten years you have been
my Mother, my son's Mother, my daughter's Mother . . .
and this Spring has brought new fertility
to your blessing of Motherhood so that now
you are the Mother of my second daughter.*

*To use mere words to express the love that fills me
when I realize the treasure that I have
merely points out the inadequacy of the language we speak.
Many times there are things that I feel I am unable to say
because there are no words to express certain feelings.
Maybe, because of my profession, I have learned to depend more upon music to say the
things that words cannot. So, I use this music . . . "The Rite of Spring" . . . which depicts
everything that is beautiful in Motherhood and Fertility,
to express (I hope) what I feel.*

*This is music that will last throughout eternity. For it is great music . . . the greatest,
composed by an immortal. So then, its description of nature and the fertility of the Earth
is not the only thing that is appropriate. It is also appropriate because
it matches my love for you in that my love is also eternal. My love is also very great . . . the
greatest, and shall last forever . . . regardless of what is to come.*

*So . . . let these, Alviette, be my expressions to you . . . my Mother's Day card to you on this
Mother's Day of Mother's Days for us.
I hope in some small way you may be able to get more out of it than I could put into
words. I hope that the music may suggest things that are beyond my vocabulary of
expression, and that you may feel, in some small way, what I feel for you, Alviette, first
the Woman, second the Wife, and third and most important THE MOTHER.*

The Executives in L.A.

The summer of 1963 would be AFO's finale. The executives planned to attend the National Association of Television & Radio Announcers (NATRA) convention in Los Angeles, and, if things were favorable, we would drop anchor and see what we could do as a band. We had attended the convention in St. Louis the year before and had gotten to know a lot of radio people from around the country. They all sort of knew about AFO because of Barbara's hit "I Know."

Larry McKinley (known today as "the voice of Jazz Fest") was a disc jockey at radio station WMRY/WYLD in New Orleans and president of the local chapter of NATRA. He was also the first cat to play AFO's first release on the air, Prince La La's "You Put the Hurt on Me." The chapter was created by and for Black radio personalities with a mission aimed at improving the status and conditions of the industry. Many of the cats that knew what AFO was about admired our efforts and saw us as role models.

We drove to Los Angeles in two cars. John Boudreaux and Chuck Badie rode in Red's Cadillac, and Melvin and Tami rode with me in AFO's Ford station wagon. Those were the days when musicians were used to packing for road gigs, so we were as comfortable as we needed to be. Since we intended to stay in Los Angeles after the convention, we made a deal with the El Reposo Motel for three rooms for the six of us.

The Poso, as Chuck called it, was in west L.A. near the corner of Washington and La Brea, down the block from the Parisian Room night club, which featured a variety of local jazz artists throughout the week. About four blocks east on Washington, the It Club occasionally brought in the heavy jazz acts: Miles Davis, John Coltrane, cats on that level.

When we arrived at the convention, we were approached by someone who remembered us from the previous year in St. Louis, wanting to know if we were going to do a show this year. Well, we hadn't

COMPENDIUM

THE AFO EXECUTIVES & TAMMY LYNN

Keeping the Music Alive!...
...since 1961

planned on it, but we were always ready. We were slotted for the next night, along with Dionne Warwick; we would be her backup band for her new hit, "Don't Make Me Over." It was a great night for her, and for the AFO Executives and Tami Lynn, who really tore it up. Tami is a natural competitor, and she just would not be outdone.

Feeling real strong about ourselves after that night, the band decided to give Los Angeles a chance. Some serious plans needed to be thought through: all of us had families back home, and each of us had to deal individually with that fact. We had to think about closing the office and the record shop we had started, and we would need to find places to live in California.

The rest of the band stayed at the Poso while I returned to New Orleans to begin to shut down that part of the AFO dream. Joyce, our secretary, had been vital in this operation, and she was quite sad to hear about its demise. She was very much into the spirit of the AFO mission and did not want to let it go. I tried to assure her that the spirit was in no way going, that this was just part of the beginning—our baby steps. When I got back to L.A. we located an apartment complex just off Washington on Mariposa. Once again we took three units for six of us.

Melvin and I began to scout the clubs in search of possible gigs for the AFO Executives and Tami Lynn. At one of the first few places we checked out, the proprietor had heard talk of "some cats from New Orleans." The Hideaway Club was at the west end of Adams Boulevard, where it merged into Washington nearly to La Cienega. We wanted him to hear us, so we asked to have a rehearsal at the club one afternoon. He must have liked what he heard because we played the club for two solid weeks. Our gig followed a stint by Coleman Hawkins and his band.

L.A.'s local 47 of the American Federation of Musicians had a law that prohibited new members of that local from working steady engagements during the first six months of their membership. We were only allowed to do casual (one-off) shows, which provided a buffer against migrant musicians taking gigs from the Los Angeles cats, so we were always having to find the next show. Melvin and I went out pounding the bricks again, but in Hollywood this time.

Getting into Sam's Orbit

By 1963 Sam Cooke had blown up from a gospel singer in the Soul Stirrers into a major pop star. Since "You Send Me" lifted him into orbit in 1957, he had a string of hits that kept taking him higher and higher. Melvin and I popped into his Hollywood office unannounced. The attractive Black lady who greeted us made us feel comfortable. She seemed as though she was glad to see some brothers out there. Melvin—Charisma Man—leaned over the counter in his rap mode and told her some stuff about who we were. Well, Sam was not in, but we were. She immediately started looking for ways to hook us up.

There were two other men in offices within the suite: Ernie Farrell and J. W. Alexander. Ernie seemed to be a public-relations person, always on the phone making deals or asking for favors on behalf of Sam. J. W. was Sam's personal manager and confidante going all the way back to the Soul Stirrers. But it was Zelda Samuels (a Jewish woman who was known professionally as Zelda Sands) who had the fire on that team. From her position as secretary, she knew everything and was the stealth mover and shaker. She loved Sam Cooke with an obvious passion, but she kept her hands off! She clearly admired Sam as a major talent and a professional but never let anything get to the personal level.

Zelda went into J. W.'s office, then came out to ask Melvin if he could write lead sheets. Melvin pointed to me, saying something like, "He can write anything you want!" J. W. was handling their publishing company, Kags Music, and needed lead sheets for copyright registration.

That was the start—or restart—of my association with Sam. We hadn't gotten to know much about each other when we worked together back in 1957, because right after the "You Send Me" session I left for my father's funeral in New Orleans, and Sam, Art, and Bumps got into a squabble about the session masters. But when he learned about AFO and its mission, Sam felt a real connection to us and our thinking. He had started his own company, SAR Records, along similar lines, with Black ownership a priority. When I approached him about a new concept I had for a project in L.A., he didn't hesitate—he was ready to finance it.

Recognizing that much of the talent in the African-American community did not have convenient access to Hollywood, I had the idea for a place that would provide a relaxed, at-home environment where talent could be developed for presentation to major companies. It was conceived to be a place where we could immerse ourselves in music, be ourselves, and be a part of the neighborhood. It was my idea, but the AFO Executives were a part of it, giving their blessing.

We found and rented a small storefront on South Vermont, between Adams and Jefferson across from the University of Southern California. This would be Soul Station #1, what we hoped would be the first in a series of future locations deeper into South Central Los Angeles. With Chuck Badie and Melvin—along with some paint brushes, hammers and nails, salvaged carpet for soundproofing, desks, chairs, a tape recorder, and a piano—in four days we had the place ready to move in. We were making music by the second week.

Our first work in the studio, in early 1964, was with Sam recording "Tennessee Waltz" for RCA. He was very much into the spirit generated by the Soul Station group and seemed to want to bring us in on everything. In addition to doing several of his own recordings, such as "Shake," "A Change Is Gonna Come," and "Ain't That Good News," his SAR artists used the Soul Station to prepare for their other sessions. Those artists included Johnnie Taylor, Billy Preston, Mel Carter, the Valentinos with Bobby Womack, Linda Carr, Patience Valentine, and the Sims Twins, among others. Then I got a call from Earl Palmer, homeboy and top session drummer in L.A., asking could I do a chart for producer Tommy LiPuma, who was at United Studios doing the O'Jays. The chart was a cover of a New Orleans tune, "Lipstick Traces," written by Allen Toussaint, and it gave the O'Jays their first hit.

We really had our hands full. In the midst of all of that soulful music, who pops into the Soul Station? Sonny Bono! It's ironic that of all the artists and songwriters involved in the Soul Station, Sonny & Cher would be the most successful.

Cher, Sonny, and Harold recording
the theme song for *Alfie*, 1965 (THNOC)

chapter **6** **sonny & cher**

Sonny's dream got the best years of my dream. He didn't take them; I gave them away. Sometimes now, in retrospect, I can see how, when, and why I lost track of the vision of what I wanted to do when I first left New Orleans—how I had allowed circumstances to gradually derail me. Responsibilities, a need for security, my position as head of household had the final word in my career decisions ("got to feed my family, and jazz ain't doin' it"). It had started back in 1956, with Specialty's temptation.

My 1963 return to Los Angeles was in no way related to Sonny's letters to me three years before, particularly not the "great team" letter of March 22, 1960. I had been so focused on the AFO project and my struggling family that I had forgotten all about his plea. When Sonny got in touch with me in Los Angeles in '63, he was working for Phil Spector; he got Phil to call me to play piano on his sessions.

I had met Phil a couple of years back with AFO. His partner at that time, Lester Sill, had approached me to produce some New Orleans–type music on the heels of "I Know" and "Ya Ya." He also asked me to go to New York, where Phil was producing a guy named Ray Sharpe, an R&B singer out of Texas who sounded a lot like Chuck Berry (Sharpe's career never really took off). The meeting was strange. I never figured out what I was supposed to do. Phil would pluck out his ideas on the guitar or piano and was happy to record little chunks of his ideas at a time, then overdub and splice. I don't remember doing anything, and I don't remember ever hearing the finished record.

These new sessions with Phil—I played on hits from 1963 to 1965 for the Righteous Brothers ("You've Lost That Lovin' Feeling"), Ike & Tina Turner ("Proud Mary"), and the Ronettes—were wildly different from anything with which I had been involved before. We were at Gold Star Recording Studios in Hollywood, on Santa Monica and Vine, and the room was full of rhythm sections: three or four guitars, two or three basses, drums and percussion all around, and three pianos. I was the designated free piano, meaning I didn't have to play what was on the music sheet—Phil wanted me to ad lib whatever I thought would fit. He would add other instruments—horns, strings, singers, etc.—later. He never seemed to be prepared, or maybe he was creating as he went along. The last few sessions I remember, he seemed to be taking longer to find what he was looking for. The Spector sessions were too long and boring for me. Since then, we have all realized his genius and marveled at the complex simplicity of his productions.

I think it was during this period that Sonny met Cher. One day he came to the Soul Station #1 with a project he wanted my help on. The following transcript—from a 1976 episode of the *Sonny & Cher Show* called "The Hungry Years"—tells the story of the beginning of Sonny and Cher:

> **Sonny:** [*looking at an old photo*] We dressed this way in 1963. I guess it's a little too late to say I'm sorry. [*audience laughter*] But this is what we looked like when we made our first record and we thought it'd be fun to talk about it.
>
> **Cher:** We should introduce the . . .
>
> **Sonny:** Oh yes, folks . . . ladies and gentlemen, I'd like you to meet Harold Battiste. [*audience applause*] Harold is our musical director and our arranger and [*hesitates*] uh, producer sometimes, and Harold and I have been together longer than you and I . . .
>
> **Cher:** I know that . . .
>
> **Sonny:** . . . have been together. Harold and I started out as producers for a record company, and he was the East Coast producer and I was the West Coast producer, and every now and then we used to pop into each others' lives, and Harold would arrange the records, and then later on I met Cher, and then Cher and I went on to become infamous background singers. [*audience laughter*] We sang backgrounds for the Crystals . . .
>
> **Cher:** And the Ronettes.
>
> **Sonny:** Who else? Do you remember?
>
> **Cher:** The Righteous Brothers. The last song that we did backgrounds on was a song that the Righteous Brothers did that became number one. That was "You've Lost That Lovin' Feelin."
>
> **Sonny:** Then one day I came up with it. I played a riff on the piano, and well, see, folks, I don't play piano well, I was fooling around, and I came up with these three chords [*audience laughter as Harold holds up two fingers*]. I was playing these, these three chords on the piano [*more audience laughter as Harold holds up two fingers—repeating the gesture*] [*looking at Harold*] What?! [*Harold repeats the gesture once more*]
>
> **Harold:** Two. That came next year. [*audience laughter*]
>
> **Sonny:** Oh. Anyway, we wrote this song ["The Letter"] and we played it for everybody and everybody liked it and we wanted to make a record of it. Well, we had one problem.
>
> **Cher:** Yeah, we had no money. [*audience laughter*]
>
> **Sonny:** Yeah. So I said, "Harold, I need you to do the arrangement and I want you to help produce the record. And I'd love it if you'd play the clavinet for me and . . ."
>
> **Cher:** [*turning to Harold*] Do you remember what you said?
>
> **Harold:** I was quite flattered.
>
> **Sonny:** ". . . yeah, and one little problem, uh, you have to do it for free."
>
> **Harold:** Yeah, I remember that too. [*audience laughter*]
>
> **Sonny:** But anyway, Harold is a sucker for sweet talk.
>
> **Cher:** [*rolling her eyes*] Aren't we all? . . .

The dialogue went on, then transitioned to me leading into "Baby Don't Go" on the clavinet. But that was actually the *second* song with which I was involved. The collaboration when Sonny first came to the Soul Station resulted in me writing charts for him and Cher to record "The Letter" for Vault Records. They called themselves Caesar & Cleo, hoping to coattail on the success of the Richard Burton–Elizabeth Taylor movie *Cleopatra*. Sonny's promotion experience and reputation got the record a little airplay, and they made a few gigs (probably for very little bread, or for free!). A couple of times I got the AFO Executives to back them when they needed to make an impression. Of course, we had to fit it into the schedule of our work at the Soul Station with Sam Cooke's artists.

"Baby Don't Go" was their debut as Sonny & Cher. That record got much more attention than anything they'd done before, and so did they. It seemed as though the time was right for the public to find out what they represented to the music world, and what they as a duo had to offer musically. I was getting caught up in Sonny's dream, and because I failed to recognize it, I was also slipping further away from my own.

Giving Up Something to Gain?

My family, too, had made several major transitions over the last few years. The lovely home on Hickory Street, which we'd purchased in 1958 before Andrea was born, had been sacrificed in 1961 in favor of my effort to launch AFO. The company had actually started in that house, but with no dependable income, we reluctantly had to give it up. The upside of that situation was that at the same time we were looking to sell, Mr. and Mrs. Ellis Marsalis Sr. were in the market for a house. That was the first of several times that the Marsalis family showed up to help us in the nick of time. The senior Marsalises lived there for years. At some point after Mrs. Marsalis died, Ellis Jr. and his heroic wife, Dolores, came to assist and comfort Ellis Sr. As of this writing, Ellis and Dolores are still living in the house.

When AFO went to the NATRA convention that summer in 1963, I'd left my wife and three children in New Orleans living in one side of a shotgun double with the hope that I would (if I could) get something going in Los Angeles and bring them out there. I made a couple of attempts to buy some of that attractive, "easy to get" California real estate, which ended in near financial disaster. Finally I managed to land a nice house in an even nicer neighborhood, on South Mansfield Avenue. This west-side address was in the area where the AFO Executives first landed when we arrived in L.A. in 1963, and it was our first real home environment in the city. Well-maintained streets, nicely manicured front lawns, a tree and some bushes in front of our own house. We had a backyard large enough to build a two-car garage. Three bedrooms, two baths, living room, dining room, den, and kitchen—this was almost as exciting as the Hickory Street house had been. It was going to be a great place to raise a family. Our first three children had come four years apart, but Harlis Ray couldn't wait: he arrived November 29, 1964, only eighteen months after Marzique.

Dec. 7, 1963

My Dearest Yette,

It is Saturday evening and I have just finished getting myself ready to go play a gig. At present I don't know whether I will mail this letter, but I'm writing it so as to release from inside me some of the anxiety, anticipation and emotional frustration I have stored up.

 This has been a very swift week on one hand and an extremely long one on the other. Between running to the real estate office that sold me the house, and calling the loan co. who had foreclosed on the previous owners and talking to the lawyers of both parties and finally employing a lawyer myself . . . the week's time flew by. But every night when it was time to retire and prepare myself for the next day's hustle, I found my mind and thoughts begin to focus on the 2,000 miles and 4 months that separate me from what I want most . . . YOU.

 Loneliness never seems to show outwardly on me . . . but then, none of the negative emotions like sadness, grief, anger, hate, etc. register noticeably in my personality. Nevertheless, they seem to have a way (mainly loneliness) of attacking me in my lowest moments when everything is going wrong and everybody seems to have turned their backs on me, then loneliness steps in to try to finish me off. I hate this even more because at that point I begin to feel sorry for myself, and self pity is a very detestable state of mind.

 Yette, I need you to be with me. I need you because I love you and need you to love me. And, even more so, I need you to talk to. I need desperately to talk to someone, and you, Yette, are the only person on this planet Earth that I have. I am so alone in this world and my only true spiritual communication with any human being is with you. If you were my sister or my mother, then only death could end our relationship. But you are my wife and you could get tired of me: tired of the unstable profession I have, tired of my absence, tired of any one of many things. And if you should, then you would leave me . . . and I would be a dead man.

But now I'm feeling sorry for myself and that's no good. So I'll stop. At any rate remember Yette, I love you and need you. Please . . . "Save your Love for Me."

Harold

Losing Sam

Sam Cooke's tragic and scandalous death in late 1964 upset the entire music world (a good source of information about Sam's life and death is Daniel Wolff's 1995 biography, *You Send Me: The Life and Times of Sam Cooke*). All of the AFO Executives had come to be quite close to Sam and his wife, Barbara. It was very hard for me to accept the circumstances under which he died. He was too good a person to go out like that. With the loss of Sam's financial support, the Soul Station project ended. Things were also falling apart for the Executives. Red Tyler had decided to go back to New Orleans. Melvin Lastie got a call from Joe Jones to come to New York for a gig, and Tami Lynn went with him. And though I still did not think of working with Sonny as a job—I was just helping him do his thing, and I was not anxious to be identified with his music—it was beginning to pay some bills.

Sonny & Cher really started moving after they met Charlie Green and Brian Stone. Charlie and Brian both fit the stereotype of the smart, slick, pushy New Yorker. I heard that when they got to Hollywood, they went on the lot of a major movie studio, took an office that wasn't in use, and began to operate their business as though they belonged there. They were hustlers. They got Sonny a record deal with Atlantic, which brought about my first big session with Sonny & Cher. Sonny was greatly influenced by Phil Spector, so we had five guitars, two basses, three pianos, etc. "Just You" had the Spector sound Sonny was looking for, and I think he had one of his buddies from our Specialty Records days, Jack Nitzsche, to add a string line. Jack used to copy for me (transcribing score sheets by hand) so he could study my arrangements.

I must admit that I was somewhat uncomfortable in this new situation. Before, I had been just a sideman on the Phil Spector record dates, and even the Sam Cooke and Sonny & Cher dates; I wrote charts and played piano or whatever. I was still low profile. I did not see myself as a real part of that music. In my soul, I was a jazz musician, or soul, R&B, or blues even. But suddenly I was sliding across the line musically and getting put up front in the studio. I had known and had worked with several of the musicians from the Spector sessions, but now I was in charge.

One day in late May or early June 1965, Sonny called and came over to my house on Mansfield. He was really excited, wearing his jackpot smile. He knew that this was it—he'd come up with the song that would define a place in history for Sonny & Cher! He went to my piano and plunked out his new song with those soon-to-be famous three chords: "It's like a waltz," he said. I got to the piano and he sang while we played with it a while, until he felt comfortable. I agreed that the lyrics were cute and catchy, but I wasn't too sure about the waltz thing. He kept singing the "oompah-pah, oompah-pah," like a tuba and trombone thing.

He wanted to go into the studio quickly—like tomorrow. As I thought about how to make this come off like he wanted, I figured out how to change the waltz feeling to a 6/8, with a little brighter tempo, and to soften the "oompah-pah" with woodwinds—bassoon and oboe—in place of brass.

The musicians we assembled for that day came to the studio routinely—they just did what they did all the time: Frank Kapp on drums; Lyle Ritz and Cliff Hills on bass; Don Randi and I on piano; Don Peake, Steve Mann, Barney Kessel, and Ervin Coleman on guitar; Morris Crawford on bassoon; and

The Battiste home on Mansfield Avenue, their first house in L.A. (THNOC)

Warren Webb on oboe. Sonny managed the orchestra, and I served as arranger, copyist, and bandleader. For the studio guys, it was just a day's work; for Salvatore and Cherilyn, a new life. Although I didn't get it at the time, "I Got You Babe" was changing my life, too.

Family Readjustments

At home, among my family, there was only a mild awareness of what I was doing and with whom. Bunny, now ten, was already thumping a basketball around the house; he had no apparent interest in music. The other three—Andrea, six; Marzique, two; and Harlis, just one year old—were in their own wonder world. I have precious footage I captured with a Super 8 movie camera at Christmas: Harlis experimenting with walking while Bunny gives him and Marzique a hard time.

Things were fairly stable at home between Yette and me, although she had mentioned getting a job or going back to school. Over the past three years, I had become aware that my work, with its uncertainty, instability, and absence from home, was having some effect on our relationship. I was still thinking as though I was in my mother and father's generation, when the man was the breadwinner and the woman stayed at home. The Women's Liberation Movement hadn't reached us yet.

Wheeling and Dealing: Hard Lessons

Charlie Green and Brian Stone left no stone unturned and let no grass grow under their feet in their relentless efforts to wheel and deal for Sonny & Cher. They made a deal with Ahmet Ertegun at Atlantic Records: the Sonny & Cher product would be released on Atlantic's subsidiary label ATCO. In a very short time, Charlie and Brian had created a buzz in music-business circles in Los Angeles and New York. It also helped that Sonny had been a promotion man for a few years and was known by the record people.

Labels were curious and interested. Bob Scaff from Liberty Records, along with Charlie and Brian, came up with the idea that even though Atlantic had an artist contract with Sonny & Cher the duo, Cher was free as a single artist. Bob signed her with Imperial Records, a Liberty subsidiary.

So I was back in the studio again. I was slipping and sliding down the rock-and-roll slope . . . maybe I was rollin'. This time, Cher and I were doing a cover of a Bob Dylan song that was out by a group called

Harold, Cher, and Sonny at Gold Star Studios, L.A.; PHOTOS BY JASPER DAILY (THNOC)

the Byrds. "All I Really Want to Do" hit the charts along with the previous stuff. By the time "Babe" reached number one on *Billboard*, we had three or four songs on the charts.

I spent most of that June and some of July in Gold Star Studios recording tunes for Sonny & Cher's first album. Everything seemed too rushed—there was no time for thoughtful selection of material, arrangements, or production. Sonny & Cher were moving up the *Billboard* and *Cash Box* charts fast, and although they had done a few gigs and had a few songs they could perform on stage live, the studio was much more critical. They elected to cover several songs that were already in the market and that Cher liked, plus the tunes that we had recorded and released ("Just You" and "The Letter"). "Look at Us" marked another exciting leap up the ladder for them. Meanwhile, I was trying to hold on to some parts of Harold Battiste: father, husband, jazz musician?

A Special Studio Guest

Two or three years later, while I was at Gold Star doing a Sonny & Cher session, there was an interruption by a Black man dressed like a celebrity—his wardrobe was a cross between California hippie and threads from India. He had on a ruffled shirt, beads, and tight pants, and his afro looked like it hadn't been picked out (combed) and groomed. Someone said that it was Jimi Hendrix. He visited with Sonny and Cher for a while, then things got back to business.

A few days later, I was shocked to realize that the Jimi at the studio was the same "Jimmy" I had known in my Specialty days! I hadn't made the connection at Gold Star because the two of us didn't have a conversation there. It dawned on me later that we crossed paths around the late '50s or early '60s, during the latter part of Little Richard's early stardom. Art Rupe was doing a session for Richard, and he got me to do the charts for "Without Love" and a couple of other numbers—to add the strings and things. Art also wanted me to be Richard's musical director for a gig at a club on Sunset Boulevard in Hollywood.

Richard's band was not the expected New Orleans cats but some young guys I didn't know. I remember two guitarists in the group, both named Jimmy. Jimmy number one was a great rhythm player—accurate and dependable. Jimmy number two was wild, unpredictable, and playing left-handed. Richard was having problems with Jimmy number two stealing the show when they were on stage. He was the Jimmy who would go on to become *the* Jimi Hendrix! The music business can be such a small world; it's amazing.

First Tour

As I prepared to go on tour with Sonny & Cher that summer (1965), I once again had a little anxiety about the job I was about to do. I had never done an extended tour as musical director of a rock/pop artist, especially flying from gig to gig. Back in the day, whenever we went on the road for a gig, we were literally on the road, burning rubber. For me it was rarely more than one night out, then back the next morning to New Orleans. There was the time I went out with Lloyd Price for a couple of weeks back in 1959, but that was on a bus.

In late August 1965 we flew to our first gig, in Phoenix, Arizona. I had prepared rhythm-section charts for the songs Sonny & Cher wanted to sing in the shows, mostly tunes that were simple—recent pop and R&B hits by other artists, such as Shirley and Lee's "(Come on Baby) Let the Good Times Roll." And of course I brought "Just You," "Baby Don't Go," and "I Got You Babe."

We didn't bring our own musicians, so at each gig I had to work with new local players. I still don't know who was responsible for picking these guys, but they offered me exciting challenges on a regular basis. Often I had to play the piano or the bass myself in order to hold things together. In some small towns, the musicians were so in awe of being on stage with Sonny & Cher that they couldn't stop gawking.

Next we went to the East and did New York City, Rochester, Asbury Park, Toronto, and Boston. There were two isolated gigs in late September and early October, one in San Jose and the other in San Francisco at the Cow Palace. We finished 1965 with shows in Omaha, Denver, Moline, Madison, Boston, Philadelphia, and Albany—whew! It was an eye-opening four months for all of us. I believe that my career crossed the line from jazz to rock and roll during that time.

The Score

Before December was over, we were back in the studio recording. From the beginning with Sonny, I had learned to withhold subjective judgment about his songs. My job was to take what he brought, look for the good, and develop it as best I could. I needed to use that approach regularly in arranging music because often people had dreams, ambition, a little money, and they wanted to go for it. Who was I to sit in judgment about who was "good" or not? The most successful songs came from the oddest approaches, and I didn't want to stand in anyone's way. I was just the hired hand. I know that I've done it (withheld judgment), and so did Sonny.

"What Now My Love" surprised me by hitting the charts so quickly: forty-seven days after we left the studio, it was at number fourteen! Recording studios would become my full-time workplace during the first half of 1966. Although my name was not on those early releases, people in the business knew, and they began to seek me out for their projects. This was unexpected, but the extra income was welcomed. I began to think about the things I could do for my family, for the house, maybe a second car. Yeah, I had crossed the line. I already had a full plate, but I took on the added chore of typing the musicians' union contracts for each session I directed. I wanted to be certain the musicians (including me) got paid on time. It seemed like ATCO and Imperial were releasing records as fast as we recorded them. Following "What Now My Love" there was "Bang Bang," which reached number two, and the title track for the movie *Alfie*, which got to thirty-two. But neither of them repeated what "Babe" had done.

Sonny was watching the numbers, and he was beginning to worry. He met a young filmmaker, William Friedkin, and along with some other guys started talking about doing a Sonny & Cher movie—the exposure could bump them up a notch or two. Sonny approached me about scoring the film. I declined. I had never scored a movie—never even really thought about it. Sonny had always had confidence in my talent and skills, but this was out of my league. He told me that he knew some film composers and he swore that I was as good or better than they. Sonny's talent and skills as a con man prevailed: I said I would think about it.

I bought a small book (I think it was *Underscore*, by the composer Frank Skinner) to acquaint myself

Harold with guitarist Don Peake (*left*) and Sonny on the stage at the Hollywood Bowl; PHOTO BY JASPER DAILY (THNOC)

with some of the basics of film scoring—the tools, the language, the process, etc. But what I really needed was to see it being done. I had Sonny's office contact Steve Brody at Motion Pictures International (MPI) and set me up to visit a scoring session. Phil Kahgan, the contractor for the musicians that day in February 1966, brought me into the soundstage on the Paramount lot to observe composer Leith Stevens. Kahgan also made it possible for me to observe Igor Stravinsky at work at Columbia Studios. I sat in the soundstage booth with the engineers and director, watching, listening, and taking notes as they did what they did. After that two-hour workshop, the process became clear, and I knew I could do it—and probably would like it.

William Friedkin invited me to start viewing the dailies—raw, unedited footage reviewed at the end of each day of shooting—from the Sonny & Cher movie with him. The first footage I saw was of Sonny walking down an endlessly long hall in an office building. For practice, I noted the tempo of Sonny's pace and the approximate length of the walk. At home that evening I wrote a cue for that scene—my first! As the weeks went on, I sat in on more dailies and began to really get involved in the challenge that cues presented. The work revitalized my interest in composing. An unexpected perk was that I was given an orchestrator to arrange my compositions for performance. I had never had one before; I'd always done that myself.

In the meantime, we went into Gold Star to start recording the soundtrack album. The movie—titled *Good Times*—was not a musical, but more of a romantic fantasy with songs. Sonny wrote several songs for various scenes in the script: "It's the Little Things," "Good Times," "Trust Me/Hey," "Big Friend/ Things I'd Like to Be," "Don't Talk to Strangers," "I've Got to Have You," and "Just a Name." My job was to make them work musically. The fantastical nature of the film required a variety of styles, which made my job very interesting. The title song was the Sonny & Cher identity—"I Got You Babe"—which I turned into a hip jazz waltz arranged for a full orchestra. The cats on the session were pleasantly surprised. These were the musicians I usually used on Sonny & Cher dates, and they had never heard me write like that. One of them, drummer Frankie Kapp, actually asked me, "Man, did you really write all that?"

I was almost insulted, but I understood. Some years later, I was reading the liner notes of the album and discovered that Friedkin had credited Sonny:

A word about the music . . . the first time I heard these songs after Sonny had recorded them, I remember grasping him by the shoulders and hugging him. I was stunned at the richness and variety and at the tremendous opportunities they presented for visualization. I've heard them at least a hundred times since and they still gas me. They include a jazz waltz, a Bossa Nova, a traditional blues, a Dixieland can-can, a Gershwinesque ballet in 6/8 time and finally a pair of contemporary pop songs. All by the same writer. Pop music has come a long way.

By the time the shooting was done and I had all the information from the director, I had become a film composer. I knew enough of their language to be conversant with them and to have a clear vision of what the music should accomplish. The day before the scoring was to begin, I was very nervous. I was thinking, *Tomorrow I am going to be on the conductor's stand, baton in hand, in front of some of the best and best-paid professional musicians in Hollywood. On their music stands will be my music, which I have heard only in my head. What if . . .* I was scared! I took my family out to Griffith Park that Sunday. Playing with my kids cooled me out.

Monday came, and there I was—anxious to hear that first downbeat. Phil Kahgan had arranged the order in which the cues would be done, starting with the largest (those that required the most musicians) and longest. First up was "Show Down, Shoot Out." After the first few measures were performed just the way I had heard them in my head, I was happy! After we finished that first one, I could feel and see that the musicians accepted me. I could see Sonny in the booth wearing his proud "I told you so" grin.

The rest of the day's recording went just as well. It was an impressive debut. When all the scoring was finished, I was contacted by two of the executives of Paramount Pictures to have lunch. We met on the lot the next day. They were impressed with my work, especially when they learned that this was my first time. They wanted to know if I was affiliated with a manager. I saw where they were headed but was not ready to get any further involved in this business.

I had signed a contract with MPI to do the music for Sonny's movie. Because of my reluctant attitude about doing it, along with my naïveté of the business, I allowed the following paragraphs to be put in the contract:

P-8 . . . Even though Battiste renders services in connection with the Picture as a composer or conductor or both, nevertheless Battiste agrees that the Corporation shall not be obligated to give him any credit as a composer or conductor, but may, if the Corporation so desires, give such credit to such one or more other persons as the Corporation in its sole absolute discretion may determine from time to time.

P-10 . . . The Corporation may add to, subtract from, arrange, rearrange, revise and adapt such material and the Picture in any manner, and Battiste hereby waives his "moral Rights" (as such term is commonly understood) of authors and composers. All material composed, submitted, added or interpreted by Battiste pursuant to this agreement, and the copyright therein and all the renewals thereof, shall automatically become the property of the Corporation, which, for this purpose, shall be the author thereof.

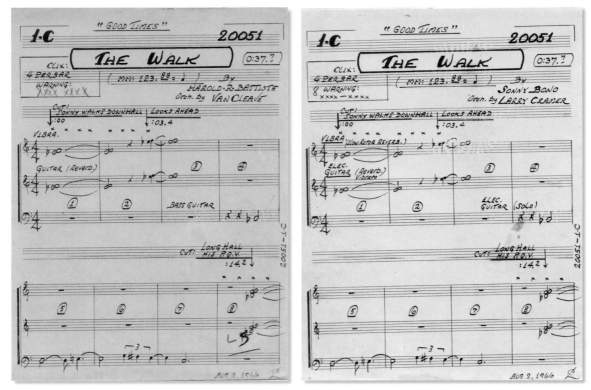

Two cue sheets for "The Walk," from the Sonny & Cher film *Good Times*. one credits Harold, the other Sonny Bono
(AMISTAD RESEARCH CENTER)

These caveats would have consequences. I missed the long-term significance at the time, but the issues with this contract would come up again.

Europe

We went to London that August, after the movie was finished—another premiere for me. The trip revealed the small but growing trouble in my marriage. On the one hand, my work was taking me away from my social and spiritual foundations, yet on the other hand, it allowed me the opportunity to provide some security for my family, for our future. The glitz and glamour of the music industry can disguise a loneliness always there, waiting. Sometimes I needed Alviette to be with me, to smile at me from the wings, to have breakfast with me in the fancy hotels. The Sonny & Cher world was their world, not mine.

Although we did a show at the Palladium I think Sonny & Cher went to London mainly to promote the movie. They made an appearance at Rediffusion Television and dealt with hordes of reporters and photographers. I caught some of the action with my little Super 8 camera. While there, we went into the studio to do a Sonny & Cher single called "Little Man." Like lots of Sonny's tunes, I didn't think much of it, but I just did what I knew how to do to make it be the best that I could. When it was released, it was very well received in Europe but not in the United States.

A notable development on this trip was when Sonny met Denis Pregnolato and made an addition to his team. When I first met him, he was leaving the hotel with several people who handled Sonny and Cher's clothes; he asked me if I had anything to send to the cleaners. He was a young man from South Africa who was on a mission to get to America and become a star. He made all the right moves with Sonny and Cher, and, I must admit, he impressed me too.

I met a few more industry people while in England: Tony Frank and Michel Taittinger, photographers; Ron Kass of Liberty Records, London; Jon Fenton, public relations for Island Records; André

Poulain of Polydor Records; and Eddie Barclay, ATCO's distributor in Paris. I also visited the Mechanical Copyright Protection Society (MCPS) to check on the status of At Last Publishing Co., which, as an affiliate of AFO Records, had copyrights at MCPS.

Next we flew to Paris (Denis included), where I encountered the "French connection" to New Orleans for the first time. There were so many little things that reminded me of home: words, like *rue* for *street*, *banquette* for *sidewalk*, *cher* for *dear*. Most of the parts I saw looked like the French Quarter. I met several men from Senegal, Africa, who had established a community in Paris. One of them, a saxophone student named Dumme Amadee, escorted me around town. Sonny & Cher were to appear at the Olympia Theater, where Otis Redding was appearing a day earlier. Over lunch Otis told me he was worried because he couldn't sing his songs in French. I told him, "Don't worry, they know them in your language!" I caught some of his show with my Super 8, too. That was the highlight of my trip.

Before the year was out we were back in the States, where we did a few more shows on the road: Portland, Oregon; Pittsburgh, Pennsylvania; Montgomery, Alabama. About twenty minutes before the end of the Montgomery show, I saw Denis in the wings, desperately waving his arms over his head. I was busy conducting the orchestra and didn't respond to him. He started pointing to me. I thought, "What's going on?" He came on stage, grabbed my arm, and ushered me backstage, where two security police escorted me to their car and took off. They had gotten word of a gang planning to "teach this nigger up there where his place was." That same night at the hotel, I met Governor George Wallace.

We closed out 1966 in the studio, working on a Sonny & Cher album that included a single that would bring them back up on the charts. "The Beat Goes On" was the biggest thing since "I Got You Babe." Not as big, but big enough to ease Sonny's mind. During this session I met a spunky young guitar player—one of the three, four, or maybe five players on the date. Curious, talented, and ambitious, he became a regular cat on the set. He also seemed to have a thing for New Orleans–style music. Leland Michael Postil became the Grammy-winning composer Mike Post, who provided themes for many of my favorite TV shows: *Hill Street Blues, The White Shadow,* and *Law & Order,* to name a few.

A New Homestead

The year had been quite exciting on the home front, as well. We bought a brand-new 1966 Pontiac Catalina. I had never before gotten beyond the "low-priced three": Plymouth, Ford, and Chevrolet. My first new car— the '53 Chevy 210—had survived three years until the new '56 210s came out. That's the one that took Blackwell, Ellis, and me out to California. Then, in 1961, when AFO got started, I got a Ford station wagon, which served as a company car for the AFO Executives and a family car for the growing Battistes.

But our really big move was into our beautiful home in Baldwin Village, on Bowcroft Street in West Los Angeles near La Cienega Boulevard. I even had my own little office—a little shed attached to the garage. I equipped it with a desk and a piano. I wrote music there and would sometimes rehearse with a musician or two.

For me this was an accomplishment that filled me with joy and pride. This was what defined me as a father and husband, and as a man. Our block had nine or ten homes on each side of the street, each with immaculate green lawns and shrubbery and driveways for off-street parking. Ours was the only front yard that was completely planted with flowering plants—birds of paradise and other exotic foliage.

The neighborhood was in transition, with Whites and Jews leaving, African Americans, Asians, and Latin Americans coming. Our house was between two of the remaining Whites, which was an interesting first for us. The people next door seemed to be cursing and fighting every other night. I learned from that experience. It was obvious to me that these White folks acted like they claimed Black folks acted—in a loud and common way. I had never lived among people that behaved like that.

Clockwise, from top left: The Battiste family house on Bowcroft Street, L.A.; Harold's backyard studio; Harold and Marzique on Venice Beach; Harlis on Santa Monica Beach; a Battiste family portrait, ca. 1968 (COURTESY OF THE BATTISTE FAMILY)

Progress Records

Sometime in late 1966 or early 1967, I suggested to Sonny that we should spread out and produce artists other than Sonny & Cher. I was anticipating the fact that they would not last forever in their current status as top record sellers. After months of evading my continuous inquiries about the project, Sonny (as I had suspected he might) said to me, as though it was a new idea, "Man, we're gonna set up a company

Sonny and Cher with Andrea and
Bunny Battiste, ca. 1967; PHOTO
BY JASPER DAILEY (THNOC)

and produce some artists!" (This sort of business dealing between Sonny and me would eventually lead
to our first separation.)

The plan as suggested by Sonny was for me to take the major responsibility, including but not limited
to approval of artists and material, music preparation and/or supervision, production and postproduction
supervision, and sale of masters. In the meantime, I was to school Denis Pregnolato in the business, so that
some time in the future he could free me to devote more time to creative work. Sonny said he didn't want
to be bothered with it, because he wanted to get involved in the motion picture business. He just wanted
a piece of it—a share of the profits—and once in a while he might want to record somebody.

Early in June 1967 Sonny asked me to listen to the material of Keith Allison, a guy Sonny liked and
wanted to record. On June 13 I supervised the session, did the charts, contracted the musicians, etc.
(American Federation of Musicians contract #411457). In July a similar sequence of events occurred,
this time involving Bill Rinehart (AFM contracts #411458 and #412463). I was later informed by Sonny
that these masters would be sent to Atlantic Records as "Harold Battiste productions." I didn't want
Sonny sending material to Atlantic without my permission. I felt that he was taking liberties with my work
and my services. I did not like the way the subject was broached nor the fact that it was being done this
way, but I didn't speak up and object. I was told that the masters would be owned by Progress Records,
a company that we would control.

I was not aware that a company name had been selected, or even that a company had been formed.
I hadn't seen any papers indicating any particulars about Progress Records. In light of what I thought
was happening with the Allison and Rinehart productions, I decided that I would introduce an artist and
a concept of *my* choosing: if Ahmet and Jerry Wexler at Atlantic were being told that these were Harold
Battiste productions, then I might as well choose. My first choice was Mac Rebennack.

In the meantime Sonny had begun work on a new motion picture project, *Chastity*. He asked me—and
expected me—to do the score. My experience scoring *Good Times* prompted certain demands: I wanted all
rights to the music composed, screen credit as composer, travel and location pay, etc. On Tuesday, May 14,
1968, I had a meeting with Joe DeCarlo, Sonny's manager. I told Joe that attorney Murray Gomer had
taken over all my affairs and that he advised me to have all business and projects in which I was involved
turned over to him. Murray had to see the papers regarding *Chastity*, Progress Records, and our other
pending projects: a month of shows in Las Vegas and a concert at the Greek Theater in Los Angeles,

around Griffith Park. I asked him when he could get all the papers to my attorney, and he said some time the next week. I demanded that we consummate the money deals regarding each pending project. I again named each one and indicated that I had already begun work on *Chastity*, having viewed dailies that day. I asked him if Wednesday, May 22, gave him enough time to get these papers to my attorney. He said yes.

Joe seemed anxious to explain that he agreed things should be done in a more organized manner, but he was full of excuses. He asked that I give him a few days to send Murray anything he needed, and he explained that the reason everything was so confused at the office was because of poor secretarial help, but that the girl they had just gotten was an expert. "I'm payin' her a hundred fifty dollars a week, but she's worth it," he said. He also said that Sonny wouldn't let him and Harvey Kresky, Joe's partner and half of Sonny's management team, do all they really wanted to do because he wanted them all to himself. Joe mentioned all the things he wanted to do—or could have done—if Sonny would have let him, like sign the Righteous Brothers before they split. He complained that Sonny had stopped recording and making public appearances because he was "all wrapped up" in his movie. "Maybe when he gets that out of his head, he'll come down to earth again and we can get somethin' goin' around here."

I met with Joe DeCarlo again on May 23. When I requested papers for my lawyer regarding the Progress Records deal between Sonny and me, he said there were none. I had been suspicious that, since my first meeting with Joe, they had been trying to set up a deal between Progress and Atlantic Records without my knowledge. Joe did a lot of talking about his desire to get things formalized. He suggested that I call Sonny in Phoenix and set up a meeting to negotiate. I said I would call—and even go there if necessary—to finalize settlement on all projects. When I called, at 1:00 a.m., the hotel operator said, "Mr. Bono doesn't receive calls at this hour. These people work hard all day and don't like to be disturbed at night." The operator let it ring for about two seconds, then said, "He doesn't answer." I asked him to leave a message for the morning. I then called Western Union and sent a night letter.

Such inequities had been accumulating. Until now I had ignored them in deference to Sonny's needs. But it was becoming quite clear that circumstances had deteriorated to a point where I had little choice but to walk away. I had to get back to my own career, family, and life.

chapter **7** **gris-gris**

Los Angeles had a large population of New Orleans natives, many of whom had been there for generations. For the homeboys, I had become, by this time, a person to call when you got to L.A. Often I was
able to help cats get some kind of gigs. Such was the case with Mac Rebennack, whom I knew was a very
talented musician. I had known Mac since 1957—back in my Specialty Records days. He showed up in
the city around 1965. Someone in the music community told me he was in town—or it may have been
Mac himself.

Whenever he got a chance to play (guitar or piano) he would get on someone's list—get to know people
so that they would call him for studio work or other gigs. After a while I introduced him to the Sonny &
Cher operation, both for studio and stage work. Sonny seemed somewhat skeptical, but Cher liked him.
He was a great asset to me at that time when dealing with some of those local musicians on the road. Mac
was there when Sonny & Cher went on tour and was often the go-to musician, playing guitar or piano on
a professional level. He was invaluable to me when we arrived to do a show in some small town and the
local guys hired by the promoter would freeze up in the presence of Sonny & Cher and couldn't play the
right sequences or notes. But despite his talent, Mac needed to be discreet with his drug needs because,
as far as I knew, Sonny & Cher were clean, in public and in private.

When I decided to choose an artist to record on Progress Records—the side project Sonny and I got
going in 1967—I approached Mac first, asking if he had anything he wanted to record. Mac told me that
he had been reading up on this character called Dr. John from the New Orleans voodoo tradition and
wanted to work something around that. The concept appealed to me immediately. I envisioned creating a
new sound, look, and spirit to the popular psychedelic/underground wave.

We discussed the project for a few days, then Mac and me started selecting musicians, singers, and
tunes. The main character, Dr. John, was to be performed by Ronnie Barron, another New Orleans
transplant, a White guy we knew from back in the day. Ronnie had a great singing voice for R&B and

Above left, Mac (*right*) with disc jockey John Stone at WTIX in New Orleans; *above right,* Mac with Jessie Hill outside Gold Star Recording Studios in Hollywood, ca. 1967 (THNOC)

pop music, and his vocals could pass as Black; he was a performer like Tom Jones. But he had a manager who thought that the Dr. John character would not be good for his career. I felt that Mac's sound was right for the part, but he was reluctant too. He didn't see himself as an upfront artist. I saw the whole concept as a tongue-in-cheek thing.

In late summer 1967 I booked studio time at Gold Star Recording Studios and got a cat called Soulful Pete to engineer the sessions. Pete worked at the studio as an apprentice doing various things, but this was his first shot at being the man at the controls. We collected our cast of New Orleans refugees who understood the spirit of what was going down. This was not to be a proper production with music arrangements and everything by the numbers. We would have to create and develop a vibe in the studio where the spirit led the way.

The cast included Mac on guitar, keyboards, and vocals; John Boudreaux (one of the AFO Executives) on drums; Bob West on bass; Ronnie Barron, keyboards (and vocals); Ernest McLean, guitar/mandolin; Steve Mann, guitar; Plas Johnson, saxophones; Lonnie Boulden, flute; and singers Tami Lynn, Shirley Goodman, Joanie (I don't remember her last name), Dave Dixon, Jessie Hill, and Al Robinson. I filled in on bass and vocals. On percussion was a guy called Didymus; I never knew his real name. He was one of those cats who was so well known in the music community that no one ever asked for his full name. He was also a partner of Mac's in the drug life.

Looking back at this mixed bag of characters, it seems amazing that we got anything done. The studio was like a Mardi Gras reunion, everybody laughing and talking, telling stories all at the same time. But once we got settled, the vibe was there and the music just flowed. I felt better than I had felt in the studio in a long time. I was comfortable, connected spiritually to the people and the music we were making. I became more involved than I had expected, and it became more than a production to me.

When the music was all done and the master tapes sent to Atlantic Records, I focused on getting a release date for fall 1967. That didn't happen. The execs at Atlantic didn't quite know what to make of this stuff I sent to them. When I talked to Ahmet Ertegun, president of Atlantic, he wanted to know what to call this type of music. "What am I gonna tell my promotion men? What radio station gonna play this crap?" I really hadn't thought about that.

NOTES
Aug.–Sept. 1967. Produce Gris Gris album. Create Dr. John.
Sept. Meeting with Sonny re: Policies & Percentages; Own Label; Lease masters; Artist contracts;
Publishing.
Oct. Meeting with Ahmet on Dr. John. How to promote; what to call the music (for marketing)
Feb. '68 Gris Gris released. Top reviews.
Mar. '68 (request made to Sonny's office): I need to know the legal status of Progress Records. We
need to formalize our agreements with respect to: Type of business; ownership and shares thereof;
Responsibilities; Resources (personnel & equipment); Payments to me in the various capacities in
which I work.

I proceeded to work on the album liner notes, credits, and all the other stuff that needed to be there. The greatest effort was on the photo session for the album cover. I got Sadie, Cher's seamstress, to make a costume for the Doctor from odd pieces of small animal skins tacked onto colorful clothes. She made him a snakeskin crown, and he found various trinkets and accessories to validate his voodoo status. The photographer, Raphael, who did work for Sonny & Cher, set up his studio late one evening, and, as

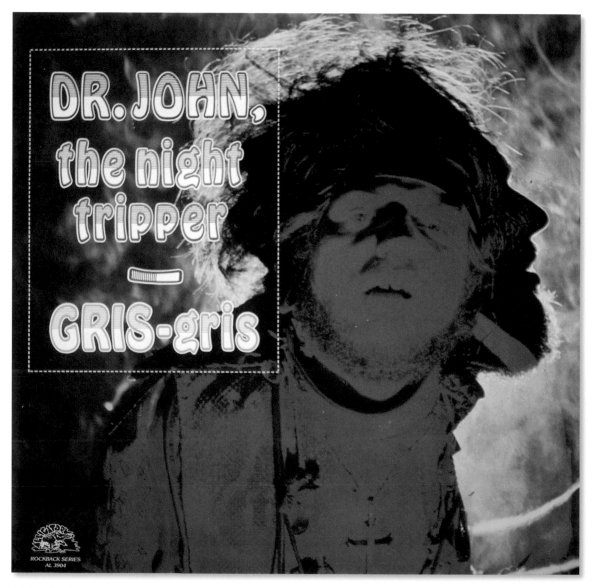

we had for the recording, we created an atmosphere that welcomed the Spirit: subdued lighting, incense burning, Dr. John music playing, Raphael creating—the image was fixed! I never had really expected serious music critics to pay that much attention to what we did. I knew it was real to us and thought it might catch on among a few hippies, underground types, flower children—but the mainstream press? I was floored at all the hype:

Dr. John is "a shadowy figure behind a strange album with a unique sound . . . The album was recorded more than a year ago but its release was delayed because the record company executives were unsure what to do with it when they heard it . . ."
—Pete Johnson, the Los Angeles Times, June 24, 1968

"Perhaps the most extraordinary feature of this mysterious note from the underground is its author's identity. No ancient Black from the Bayous, Dr. John is in fact the imaginary creation of a young, white studio musician . . ."
—Albert Goldman, the Sunday New York Times, November 10, 1968

"Boasting in another chant 'Je suis la grande Zombie,' Mack Rebbenack is obviously a man gifted with strange powers. He well may claim to be a sorcerer, for by sympathetic magic he has stolen the black man's soul."
—Albert Goldman, Life magazine, 1968

"The put-on comes with Dr. John himself: He simply cannot sing, but he covers himself with so much swamp-salt marsh-Creole-bayou mumbo-jumbo that no one will ever know the difference. Well, no meshugane appurtenances can hide the outstanding arrangements by Dr. John's producer, Harold Battiste. They overshadow what they're supposed to accompany."
—Harvey Siders, The Hollywood Reporter, April 23, 1969

"[The songs] were, in essence, toned-down variations on some common old voodoo chants, coupled with Dr. John's seemingly improvised, fascinatingly colorful vocal ramblings, the whole thing arranged and produced to absolute perfection by Harold Battiste."
—Phonograph Record Magazine, July 1973

By the time all this publicity was happening, problems had begun to brew. Mac was primarily a songwriter and studio musician. He was comfortable and confident in those environments. Now he was confronted with the idea of being an upfront stage artist, which required many adjustments, mentally and physically. He needed to put together a band. He needed to develop a show and get it ready for the road. He needed people to do these things for him—he needed managers.

Joe DeCarlo, along with Harvey Kresky, was now managing Sonny & Cher. Mac came to me saying that he had been approached about signing with them, but he was afraid to sign—and afraid to tell them he didn't want to sign. He suggested that I could be a buffer between him and them if he signed with me. I sort of understood his dilemma and went along to calm his fears.

His first major show was at the Filmore West in San Francisco, where we shared billing with none other than Thelonious Monk! I couldn't believe it—Mac and Monk? The promoters saw something I missed in putting these acts together (unless they saw them as equally weird!). I thought Mac's group was rather shabby on stage, but they got through it, and got paid.

Babylon

In June 1968 we embarked on Dr. John's second album. The material Mac came up with would take the original concept in a different direction. He would still be Dr. John, but with an observing eye on some social conditions in the country. "Babylon" would become the title track because its lyrics laid out the message of the project—"America is fucked up"—and hence the reference to the ancient city known for

DR. JOHN

Babylon is represented in the Bible by a stone. Babylon is thrown in a river and lost in a storm. Babylon—never, never, ever again will anybody want to call you they home. This is how you gonna sink now, I don't care whatever you think now. I'm gon' bring my wrath down on you now, so you'll feel the weight of truth now. I'm gonna drop you like the Rock of Ages in the sea, 'n disappear like a pebble in eternity. Nobody wants to save what's best left dead. A tidal wave is gonna dig your GRAVE!

Never again will you ever hear the sweet sound of no beautiful singer's voice, no angels playin' Guitars, or plunkin' on their Harps. No Flutes, no Trumpet players will be left by the new tone. Ain't gon' be no ditch-diggers, no construction workers, no pimps, no hustlers, no jawjerkers. No city lights, no pretty sights will ever shine on you again. No more actors, no Max Factors will smog your mind and leave you blind. No politicians, no high religions to guide you from the dark. No more love-ins, no more human beings will light up Griffith Park.

Babylon! On your hands is the blood of the Prophets and all the Holy Ones. Babylon! Everyone you executed with your machine guns. Babylon! You bringin' about your own destruction, Babylon. I'm puttin' you down, down, down, down where you can never rise up again. Watch your ashes light up the midnight skies once again. After reading the words of this old scroll to you, I hope y'all cap back on the message, Lawd, that I just told to you about Babylon!

Glowin' in the light of my life, singin' to the stars in the sky. Glowin' in the light of my life, talkin' in the way you hear. True love feelin' is the only course, yes it is, yes it is. Ain't no need for all this greed—when everything comes down to one, Thy will be done. Glowin' in the last of the best, puttin' all the charts to the test. Glowin' in the light of my life, knowin' the law for happiness.

The plan is for every man to be like a tree planted by the stream, yes it is. With good understanding and a lot of patience, you can make it, yes you can, beyond your wildest dreams. Cut out all this worryin' and complainin', you got to cut out all this fightin' and strainin'—you better know it—and just live plain old life! All the eyes of the world are on you, and they all want to see just what you gonna do—don't commit suicide, gotta keep on Glowin'.

There's a hand writing up on yonder wall, nobody seems to understand what it means at all. How can we live in a kingdom and never see the throne? Have all the riches and treasures and still feel like we're all alone? You got to keep the law of the great commandments—in the jungle of the streets, we all are defenseless.

This is not the land of Milk and Honey, this is the place where people sell their souls out for money (and you know they do!)—you got to keep on Glowin', this is the time of the Syne, yes it is, you got to keep on keepin' on, keepin' on, you got to accept it, you got to expect it, you got to keep on, keep on, keepin' on Glowin'!....

In a candlelit cafe down in New Orleans, where they play Guitars and shake Tambourines, I met a woman and we began to talk, and strange things began to happen in the dark. Hey now! I kissed her, I couldn't resist her, yeah, I discovered that I loved her—but how was I to know, as I sat beside her, that I was fallin' for the Black Widow Spider? On the very night that she found me, she began to spin her web all around me. She blinded me with kisses, so that I couldn't see how she spun her web of tragedy.

She said she loved me and put no one above me, she called me "Honey" to cop my money—but how was I to know, as I sat down beside her, I was fallin' for the Black Widow Spider? She got a heart cold as ice inside her.

Hey now! If you're ever down south in New Orleans, where the Creole ladies serve rice with red beans, take care, my friend, beware, 'cause strange things are known to happen there. You might get screwed up with the Black Widow Spider, she got a heart cold as ice inside her. Got a heart as cold as ice down inside her, the Black Widow Spider.

Onaday, onaday, onaday makiyo! Mapabay, mapabay, barazay Flamingo! Fishin' 'long the bayou, Barefoot Lady playin', comin' down the line, in and out my mind, never stays to play, comes and goes away, singin', onaday, onaday, onaday makiyo! Mapabay, mapabay, barazay Flamingo! Flashin' her design in and out my mind. Five can never catch her, ten can never hold her. She keeps gettin' younger, I keep feelin' older. Onaday, onaday, onaday makiyo! Mapabay, mapabay, barazay Flamingo!

SIDE ONE

1. BABYLON
(By Dr. John Creaux; Marsaux-Joharv, BMI. Time: 5:13)

2. GLOWIN'
(By Dr. John Creaux; Marsaux-Joharv, BMI. Time: 5:37)

3. BLACK WIDOW SPIDER
(By Malcolm Rebennack; At Last-Joharv, BMI. Time: 4:45)

4. BAREFOOT LADY
(By Dr. John Creaux & Harold Battiste; Marsaux-Joharv, BMI. Time: 3:00)

ATCO

SD 33-270
STEREO

SIDE TWO

1. TWILIGHT ZONE
(By Malcolm Rebennack; At Last-Joharv, BMI. Time: 8:10)

2. THE PATRIOTIC FLAG-WAIVER
(By Dr. John Creaux; Marzique-Joharv, BMI. Time: 4:53)

3. THE LONESOME GUITAR STRANGLER
(By Dr. John Creaux; Marzique-Joharv, BMI. Time: 5:35)

BABYLON

Conjure woman, the Hainty man is in love with you, you Barefoot Lady! Conjure woman, you just about, just about to drive this poor fool crazy. Never remain the same, duckin' through the sugar cane. Help me, conjure woman, give this Hainty man a hand.

Onaday, onaday, pnaday makiyo! Mapabay, mapabay, barazay Flamingo! Conjure woman, the Hainty man is in love with you, Barefoot Lady, Lady. Conjure woman, you know you just about, just about to drive this poor fool crazy. Conjure woman, I need your "Come To Me" French love powder (you hear my heart beatin' louder)! Conjure woman, that strong Van Van rub will capture all her love.

When all the clouds in the sky disappear in front of your eyes, when you hear a lullaby you once knew, now you can't recognize, you've stepped into the Twilight Zone, in the outer limits of a land unknown, You're in the Twilight Zone. Martians kidnap the First Family, they gonna demand New York City for ransom money. We gonna outsmart 'em, leave a note for 'em to read—the best they can get is Milwaukee, in the Twilight Zone. John and Robert Kennedy have set the stage for you and me. The Reverend Doctor Martin Luther King lived the way Jesus would have him do his thing. But where they at!??—Somewhere in the Twilight Zone, in the outer limits of a land unknown, in the Twilight Zone.

I wear a ten-gallon hat and I carry a baseball bat, singin' 'bout "My Country 'Tis of Thee" down on the corner of Sixth & Main Street, Stick all the communists in one neighborhood, terrorize their children and we'll feel real good, singin' 'bout "My Country 'Tis of Thee" down on the corner of Sixth & Main Street.

I belong to the KKK and the NAACP, I'm a Berkeley student in the John Birch Society. A missile erector, a propaganda collector, a woman selector and a Castro defector, a medical dissector and a States' Rights protector, a professional soldier and a conscientious objector, Hell's Angel member of the Black Panther Party, a communist member since early 1940, a Digger, a Hippie, acid head and a Saint, a Daughter of the Revolution, a Minute Man in war paint. Divided we stand, multiplied we'll fall, over-population is my call. I'm black and I'm white, I come in every color, I'm a student, a teacher, and I'm dying of stone hunger. A Hawk and a Dove known as a hate-monger, old as the hills, but I feel a little younger. I'm righteously righteous, stone justly just, faithful in the need of everyone's trust. Loyal to the lodge that just painted my garage. I notice when your family see me coming they begin to duck and dodge. I'm a gourmet chef of charcoal barbecue, transplanted heart sewed to the sole of my shoe. You might think I'm crazy, you might think I'm insane, never know the secret that lies hidden in my brain. I'm a hundred per cent for Uncle Sam, a Patriotic Flag-Waiver is what I am. Send all the draft card burners back to Viet Nam, and if they protest over there, you know I won't give a damn.

I'm the Lonesome Guitar Strangler, and down the road I go, strangling Guitar players, every day I get one more. I shoot them full of fuzztone, my reverb kills them slow, I'm gonna use my G-string on a fellow named Gabor Szabo. I'm the Lonesome Guitar Strangler, so full of hate, you see, hot on the trail of all you copycats who copy Wes Montgomery. I'm a Lonesome Guitar Strangler, with all my bread I should'a been a banker, hot on the trail of incense and sitars to bury Ravi Shankar. I'm a Lonesome Guitar Strangler, smokin' psychedelic guitar picks, ready to do in every one of y'all—better get ready, Jimi Hendrix!

DR. JOHN, THE NIGHT TRIPPER

We thank the children who sang so sincerely and innocently on *The Patriotic Flag-Waiver*: Andrea, Beryl, Billy, Bunny, Butch, Dawn, Marzique, Terri, Troy, and Troy Lynn.

Recorded at Gold Star Recording Studios, Hollywood
Recording engineer: "Soulful Pete"
Album photography: Norton
Album design: Stanislaw Zagorski
ARRANGED AND PRODUCED BY HAROLD BATTISTE, JR.
A SONNY & CHER PRODUCTION

 This is a stereo recording. For best results observe the R.I.A.A. high frequency roll-off characteristic with a 500 cycle crossover.

© 1968 Atlantic Recording Corporation   Printed in U.S.A.
ATCO RECORDS, 1841 BROADWAY, NEW YORK, N.Y. 10023
DIVISION OF ATLANTIC RECORDING CORPORATION

its wealth, luxury, and wickedness. The surprise recognition we got for *Gris-gris* did not lead me to believe that we were going to have a hit commercial seller, so I saw no reason to hold back on what Mac wanted to say in his lyrics (and I liked what he was saying). The somber message of "Glowin'" or the sly contradictions in "The Patriotic Flag-Waiver" (with kids from my neighborhood singing background) staked out new territory for the doctor's rap.

Barry White and Jackie DeShannon

It was around this time that I got a call to do a production for Imperial Records. "The Weight" had been done by a rock group, and the people at Imperial wanted a new singer, Jackie DeShannon, to cover it. The session included a songwriter, arranger, and producer named Barry White. Barry was a big cat, about six foot two and three hundred fifty pounds plus. He could have easily been a linebacker for the Los Angeles Rams. His singers, who later became the girl group Love Unlimited ("Walking in the Rain"), featuring his soon-to-be wife, Glodean, were handling the backup on "The Weight." Those women had strong voices and great harmony. I was amazed and impressed by Barry's success a few years later, when he became known for his bedroom talk and sexy vocals supported by his own lush orchestrations. He went on to '70s R&B crooner/love-meister fame with "Never Gonna Give You Up," "Love's Theme," and "Can't Get Enough of Your Love, Babe." The music business is amazing!

Hal-Mac

In the meantime I had been listening to other artists and songwriters with thoughts of trying to help them get where they wanted to go. One was a duo, another, two guys with three girls as background vocals. Another wrote the kind of songs that I felt were on the level of standards that come from Broadway musicals. And there was King Floyd, who was brought to me by Leslie Milton, a drummer friend from New Orleans who was living in Seattle.

I needed a production deal that would underwrite the session costs for these acts. I got a one-shot deal at Liberty Records to produce New Orleans singer Lydia Marcelle, who was doing songs composed by a Broadway-standard writer named Jane McNealy. Al Bennett, CEO at Liberty Records, was impressed by Lydia, so I got to do two of Jane's songs with full orchestra. Jane invited her parents to the session to hear her songs. They were impressed with how the arrangements showcased their daughter's material.

I got a call from Mac about a new project he was doing for Mercury Records that might need my help. I met with him at a restaurant on Hollywood Boulevard near where Sam Cooke's office used to be. Mac had gotten involved in doing some producing for Irving Green, Mercury's CEO, but things had stalled and the recording was not getting done. I was being brought in to get the project finished. The artist on the project, singer/writer Wayne Talbert, was an old buddy of Mac's, and they shared some bad habits together that may have affected the pace of their work. I wasn't into drugs or the hard drug scene, but I could see what was happening. Despite all of that, I liked Wayne and thought him to be quite talented. I met with Irving Green's West Coast affiliate, Irwin Garr, and I would be working with Mac to produce Talbert's album for Garr's Pulsar Records.

Mac and I formed Hal-Mac Productions and signed an agreement with Pulsar. I traveled up to San Francisco, where Mac and Wayne had been recording for several months without much result. With a little organizing, discipline, and focus, we completed the music in less than a week. Garr, who usually came off as gruff and grumpy, was happy.

The Cake and Other Acts

I was keeping myself busy around this time. I managed during 1967 to do several other projects (besides Sonny & Cher): a girl group from England who called themselves the Cake had sought me out through

Sonny & Cher's former agents, Charlie Green and Brian Stone, to do their self-titled debut album for Decca Records. I think they thought of themselves as the female Beatles. I heard their songs and style as sort of baroque British folk. I enjoyed doing the music for this project, which allowed me to handle chamber music with a polite groove. It wasn't a hit, but about six months later in Los Angeles, we did a second album, *A Slice of Cake*. Some forty years later, on February 3, 2007, I received an e-mail from Chelsea Lee, one of the original slices of the Cake (she was called "Eleanor" back then). The Cake had been rediscovered and revived in England. I was really proud of them and the work that we had done: their music withstood the test of time.

That same year, Louis Prima, a high-energy New Orleans entertainer who was living and doing his show in Las Vegas, summoned me to produce a record for his group. We had a lot of fun with the Chief and Sam Butera, his bandleader and sax man, for four or five days, but that's all the time we had, so there was no record. I did a second album with Wayne Talbert (*Lord Have Mercy on My Funky Soul*) for Pulsar, plus the debut album for King Floyd (*A Man In Love*). And I did two commercials for ad agency Young & Rubicam, selling the Plymouth Roadrunner.

The Pulsar Period

Mac and I were now a production team, with a named company and a signed agreement. I didn't really think all that would change much about the way we dealt with each other—or felt about each other. We had a long history, going all the way back to Mac's teens. His mother had spoken with me before he made the trip to California and explained the dramatic circumstances under which the trip was being made. Mac had gotten into trouble and went to jail in Florida. He was shot in the hand, and the wound messed up one of his fingers, so he couldn't play guitar anymore. Soon after, Mac switched to piano as his primary instrument. To make matters worse, Louisiana authorities made it known that they didn't want Mac to return to New Orleans, so he came out to Los Angeles. Our relationship—or, I should say, *my* relationship with *him* over the years—had become somewhat parental. I functioned, at least, as a sort of responsible adult for him out in California.

Hal-Mac Productions got an office in the Pulsar Records suite on Beverly Boulevard. I would be responsible for generating, planning, and directing the work. Mac would concentrate on developing material, writing songs, and helping prepare artists. Before we came on, I don't think Pulsar had any artists other than Wayne. Of the artists available to me that I thought were ready, King Floyd was my choice.

Dr. John in the Hal-Mac production office at Pulsar Records on Beverly Boulevard, L.A., 1968 (THNOC)

He had been coming to my house working on his songs in my backyard office, and I had been helping him with his chords on the piano. I liked the stories in his songs and the way he structured them. I could hear how I would arrange them.

In those days, record companies would put out a few singles on an artist to test the market. If they got even a modest hit, then they would go for an album. But for some reason I did not understand, Irwin Garr at Pulsar wanted to do an LP on Floyd his first time out. I teamed him up with Mac and his writing buddies Jessie Hill and Al "Shine" Robinson to come up with a few more songs to fill out the album. My work habits were quite different from Mac's. I had developed procedures and methods to manage projects in ways that were efficient, with money and time—to get more bang for the buck. Sometimes I felt that putting Mac to work with Jessie and Shine was not smart. It was like the situation in San Francisco with Mac and Wayne. Garr was always on Mac's case about being late for sessions—and a host of other things. Garr's manner was gruff, irritating, and, to Mac, intimidating.

Dr. John got booked for some gigs in the Midwest, but, before he even got to his first gig, he got busted in St. Louis. Of course the shows were off. He called Atlantic Records in New York and found someone to bail him out. I wasn't there, but I found out from Mac that Charlie Green and Brian Stone went to St. Louis to grab Dr. John and lock him into a deal. For several months Mac seemed to have disappeared. I heard rumors that Jerry Wexler at Atlantic had gotten involved and put Mac on a detox program. I received a registered letter informing me that Mac had given power of attorney to Green and Stone and had dissolved his contract with me. I was upset and felt completely betrayed. I'd had my fill of dealing with Mac at this point, so I was somewhat relieved—but still angry. I had gotten into a 25 percent contract with Mac due to his concern about being taken advantage of by Joe DeCarlo, and this was how it all ended.

Hal-Mel

In 1969 I went to Cannes, France, for the MIDEM international music conference. The experience was quite different from the time I went with Sonny & Cher a couple of years before. My orientation and focus was toward the publishing business now. Of course, most of the dealings at the conference were happening over my head, out of my sight, and beyond my understanding, but I was cool. I got to meet a few of the big players, but I just watched them play.

On the way to Cannes I had a little layover time in New York. I was able to contact Mel Lastie, my business and spiritual partner since the AFO days. He insisted that I come to his Harlem apartment, which he and his new lovely lady, Elaine, had recently acquired. (A New York miracle!) There was too much for us to catch up on now, so we got right to business. I needed his help in a big way. The Hal-Mac deal with Pulsar had great possibilities, but I couldn't get it done with just Mac. I needed Mac for what he could do, but he couldn't seem to do all that was needed. I wanted Mel to think about moving to Los Angeles, but that was asking a lot. I offered to bring him and Elaine out for a couple of weeks to check it out and think about it.

When I got back to L.A. after MIDEM, Mel had decided to come out West and check out my situation. It was like in 1961 when I had approached him about the record company idea—he just got it! He understood and saw the potential. Our minds were in sync. In less than a month, he and Elaine were looking to buy a home in Los Angeles.

Hal-Mac became Hal-Mel. We began to get new artists to develop and produce for Pulsar. Garr con-

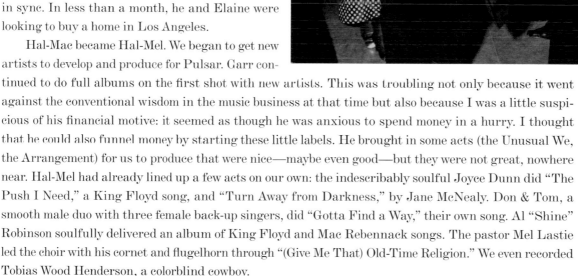

tinued to do full albums on the first shot with new artists. This was troubling not only because it went against the conventional wisdom in the music business at that time but also because I was a little suspicious of his financial motive: it seemed as though he was anxious to spend money in a hurry. I thought that he could also funnel money by starting these little labels. He brought in some acts (the Unusual We, the Arrangement) for us to produce that were nice—maybe even good—but they were not great, nowhere near. Hal-Mel had already lined up a few acts on our own: the indescribably soulful Joyce Dunn did "The Push I Need," a King Floyd song, and "Turn Away from Darkness," by Jane McNealy. Don & Tom, a smooth male duo with three female back-up singers, did "Gotta Find a Way," their own song. Al "Shine" Robinson soulfully delivered an album of King Floyd and Mac Rebennack songs. The pastor Mel Lastie led the choir with his cornet and flugelhorn through "(Give Me That) Old-Time Religion." We even recorded Tobias Wood Henderson, a colorblind cowboy.

I didn't know that while my head and heart were buried in Pulsar's future, Garr was closing the whole thing down. It seemed that Pulsar was part of a larger plan in which Hal-Mac-Mel was not included beyond a certain point. We had evidently served our purpose as producers; Garr and Green were off to other things. Still, I had enjoyed the musical experiences I'd had—working with the variety of artists we produced—especially after having been with Sonny & Cher since 1964. I was concerned that I had gotten Melvin to leave New York for nothing, but he and Elaine were glad to have made the move.

Mel and I worked out a plan to buy back the masters Hal-Mel had produced for Pulsar. Garr wanted only five thousand dollars for them, which confirmed to me that he really never did have the kind of plans

Mel Lastie and Harold in the
Hal-Mel office at Pulsar, 1969
(AMISTAD RESEARCH CENTER)

for us with Pulsar that I had thought. Mel and I also got connected to some MCA Records people through a brother with a recording studio in South Central L.A. The studio was owned by the Electrodyne Corporation, which was affiliated somehow with MCA and other record companies—Decca, Coral, Kapp, Brunswick, Uni, and others. We had started talking business with MCA at the end of 1969, and in December I submitted a document with a proposal for a merger:

In approaching the problem of restructuring the various companies of Hal-Mel Enterprises in such manner as would give them the flexibility necessary to work in conjunction with the existing structure of M.C.A. and its affiliates, (more specifically and directly with Electrodyne and Soul, Inc.), I shall proceed as follows:

I. Outline the Hal-Mel structure;
II. Outline, to the extent of my knowledge thereof, the M.C.A. structure;
III. Determine and evaluate the alternatives of profitable correlations between the two; and
IV. Set estimates of operating cost of one alternative which, in my opinion, such alternative shall represent the medium between the ideal (most costly) and impractical (least costly) alternatives.

Listed in the order of age, with a brief description of their present legal status, the companies of H.M.E. are:

1. A.F.O. Records, Inc.—(1961 Louisiana) A.F.O.
Present status: Sole proprietorship by Harold Battiste.
Assets: 81 master sides.
A.F.M. Signatory

2. At Last Publishing Company (1961) A.L.P.C
Present status: Sole proprietorship by Harold Battiste.
Assets: 222 Copyrights, recently transferred to M.M.C.I.
Mechanical license issued on approximately 64% of catalog.

3. Adormel Music, Inc.—(1966) New York A.M.I.
Present status: President, Melvin Lastie
Assets: 35 Copyrights.
Mechanical license issued on approximately 45% of catalog.

4. Marzique Music Company, Inc.—(1967 California) M.M.C.I.
Present status: President, Harold Battiste.
Assets: 145 Copyrights (plus At Last catalog)
Mechanical license on approximately 47% of catalog.

5. Marzique Music Company—(1967) M.M.C.
Present status: Sole proprietorship by Harold Battiste.
Assets: A.F.M. Television Commercial Packaging Licensee
Artist Management Contracts—Dr. John, The Night Tripper; Tami Lynn.

6. Hal-Mel Productions—(1969) H.M.P
Present status: Partnership—Harold Battiste, 62½% Melvin Lastie, 37½%.
Assets: The Cream of The Crop, female vocal group; The Individuals, male vocal group and writers; Tami Lynn, female vocalist; Troy Randall, writer and male vocalist; Shine, male vocalist and writer; and Jane McNealy, writer.
(These artists and writers are not presently under exclusive contract to H.M.P., and H.M.P. has not responded to their willingness to sign because we do not wish to impede their freedom to negotiate with other companies.)

As is evidenced by examination of the chart (page 5), it is quite obvious that the possible alternatives for merging the companies of H.M.E. with those of M.C.A. in such manner(s) as would be mutually profitable are practically infinite. H.M.E.'s most apparent assets are the experience and capability in the various facets of the music industry of its principals, Harold Battiste and Melvin Lastie (see resumes).

The physical assets (copyrights, artists, writers, etc.) of the companies under the H.M.E. banner have been acquired as a result of, and under the expert scrutiny of the principals over the past 15 years. Let's examine the possibilities.

1. M.C.A. Record Division at large;
2. any one of the existing labels of M.C.A;
3. be leased to labels outside the M.C.A. organization;
4. Manufacture on our labels for independent distribution;
5. number 1 and 2, above, on M.C.A.'s artists; and,
6. number 1 and 2, above, using M.C.A.'s copyrights.
7. Etc.

Harold R. Battiste, Jr.

We were quite ambitious and optimistic. Our grand notion of a merger between MCA and Hal-Mel Enterprises (HME) was also quite naïve. We knew we were walking in tall grass but had no idea how short we were. After a week or so of run-arounds, we got the message that we were not going to get a contract with MCA. We were glad that it didn't take longer.

The Dawn of a New Decade

In January 1970 Sonny had acquired a script done by Sandy Baron and Neal Marshall for a show to be called *Sonny & Cher's Nitty-Gritty Comedy Hour.* I passed on the offer to be musical director, but the idea never really got off the ground anyway. It ended up as a one-time special—*Sonny & Cher: Nitty Gritty Hour*—that aired in the summer of 1970.

That same month I got another shot at producing a session for Louis Prima, and we actually made a record this time—the single "I'm Gonna Sit Right Down and Write Myself a Letter." In February, J. W. Alexander, Sam Cooke's mentor and manager since his gospel days, got the urge to revive his own singing career and asked me to coproduce and arrange his album. In May, film composer Stu Phillips called me in to compose some cues for *Beyond the Valley of the Dolls*—and I still get a few pennies in royalties! I don't know why they bother to send those few pennies. I actually received a check once for a penny, and I framed it. It cost them accountants' fees, plus thirty-nine cents to mail the check, then I had to travel to the bank to deposit it. I'm imagining that the tellers get a laugh from those checks.

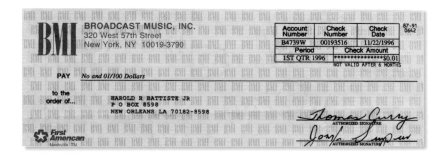

In the midst of all this action, Melvin and I had developed a great relationship with Lowell Jordan, the engineer at Hollywood Central Recording Studio. This is where we had done some of the Hal-Mel productions for Pulsar. Jordan was also a singer/songwriter/piano man who enjoyed hanging with us. We got a lot of free studio time and decided to put some things down just for fun. We played all the parts: Melvin on trumpet, cornet, flugelhorn, drums, and percussion; me on tenor and alto sax, piano, B3 organ, and bass. The record, *Hal-Mel, Alone Together*, was finally released on Opus 43 Records in 1976. I love this album so much; it was just the two of us working together and having a lot of fun. My handwritten note to the listeners appears on the back of the album jacket.

> The music in this package represents more than the sounds you hear . . . it represents the relationship between two men—myself and Mel Lastie. In the late spring and early summer of 1970, Melvin and I, along with engineer Lowell Jordan, embarked spontaneously upon making some music in the studio. There was no pre-conceived notion of what the "concept" of the album would be . . . in fact, we never thought we were doing an "ALBUM." Instead, we were just "RELAXING" . . . running <u>from</u> the pressure-ridden record-biz to a place where we felt <u>secure</u> and <u>happy.</u> The relationship between Melvin and I started in the late 50's and we solidified that relationship in 1961 when we formed A.F.O. Records. It became evident to me that our thinking and personalities were compatible. The strengths of each of us made up for each of our weaknesses.

At the beginning of 1970, I had thought the Sonny & Cher thing was over. Not so easy. Sonny still needed me near, and, frankly, I still needed him a little. While I had been busy setting up a new future for my career, Sonny had been trying to finish his *Chastity* movie. He and I had not been able to agree on terms, so I was not involved with that project. By the time he finished, sometime in late 1969 or early 1970, he had lost a lot of money. Sonny & Cher needed to do some gigs, so they called and asked me to go on the road with them again.

Harold on tour with Sonny & Cher during a stint at the Blue Room in the Fairmont Hotel, New Orleans, 1970; PHOTO BY PORTER NEWS SERVICE (THNOC)

chapter **8 up & down the scales**

Though I was a bit reluctant to get back on with Sonny & Cher, there were some developments that attracted me to the 1970 tour: they had assembled a new rhythm section, some of whom had come out of the new jazz studies program at North Texas State University. They also had some new charts done by a fine guitarist named Dean Parks. This was the best-trained section I had ever had on the road with Sonny & Cher. Standouts were drummer Matt Betton, whose father was one of the founders of the National Association of Jazz Educators, and Tom Canning, who became pianist for jazz vocalist Al Jarreau after leaving Sonny & Cher. Another attraction for me was that the tour included a three-week stint in New Orleans. I had my list of family, friends, people, places, and things to see back home—more than I could possibly do, but I was ready. Among the musician friends on the list were James Black, Ellis Marsalis, Willie Tee, Alvin Batiste, and Red Tyler.

The shows were at the Fairmont Hotel, formerly the Roosevelt. When I left New Orleans in 1963, this was the premier hotel in the city, and, of course, it was for Whites only. I had never seen the famous and popular Blue Room, where we would perform nightly. Sonny & Cher did not go over well at the Fairmont (no surprise to me), but we worked hard every night. The Blue Room was one of those elegant but conservative (and upscale) venues. Sonny & Cher represented "Young America," a hip way of being—not the feeling associated with Blue Room patrons. Their kind of pop music just didn't click with that audience. These poorly attended shows were, if nothing else, a good dress rehearsal for the rest of the tour. All was well until I got overenergized and threw my back out. I was flown to New York the next morning to see Dr. Milton Reder, a specialist with a remedy. He dipped two long Q-tips in clear liquid and stuck them up my nose. He then told me to stand up. The pain and discomfort were over!

On September 7 we said bye-bye to the Big Easy. I was back in Los Angeles for a short while, just in time to celebrate Yette's birthday. Then I was off again with the tour, to Vancouver, Philadelphia, and Las Vegas.

I enjoyed a truly bright moment when we were in Vegas. In the lounge at the Flamingo, I saw a familiar face that turned out to be Johnny Hodges, a.k.a. "Rabbit," the famous lead alto sax in the Duke Ellington orchestra. He looked a little intimidating, but I introduced myself anyway. After a little musician talk and a couple of drinks, he invited me to a studio where they were doing a session. I couldn't believe this was really happening! The scene at the studio was very relaxed, casual. I was expecting the whole band, but that was not to be: only about two or three of the cats were there. After a while, about four more showed up, among them the brilliant tenor man Paul Gonsalves—drunk, but still brilliant! Duke never made it to the studio, but after the session I went with the cats to the hotel, where Duke was downing a big steak in his suite at three in the morning.

Still, I felt like my career was again stalled in the Sonny & Cher mode.

Daily Reminders

With all the activity happening in my work life, it was hard to imagine that equally as much—maybe more—was going on at home. In 1970 I bought a Daily Reminder journal to try to keep track of my activities. I began to see just how busy and scattered my life was (and keeping up the Daily Reminder added another activity!). The Reminder became a sort of diary where, in addition to business stuff, appointments, phone numbers, etc., I would write thoughts on various subjects, incidents, and people. I got a new one every year for twenty years.

At the start of 1971, I reflected on what had been going on in my family for the last year:

DAILY REMINDER / 1-1-71

I see that the entries in the Daily Reminder are, in many places, speaking of the obvious confusion in my life. Many of the things I wrote on these pages were conclusions arrived at about problems to which I had given much thought. The problems had no particular relation to one another nor to any one subject, but rather to general life, living and surviving, understanding self and surroundings.

I have arrived at an awareness which contains the key to understanding and operating my life. This awareness has taken many of the things out of my life upon which I could lean for "moral support." The "Goodness of Man," "Hope, Faith and Love," ". . . Meek shall inherit . . ." and other such beliefs which I held deeply and attempted to live by, no longer occupy the same priority. They are replaced by a less pleasant, but more realistic understanding of such things.

Without question, the most significant event, and the most traumatic, was leaving home and attempting to play out the role of separating from Yette. This episode happened in the middle of 1971 and lasted a little over two months. The physical absence from home, and the manner in which it happened, was both necessary and unavoidable. Entries in the "Daily Reminder" bear out this fact.

The play ended when I decided to go on the road with Sonny & Cher. By then, I had bought a Cadillac convertible for the wrong reasons. I was going through the clichéd midlife crisis and moved into a "single's" apartment in the summer, feeling quite irrational. I gave up the Cadillac and moved back home by the fall, thinking that I was quite a different man. I knew that my family filled a great need in my life, one which I could not, for long, do without. I also discovered that the basic laws of self-preservation abided strongly in Yette. This was one of the unpleasant facts that I avoided facing.

African Genesis

While I was on the road with Sonny & Cher, I was introduced to a book that became a very important part of my understanding of history—well, not so much HIStory as maybe A story—*African Genesis: A Personal Investigation into the Animal Origins and Nature of Man,* by Robert Ardrey. Although he had formally studied the natural sciences, Ardrey had become a playwright and was absorbed in theater for twenty years. On assignment in Africa to do a story about the work of anthropologists Louis and Mary Leakey, Ardrey became reabsorbed in anthropology. His storylike writing style kept me involved in the book, which ran to nearly four hundred pages (big for me). Most satisfying to me were the numerous times the information verified thoughts and notions I had written about in my notes.

So when Sonny and Denis Pregnolato approached me to discuss where I thought music was heading, I just told them that all the music was going back to Africa. I was not surprised when, about a month later, in November 1971, Sonny came to me with an idea to do something "African"; he may have already

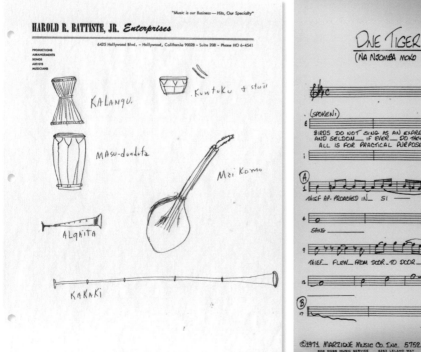
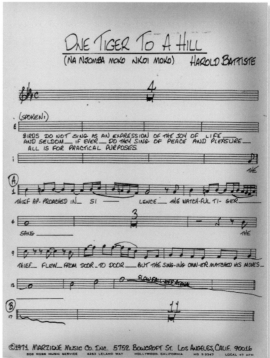

Left, Sketches of African instruments to be used in the recording of the *African Genesis Suite; right,* chart for "One Tiger to a Hill"
(AMISTAD RESEARCH CENTER)

set a deal with Johnny Musso, president of Kapp Records. I had some thoughts based on the *African Genesis* book. Some of the chapter titles gave me ideas—"One Tiger to a Hill," "A Romantic Fallacy." I did some research on languages and musical instruments at UCLA, and I also found a homeboy in Los Angeles, Juno Lewis, who was deep into making and playing African percussion instruments. He was the featured percussionist and composer on the John Coltrane *Kulu Sé Mama* album.

The *African Genesis Suite* was unique in its conception and its production. Juno created the Daka d'Belah for this music, along with several other drums for the players. Melvin Lastie had a group of talented young percussionists who were also part of the mix. The group included the brilliant John Barnes on piano/keyboard. Barnes went on to work with Quincy Jones's production company and coproduced a number of projects, including Michael Jackson's *Off the Wall* album. Add Tami Lynn on vocals, three soulful background singers, plus kids from the Baldwin Hills Elementary School choir. Everything came together. It was like that first great Dr. John session, but based in Africa.

But it was too good to be true. By the third session, about midway into the production, Sonny and I started having differing views on where the music was going. I think he was used to my being there just to support his ideas, but this was different. I don't think he knew how to switch roles, and I couldn't let him take this down the wrong path. We never finished the project. I still have the four tracks we did do, and someday they may see the light.

Tami and Me in England

In June 1971 Tami Lynn contacted me to say that she'd been asked to tour England and she wanted me to go along as a manager, of sorts, to deal with some of the things that would come up. (Neither of us knew much about managing a tour: negotiating contracts, receiving payments, setting up travel, etc.) The offer to tour had come about under unusual circumstances. A few years back, maybe 1968 or so, when Tami was in New York working with Melvin Lastie, she recorded a song for Atlantic Records called "I'm Gonna Run Away from You." Producer Jerry Wexler had always been fascinated by Tami's talent and energy. This song, however, was a quiet, pop-type number, not at all what Jerry expected. Tami didn't think much of it either. Sometime during the next couple of years, John Abbey, editor of *Blues & Soul* magazine in England, had acquired some masters from Atlantic, one of which was Tami's "I'm Gonna Run Away." Abbey liked it well enough to get it played at some places in London. It caught on and went up to the top of the charts there.

We arrived in London midday on Tuesday, June 8, and were met by Abbey, Mike Clifford from Polydor Records, and Ronnie Jones of the APB booking agency that had set up the tour. They were with Pat Mulligan of Atlantic Records, who was en route to meet Jerry Wexler and Aretha Franklin in Paris. Tami and I went to the Kensington Palace Hotel, where reservations had been made for us. I was getting a little nervous because nobody had talked about money: John, Mike, and Ronnie all seemed reluctant to talk about work or business. We all had dinner at the hotel, and, when the waiter brought the check, I thought John would take it; instead, he told me to put it on my bill.

The next day, things were quite different: lots of activities were scheduled and there was a more hectic vibe. There was a TV appearance, press interviews, band rehearsal—which fell to me even though I was not there as a musical director. Once again I found a situation similar to the one I had with Sonny & Cher: not the greatest musicians in the road band. I managed to put together a fairly nice show using some popular songs of the day—"What's Goin' On," "Close to You"—and Tami's London hit. Our first gig on the tour was in Scarborough, a town in the north that looked just like a typical small town in England, based on stuff I had seen about England in various movies, like *Georgy Girl*. It was interesting to see the same in reality. From there, we played Manchester, then returned to London.

Left London 12 Noon. Hotel paid by Leo of A.P.B. I asked for a copy of the bill. He said he had it in his case. So far, I have allowed events to progress in a [manner] contrary to practices of what I understand as 'good' business procedures. Several factors contributed to my decision to 'go along.' First, Tami's need to have this dream fulfilled. Secondly, the publicity value and press can be used later in the States. Then, the possibility of recording without obligation, in England. However, at this point it has become necessary to tighten up a bit . . . particularly on the agency. Tami has no legal commitment to them, nor they to her, except that they have illegally used her name and likeness to promote these dances and engagements.

I paid another visit to the Mechanical Copyright Protection Society (MCPS) while in London to check on tracks owned by At Last Publishing and Marzique Music. I was shocked to discover that for nearly ten years, the royalty earnings for At Last's hit "I Know" had been paid to another company. I had to accept responsibility, though, because of my ignorance of the business from the beginning. With the help of some of the people at MCPS, I was able to get some of the information corrected, which enabled At Last Publishing to begin receiving royalties. But by now, years after the song hit, there wasn't much left.

We left for home on June 24. Overall, the trip was a good one for both Tami and for me. We met several wonderfully nice people, and some important business contacts too. I still have copies of magazine stories from *Melody Maker, Blues & Soul,* and *Cream* that reviewed Tami's performances and shined a bit of a spotlight on our work. It was good to get some recognition for what we were doing musically.

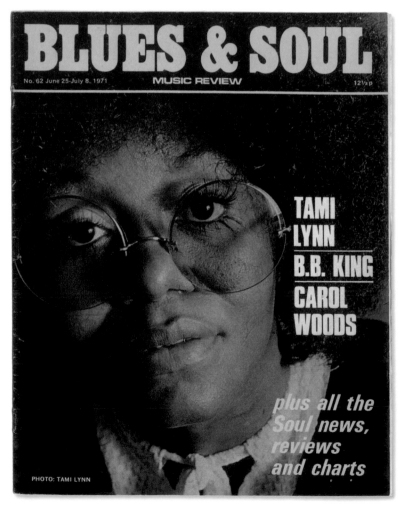

Cover of *Blues & Soul,* No. 62, June 25–July 8, 1971 (AMISTAD RESEARCH CENTER)

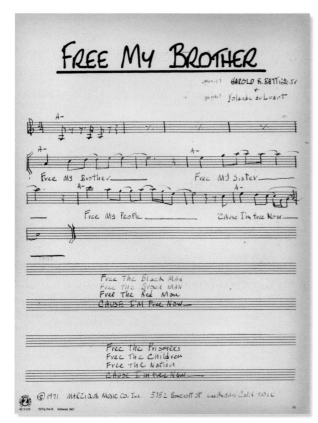

Portrait of a Revolutionary

Before the summer of 1971 was over, I had the opportunity to collaborate with director Yolande DuLuart on composing a theme for a film about Angela Davis and the Soledad Brothers, *Angela Davis: Portrait of a Revolutionary*. Davis, a young Black college professor, was acquitted in the summer of 1972 after being accused and jailed for her involvement in an incident in which Jonathan Jackson and others (including a sitting judge) were killed in a courtroom shootout. Jonathan Jackson's brother George was one of the so-called Soledad Brothers, a group of young Black revolutionaries who were in California's Soledad Prison on a variety of charges. Davis was in love with George Jackson, and their love affair was documented in Jackson's book, *Soledad Brother,* a treatise on race and politics in America. In 1970 Jonathan Jackson and several other young men kidnapped a judge in an attempt to free his brother; all died in a hail of police bullets after a standoff. Jonathan had several guns in his possession that were registered to Davis, which led to her being sought by the police and FBI; in fear for her life, she went underground. After her capture and imprisonment, Black people across the United States and around the world engaged in a "Free Angela" movement; George Jackson's death at the hands of a prison guard in August 1971 stoked the flames. Davis was (and still is) a symbol of militant Black resistance in the late '60s and early '70s. Davis's photo, sporting a huge Afro and raised fist, was seen on posters and T-shirts for many years.

It was a very refreshing experience to revisit the political side of my life after having been out of my neighborhood professionally so often. It felt good to work on some music that allowed me to go deep into my soul, with artists and musicians who shared that familiar spirit. In addition to John Barnes, Darryl Clabon, and the fellows I used on the *African Genesis Suite* project, I enlisted the help of vocalist Mae Mercer, a soulful singer with power in her tone. "Free my brother, free my sister, free my people, 'cause I'm free now!" Mae demanded. "Free the Black man, free the brown man, free the red man, 'cause I'm free now!" It felt so good!

DAILY REMINDER / 8-4-71

Yolonde DuLuart . . . filmed "Angela" documentary . . . needs music. (Fri.6) Angela film screened at U.C.L.A. for John, Darryl, Yolonde and me. Met Mae Mercer. (Tue. 10) 7417 Sunset. Tony Christian re copyright to "Free My Brother." Set meeting to discuss film for 6:00 p.m. at Mae Mercer's. Said he needed to have a concept for a film which would tell the story of the Black Man's Blues. Insisted that he wanted the Truth. Showed us their sound stage & equipment for rehearsals and a van for remote recording . . . all owned by Far-Out Productions. (6:00 pm) Tony Christian, in my opinion, needed or wanted more than an 'opinion' but needed to extract story ideas . . . (Wed. 11) Character of T.C. becoming more suspicious re his sincerity tho his act is highly developed. I have not dealt with the new generation of J.W. & A.R. (who 'luves' niggahs). So, it is quite educational to observe their performance, (when they can be detected!)

Not-Yet-Famous Amos

In October 1971 I got a call from Ira Okun at the William Morris Agency, which had begun representing producers, to discuss the possibility of his representing Hal-Mel. At our initial meeting I got acquainted with their operation and tried to determine the potential benefit to Hal-Mel, and I met Mark Turk, a young attorney with the agency who negotiated production deals. They wanted Hal-Mel to sign a three-year agreement naming the William Morris Agency as our reps, and for Mark Turk to get a label deal for the gospel album Wally Amos wanted us to produce.

I had met Wally back in 1965 when Sonny & Cher signed with William Morris. They sent two of their young agents, Wally and Harvey Kresky, out on tour with us to manage business matters. Wally had aspirations to become a music and entertainment star maker. He was a very likable, good guy—cheerful, optimistic—and he made these great cookies, which he gave to friends and people in the business.

In 1971 Wally had started managing and producing talent on his own. He was well liked and well connected. He called me to set up a meeting with John Rosica of Bell Records to hear the tapes on an artist he'd found, a gospel group called Gideon & Power. Rosica was anxious to get the right producer for Gideon, the lead, and his backup group, and he felt that I would be right. He called Mark Turk to thank him for recommending me. Larry Uttal, who owned Bell Records and was one of the music executives with whom Wally had connections, was very happy! After the expected amount of meetings, debate, and confusion between Wally, Turk, Rosica, Judy Kyle, et al., it was agreed that Hal-Mel would go to San Francisco to hear Gideon & Power. Judy was trying to become a manager in the music business. She was equally interested in becoming Mel's woman. Melvin didn't dabble in that, but let her hang around if she could help us get rolling.

The next day at Mooney's Irish Pub, on Union and Grant in San Francisco, rehearsal had been set up by TV engineers, who were there for a taping of Gideon & Power. Wally had to deal with some acoustical problems at the club, but that wasn't the real problem—it turned out that Gideon & Power weren't what we thought they were. Their show consisted mainly of visual antics and bawdy humor, which didn't quite mesh with their reputation as a gospel group, and neither of which was acceptable at that time for a mass audience. Wally displayed his typical optimism when he said that Gideon could put a band together in a "presentable form."

But the story ended right about the time Wally discovered the real star he had been producing all along: his special chocolate chip cookies! The cookies later took off in a big way and gave Wally a whole new career, while Gideon & Power suffered a natural show-business death.

Before that happened, though, I had to mix the Gideon tracks at Wally Heider's Studio. For three days I went out there in the morning, and then out to Sound City Studio in Burbank, in the San Fernando Valley, to arrange, record, and coproduce Dr. John's *Gumbo* album, from three in the afternoon until about two in the morning. On the second day, I told Jerry Wexler that Mac was not prepared, but we forged on anyway. On the third day, I told Jerry that I didn't want to participate in the way he was running this project. When I had gotten the very first call from him, I refused on the grounds of things that had happened with Mac and me before—the whole thing with the St. Louis bust and my being dropped as a manager. I didn't want to subject myself to more of the same.

Jerry (as only he can) went into his persuasive mode, assuring me that things were different now, that this was the time for us to heal, that this was the project to bring us back. So I agreed to produce Mac's project. Despite all the difficulties, I did enjoy doing the music and the spirit. The "Iko Iko" chart has survived the time test and emerged to join the parade of Mardi Gras classics. I'm happy with that!

Meet with Jerry Wexler & Mac re Gumbo LP.
3pm. Called Mac, no answer. I assumed they weren't back from San Diego yet. At 4pm, Jerry called me and asked how soon I could make it to Mac's. I got there at 5. They were listening to tapes of the tunes Mac and the band had rehearsed. Gave me a run-down of the tunes they selected (about 20), and gave me a picture of what they were attempting to achieve. Concept: Dr. John doing a compendium of New Orleans grooves e.g. Longhair, Huey Smith, Earl King, Fats . . . late 50s & early 60s funk . . . (they were both high). Jerry offered me a Co-producer deal with him, 1G up front and a 1.5% royalty. (They mentioned something about the John Abbey article in a British magazine). Jerry suggested I get Melvin Lastie for the session . . . I added Lee Allen.

Life: Winning & Losing

In 1972 I tried to take stock of my personal life. A long entry in my Daily Reminder book from that time highlights what was on my mind:

I shall do my best to take inventory of my circumstances at present. The scope of things as it is in my brain may be much larger than I am willing to encounter at this time, but some picture of my situation, I feel, is necessary. I shall briefly look at the factual analysis of my health, family, finance, business, friends, acquaintances, and whatever subject seems important.

I am in the 41st year of life. I have had high blood pressure for the last five years; however, it is kept under pretty good control. I take one Hygroton pill per day and three potassium chlorides per day to counteract the effect (negative) of the Hygroton. I have some ailments (arthritis or something) which affects my shoulder, back, ankle and knee if I miss taking at least one Indocin per day.

During the past five months, I have gained 20 pounds in excess of my normal overweight, which brings me to a grand total of 201 pounds. My chief problem regarding health is my inability to quit smoking. In spite of many serious efforts during the past year, I am still smoking a pack a day. This represents as much a psychological problem to me as it does a physical one. Psychologically, it destroys my confidence in my ability to discipline myself, and thus affects my eating habits, working habits, exercise, and in some way, all activities.

In spite of this rather dismal picture of health, I have not been stricken ill (except for a cold now and then). My body has stood up well and has thus far fought off any major disasters which I might have anticipated. (This sometimes leads me to speculate that when it does happen, it will be fatal.)

My family seems to be in good health. They too, have managed to steer clear of any major illness. This is quite fortunate considering we have no insurance – health, hospitalization or anything. Although our surface activities do not show it, I sense a deep closeness between us. I have found myself wanting to see evidence of that closeness demonstrated in our day-to-day routines, but I have not achieved that goal yet.

Yette is 36 (or 37); Bunny, 17; Andrea, 13; Marzique, 9; Harlis, 7, and they are experiencing fairly normal problems of their age, both physically and psychologically.

We are in a comfortable home with a $28,000 mortgage and a $45,000 market value. We have another home which I use for work and business. That house has an approximate $10,000 mortgage and $20,000 market value.

Me and Yette have just lost $15,000 equity in an apartment building, which was foreclosed by the bank. We are filing legal action for fraud and misrepresentation against [the woman] who sold us the building, and . . . the licensed broker handling the sale. Attorney David Kornblum is filing the action and it was on his advice that we let the bank foreclose. We have five 1½-acre parcels of land in Modoc Recreational Estates, three of which are paid for. They should be valued at not less than $5,000.

We were in the process of collecting a settlement on the Hisperia land. We had savings of nearly $10,000, which is dwindling because of my unemployment. We have an assortment of personal property ranging from automobiles to clothes to electric knives to tape recorders, which may roughly be valued at $25,000 to $40,000.

Marzique Music Co. Inc. (MMCI) is, at most, maintaining status quo. It has litigation pending against King Floyd and Malaco (Jackson, Mississippi) and possibly Atlantic Records, which could result in being awarded the royalties from one of its copyrights recorded by Floyd. MMCI needs to have a lot of paperwork brought up to date (which could be accomplished if the money can be obtained to pay for help). MMCI is contemplating action against Mac Rebennack, Charles Green, and Al Grossman for breaking the Dr. John management contract. MMCI also holds the contract on Tami Lynn. I have just reluctantly agreed with Jerry Wexler to expand the project and complete an LP with Dr. John—Gumbo. It's all just a contractual mess.

Hal-Mel has just signed with the William Morris Agency (after the Gideon & Power fiasco), who is to seek out production deals for us. Mark Turk plans to negotiate a deal with Bell Records or another entity for us to produce Lola Falana. Judy Kyle is our acting manager.

NARAS Forum on R&B

Back in the summer of 1970 I had been invited to attend a board meeting of the Los Angeles chapter of the National Academy of Recording Arts & Sciences (NARAS) by its chairman, Lee Young. I welcomed the opportunity to experience the inside of this important industry organization, which awards and hosts the Grammys. On the agenda for that meeting were discussions of how to categorize award nominees. I do not recall the details of the problem—they seemed to be having trouble agreeing on a Duke Ellington entry—but I was asked to offer some thoughts to the group. They were impressed with my ideas, and Lee Young expressed thanks and extended an invitation to me for future meetings. I became a member of the Los Angeles chapter board and served over three years.

I was concerned about the issue of categorizing artists. Great talent was being improperly labeled. For example, in 1964 jazz vocalist Nancy Wilson was awarded a Grammy for best female vocal performance in the R&B category, for "How Glad I Am." Nancy was highly insulted because her forte was jazz. She wasn't a "Chitlin' Circuit" singer; she exuded elegance and style and sang in supper clubs. I wanted to

Left to right: Mel Carter, Charles Wright, Mike Post, Harold Battiste, Warren Lanier, and J. W. Alexander, 1972 NARAS forum on R&B;
PHOTO BY WILLIAM R. EASTABROOK (THNOC)

Yette and Harold at the Grammy Awards with composer Mike Post and his wife, ca. 1973; PHOTO BY JASPER DAILY (THNOC)

start the discussion to change how the industry viewed Black artists and their work. I suggested that a forum should be held to hash out the details and set some guidelines. And by 1972 NARAS was on board. That fall I produced a major public forum dealing with these issues. The following promotion piece was published and sent along with invitations to the event:

> Some thoughts that should be considered in inviting the membership of NARAS and other concerned people to discuss R&B: What It Is . . . What Is It?: What is the primary source of the categorizing of music? Does the composer categorize it in terms of his visions and intentions for the end product? Does the producer and/or arranger determine the category as a result of treatment, sound, tempo, instrument, etc.? Does the artist, because of his particular performance, change the category? If Wilson Pickett (R&B male vocalist nominee, 1970) sang "Let It Be" (Contemporary song nominee, 1970), does his performance make that piece an R&B song or does he then become a Contemporary vocalist? Or, considering the message of that particular song, had it originally been done by the Staple Singers instead of the Beatles, would the song have been categorized as Gospel? And if so, would it have been Soul or Sacred? Are the Staple Singers still in the Gospel division? As a result of their recent hit recordings, have they moved into the R&B status? What is the anatomy of R&B? What are the racial and ethnic considerations? What are the economic factors of being in this category? When a promotion man says, "This one's got to go to the R&B station but maybe the Pop guys will get on the other one," is he really thinking, ". . . Black station . . . White guys?"

I had heard these questions asked for several years and had asked them a few times myself. I thought that maybe we were asking the questions to the wind, for there hadn't been one industrywide authority willing to face the challenge these questions offered. Our organization, NARAS, accepted the challenge. It was fitting that we did so, inasmuch as we bestowed the most prestigious award in the recording industry (categorically).

The forum took place on November 12 at A&M Studios in Hollywood. The panel was made up of a diverse mix of industry people: artist manager and publisher J. W. Alexander, publicist Warren Lanier, film and television composer Mike Post, artist and singer Mel Carter ("Hold Me, Thrill Me, Kiss Me"), artist/bandleader Charles Wright (Watts 103rd Street Rhythm Band). The event was well attended by the interested music public and the press. The topic was hot and the discussions were heated. People had been thinking about these things for a long time. NARAS had problems each year coming up with categories for the new music that didn't fit the existing genres. Publicists and music journalists created names for music, and often an artist would create a genre in order to distinguish his work from the crowd. *Hollywood Reporter* and *Variety* both ran articles on the event.

Encouraged by the positive response to the forum from the members and staff at NARAS, I began to think of addressing another one of my questions: Why isn't there a Grammy for studio musicians? Vocalists, songwriters, producers, engineers, graphic artists, even liner-note writers are recognized and awarded for excellence in their work. The excellent work that goes on in the recording studio—the skill, artistry, passion, and soul—should also be acknowledged. After all, the music is the foundation of it all.

I brought my question before the board at the next meeting, in November 1973. For a moment, no one spoke. They looked at each other, each seeming to expect that someone else had the answer. Someone gave the standard response for when there is no answer: "That's a good question!" After the laughter died down, we began to talk about some possibilities.

Once it was decided that we were going to establish the award, we had to address a few obstacles. The major one: How would we present a national award for regional work? Each of the major recording cities had its local and regional musicians. A few specialists traveled for special assignments, but mostly we stayed close to home. The Los Angeles chapter of NARAS decided to do our own award event and partner with the American Federation of Musicians Local 47 to recognize a "Most Valuable Player." We got the word out to all the major studios so that all the musicians became aware of what was in the making. Once the idea caught on, NARAS AFM 47 really got into the spirit. They took over! At times I thought they had forgotten about me (there they go again, White folks takin' our shit!), but I was wrong. They were just very enthusiastic about the idea and acting like White folks—all overexuberant and bubbly, but making it known that they wanted control. The event went over big—we had a real success. The concept was adapted and instituted as an annual event on the academy's calendar. Some years later, I was given a plaque acknowledging the creation of the MVP award.

Mel and His Disciples

Melvin Lastie had continued to work with his group of talented young percussionists, which he had begun to refer to as his "disciples." They were at his home the majority of every week. They ate there, practiced there, and I believe they worshiped there. Although I had been staying busy with a variety of projects, at the start of 1972 I noticed that Melvin seemed not to be the jovial personality he always had been. I was seeing less of him, and when I went to his home he had candles and incense burning and religious articles on an altar—something was going on.

I couldn't get Mel into the studio. Bob Ross, my copyist, had been quite beautiful about the use of his recording studio. He offered it to me to use (for free) whenever there was time open. He would not even accept money for the tape I used. Even with this studio at our disposal, I could not get Melvin and his disciples to make use of it. There always seemed to be some reluctance to going there, and I can only speculate as to why. Melvin would say discouraging things like: "They're not ready for the studio yet" or "It would just be wasting time." Those statements were just not true—they were as ready as any musicians needed to be, and more capable than many. They were quite ready when I used them on my *African Genesis Suite* project—and I was paying them like professionals. It seemed to me that Melvin was adopting a rather protective, "They belong to me" attitude. I didn't know why he was behaving in this way.

I told Melvin and his disciples that they were welcome to use our family's old house at 2229 South Mansfield (our first house in California), which we had moved out of but still owned, as a rehearsal studio. This would give them a place where their equipment could remain, they could get more hours in, and they would have many other advantages, including giving Melvin and his wife, Elaine, the privacy of their own home. It seemed as though Melvin and his disciples had thought about it and discussed it but were waiting for another offer. They talked about the possibilities enthusiastically but never said anything definite about when they wanted to start the move to Mansfield. I had noticed that they habitually operated on a sort of noncommittal level: many things were discussed and agreed upon, but the agreements were left with enough loose ends hanging so that the agreement could be cancelled without a negative statement from anyone. This could be why, after a year of meeting and rehearsing, they had made so little progress.

I soon learned that Melvin's health was declining and he was in denial. Sometime that summer or early fall, I do not remember exactly when, Melvin left Los Angeles and returned to his home in New Orleans. On December 4, 1972, he left all of us.

Sonny & Cher's Playboy Tour

In 1973 I was again called to do a special tour with Sonny & Cher, using the Playboy jet (which included the Bunnies). Sonny & Cher had a much better rhythm section than usual: David Hungate on bass, Dan Ferguson on guitar, Jeff Porcaro on drums. Jeff's father, Joe, played percussion on some of the early Sonny & Cher hits. On this tour I played organ, and Mike Rubini, a pianist from the studio session band, did my old gig directing the stage orchestra. The tour started at the Westbury Music Festival on Long Island. For me, doing this tour as a sideman was interesting and relaxing. I found myself seeing things that I had not noticed before.

An early childhood directive—"Boy, you better learn how to stay in your place!"—came back to me poolside at the Ramada Inn in Monroe, Louisiana, on May 18, 1973. Several guests at the hotel, about twenty or twenty-five people, were staring at our group: me, Sonny, and a few other men and women from the tour. Suddenly, an overwhelming feeling that I was in the wrong place came over me. In an attempt to dispel the feeling, I tried to form a picture of our group in my mind, but whenever I tried to put my image in the picture, the whole scene went blank.

A similar experience happened the next day, in Mississippi. Our (White) chauffeur had brought us to the gig for rehearsal. He approached me for instructions. "Sir, what do you want me to do now? Shall

On the Playboy jet with Sonny & Cher's 1973 tour (THNOC)

I wait here for you, or would you like me to stand by back at the hotel? I'm at your disposal." I was at a loss to give him orders. Technically, orders should have come from the road manager, but I was the only authority on hand. I knew what to tell him, but that was not relevant to the psychological position I took, which was *How could you, a White, expect me, a Black, to give you orders of that nature? It's not my place to do that!* I had never felt that way before, even though I'd been in similar circumstances many times. I could only attribute it to being in Monroe the day before, and in Jackson now, rekindling all those early stories about the South.

McNealy's Shadow

I met songwriter Jane McNealy back in 1968 through singer Lydia Marcelle and her manager, David Ezell. Over the years, Jane had continued to bring songs to me. She was impressed with the way I had arranged and recorded two of her songs for Liberty Records. I was impressed with the caliber of material she was writing and dismayed that she had not been discovered.

Marzique Music (MMCI), the publishing company I'd started in 1968, dealt mostly with new stuff from the West Coast, including the Dr. John material. Jane's songs were coming out of a theatrical bag, à la Broadway musicals. I was most impressed with her melodic and harmonic sensibilities—these tunes could morph into jazz or standards—and they were being signed into the MMCI catalog!

My interest in Jane's songs led to my becoming acquainted with some of her circle of friends, most of whom were into some form of art. The closest friend was writer and lyricist Alice Kuhns, who created the words for many of Jane's melodies. Jane also had an apartment loaded with recording equipment for creating demos of the compositions. I began to spend much of my spare time there. I had a new TEAC four-track in my living room at home, where I could do some stuff and transfer between studios.

Jane and Alice had met Yette and our children when they had been at my house working, and they had developed what I thought was a cordial relationship. Alice's family closely resembled ours—we had two boys and two girls, and the Kuhns family had three boys and two girls, with all the children around the same ages. But Yette mentioned to me a couple of times that when Jane called she felt or sensed something in Jane's voice or tone that made her uncomfortable. Yette would often accuse me of having a thing with Jane other than the music. I did not want to make too much of these incidents. But there were other problems: Yette didn't feel like she belonged in that world—she felt socially insecure. In transferring to California, we had experienced similar issues we thought were racial that turned out to be more like class differences. Both Yette and I, with our deep southern upbringings still lingering in our radar, were prone to hear stuff that way. My focus was on the potential Jane was bringing to our publishing company as a songwriter, but I also sensed something else—something that could bring problems.

chapter **9 bacon & bread**

In 1974 my children were in the midst of their adolescent years. My oldest son, Harold III (Bunny), was coming up on twenty years old. It seemed like he was just enjoying the celebrity of his moves on the Hamilton High School basketball team. He had the dream of so many young Black men of that age and time—the idea that being an athlete, that basketball, was the path to college and then the pros. Bunny was a star athlete; he even was nicknamed "Earl the Pearl" after Earl Monroe (a pro player with the Baltimore Bullets and the New York Knicks). Bunny had been thumping the basketball around the house for five years but didn't take his studies seriously, so of course he thought he was destined for a scholarship to college. When that didn't happen, he dropped out of high school in his senior year and joined the army, which was not the answer for him. Bunny found a way to get out of the military, got his GED, and then went to a small community college in San Luis Obispo. He started dabbling in music, with the electric bass, keyboards, and songwriting. Bunny had a good ear, good feeling, which is crucial for a musician. But he didn't concentrate on music either. He thought it was too late for him to switch gears.

Andrea, eighteen, finished Hamilton High and enrolled at Santa Monica College. She had always shown an exquisite, delicate taste in her selection of clothes and accessories. She was thoughtful and inquiring and kept a diary. She also wrote insightful letters to the Los Angeles *Times* critiquing art issues, and many of those letters were published. I always enjoyed conversations with her about things going on in her life and in society. Marzique and Harlis, eighteen months apart, were just emerging from childhood. 'Zique had entered Audubon Junior High, and Harlis had another year at Baldwin Hills Elementary.

Things between Yette and me were not going well. The years had put us to the test—our backgrounds, our upbringing, education, values—all the things that shaped us before we knew each other. For the past fifteen-plus years, we had been trying to maintain the magic of our youth while trying to reconcile the differences in our childhoods. Our lives were a lot more complicated in the early 1970s. Over the last four or five years, I had been extremely busy—much busier than I had been in the late '60s. I was pursuing a variety of projects with potential brought by a variety of people with possibilities—recording with King Floyd, composing and arranging with Jane McNealy. I didn't notice that my income had dropped significantly. I did notice that Yette was being more assertive about getting a job.

From the beginning of our marriage, Yette had always had the mindset of a working wife. When we returned to New Orleans in 1954 from DeRidder, she got a cashier's job at the corner store. When we moved to Los Angeles in 1956, she worked at a Dairy Queen parlor. I was never comfortable with it, but I knew that it was important to her and that this was how she wanted to help—and in those early days, she really did help. But I had a real problem with the "working wife" in the context that it was being propagated and interpreted. In my mind, the concept was an assault on the traditional family and family roles. I knew it was my responsibility to provide for the family. The differences came about because Yette always wanted to work. Although we were not actively involved in the Feminist/Women's Movement as it grew around the nation, we did discuss it between us and among our friends. I had always thought that the position of wife was second in prestige and reverence only to that of mother. As for work, what job is more important than those positions? My childhood was spent in a home with my grandmother and grandfather, and my mother and father, who showed me daily how well that set-up worked.

So I was torn when Yette began doing volunteer work at the YMCA in 1972. I agreed that she needed contact with different people and environments outside of family, neighbors, and regular friends. But I was bothered by her insistence on pretending to some people that she had a paying job. Why did she feel it necessary to have people think she was working? Did she envy the working wives in our group?

I was also disturbed because I desperately needed a "volunteer" worker for my businesses, MMCI and At Last. I had tons of work that needed to be done but the company couldn't afford to pay for. Since the business was "all in the family," it seemed to me that the members of the family should put in some volunteer time. If I should die, everything that I worked for would be lost, because no one in the family had the slightest interest in or knowledge of how the businesses ran. I probably felt uncertain about where I was going with my work—and a little defensive. I needed Yette's help, but she didn't see where or how I needed it.

The first sign that Yette was ready to make a strong move to reset her goals was in 1972, when she enrolled at West Los Angeles College. My brain got very hyped up. I was excited about her being in school; I thought it was wonderful. Yette was taking a sociology course. I studied with her, and we had interesting conversations both on the subject matter in the course and on current sociological phenomena. She had as required reading a paperback entitled *Man Alone: Alienation in Modern Society*. The book awakened, provoked, and confirmed thoughts that I had filed away in the "useless" section. We had a lot of discussions about this book. I felt that our new discourse could improve things between us, but I knew that it wouldn't change me—I was still an old-fashioned guy, as my Daily Reminder notes show:

> *I'm so happy and enthusiastic about these developments until I can hardly contain my thoughts; they are just running wild and that is an understatement! They are more like insights and revelations on a whole spectrum of subjects. I must control this thing so that it can be channeled into the direction I want it and not spend itself out too quickly. With Yette's help, I feel that I can at last begin to organize our philosophy and experiences into a communicable form. To that end, the course Yette took last year will be an indispensable asset.*

Back to Work

Come 1975, I had to face reality: I knew I had to make some money. What should I do? What would I do? I was a teacher and a sax player some time ago. I learned a little about the record business—very little— just enough to make me *think* I knew enough, but I didn't. Since high school I'd known how to arrange music, so when a friend asked me to help him make a record, then another and another, I wound up giving my career away to other artists, like Sonny & Cher. I made some money—not much, but some. I had to write some music again!

Before the first month of 1975 was over, I had lots of music to write and hoped to make a little bacon and bread. Jane McNealy and Alice Kuhns were writing a musical, *To Be Fred.* Jane composed music that knocked me out, but she couldn't score it or write it out. They asked me, could I? would I? Right on time! I needed a project like that to refresh my writing skills and try a new genre. In the meantime, I got a call from Denis Pregnolato asking me to meet with him at the Hamburger Hamlet on Hollywood Boulevard. He filled me in on Sonny's situation: lots of stuff had been going down between him and Cher while I was disconnected. The marriage had fallen apart. They both were trying to do television alone. Sonny's money was sort of funny, but he had a plan: he wanted to develop a new act from scratch and go on tour to get his confidence back. I could really relate, because that's what I was doing with *To Be Fred.* We figured on one year to "get over" and make the public accept him without Cher. Sonny had hired a director-type person to help him write the show, and a choreographer to teach him some stage and dance moves. He also got Darlene Love, a singer who had been associated with Phil Spector and had done some studio background singing for me, and her sister Edna to be part of his act.

Both projects needed to be on their feet and ready to go by mid-March—about sixty days! One day I met with Jane to prepare a music cue sheet for *Fred.* The next day I started writing the overture. That same afternoon I got a call from Sonny's road manager, Jerry Ridgeway, who brought me a tape and lead sheet of a medley to arrange for Sonny's act. That's the way it started, and for the next two months, I sharpened many number-two pencils.

Of the two projects, I was drawn to the one where there would be little if any bacon. *To Be Fred* was to be produced for a small theater (ninety-nine seats), a small orchestra (five musicians), a small cast (four actors/singers), and a very small budget. But I loved the music and the challenge. The orchestra comprised a rhythm section—drums, bass, guitar, and piano—so most of the detailed scoring was in the piano part. That was where the challenge lay. Usually, for a larger group, I could write a simple chord/rhythm chart for the piano, and the player could follow that, but in this situation the pianist *was* the orchestra, and I had to streamline all the information that would be distributed to other instruments. By mid-February I had just about finished *Fred*'s charts, and the show went into rehearsals. In just over two weeks, I wrote the charts for thirteen songs: "I Don't Exist," "I Can't Wait to Be There," "That's Romance," "Glorious," "Starting Today," "To Be Fred," "Did I Really Try?" "Cinderella Ballet," "You'd Better Live While You Can," "Do You Know What You've Done?" "The Last Impression," "It's Not the Same Anymore," and "What Is Today Without You?" The production opened in early March.

Two days later, I turned my attention to Sonny's project. I had been working on some of his charts, all of which were written for a large stage orchestra: five saxophones (who also doubled on flute, clarinet, and other woodwinds), four trumpets, two trombones, one flugelhorn, and a full rhythm section. All through March I was writing, changing, fixing, and rewriting the charts. Then we started having rehearsals. One number in the show, "Long Tall Glasses," called for Sonny to do some solo dancing Gene Kelly–style, so we needed a lot of rehearsal time. And how would we use the Love sisters and avoid looking like Tony Orlando & Dawn (who happened to be quite popular at that time)? Sonny was always aware of his limitations but was bold and smart enough to use them to his advantage. Something was added or something was cut out at almost every rehearsal.

We took the show out in early April, to Two Rivers, Wisconsin. I don't remember much about the town, but I remember that it was C-O-L-D! Thirty degrees! The audience for our opening show was a little warmer. The following day, the local paper had a review. The reviewer was kind and, in my opinion, sort of generous. Jean Lokker, staff writer for the Manitowoc *Herald Times Reporter,* managed to mention every aspect of the show, even moi!

Here's how the show finally came together:

THE SONNY BONO SHOW

1.   Overture (Piano background under short monologue)
2.   You Are So Beautiful (Rhythm section vamp under short monologue)
3.   Medley #1
       (a) Boogie on Reggae Woman
       (b) Love Song
       (c) Hang on in There Baby
Monologue (extended) + Introduction of Darlene & Edna
4.   Medley #2
       (a) If You Could Read My Mind
       (b) Never Can Say Goodbye
       (c) The Best of My Love
Piano background
5.   You're the Best Thing that Ever Happened to Me
     (underscore to a film featuring Sonny's daughter Chastity)
6.   Long Tall Glasses
7.   Three song set with Darlene and Edna
       (a) Evil
       (b) You've Got the Love
       (c) All in Love Is Fair
Rhythm section vamp under short monologue
8.   Bang, Bang
Piano under monologue
9.   You Better Sit Down Kids
Rhythm section vamp, acknowledgement of personnel
10. I Got You Babe
11. Our Last Show

Heart Attack

The next gig, in Lake Geneva, Wisconsin, had something surprising in store for me. On about the third day, I experienced the worst chest pains I had ever felt. I couldn't lie down; there was no position that relieved what seemed to be pressure on my breastbone. A doctor at the hotel took my blood pressure and said it was OK. He did an EKG and said it was OK. Chest x-ray, OK. He recommended I go to the hospital for a series of EKGs. Afterward I returned to the hotel to sleep. I felt a little better, but not much. I walked to the lobby to find Denis, and to see how I would feel, trying to prepare for that night's show. I felt fair. I went back to my room and put on my back brace, which I'd been using on and off for a few years, since hurting my back on tour with Sonny & Cher in 1970. The support felt good, but when I took it off after about two minutes, I nearly passed out.

The rest of the story is recorded in my Daily Reminder:

9:00pm Did the show and went straight to bed. Woke up about 5:50am. Pain still there . . . not as frightening as yesterday but just as severe. Called Dennis and told him I'd better go to the hospital. Called Dr. Doreza. Told me to go to Elkhorn. 8:00 Admitted to Lakeland Hospital. Dr. Doreza was there. I was put in ICU. Later that day, after all the tests and a blood enzyme analysis, was told I had suffered a 'mild' coronary.

Sonny, Denis, and some other guys from the tour came over to see me. I must have looked a mess with oxygen tubes in my nose, an I.V. in my arm, disk monitors all over my chest. They assured me that they would see that I was well taken care of. I was released from ICU and put in a private room. The doctor said I should stay in the hospital for five or six more days, and that made me feel sad—the thought of being left there—even though the people could not have been nicer. But my life was on Bowcroft Street, and somehow, without my actual family around, when Sonny and Denis and the troop left, it was like all connection with home was cut.

I was discharged and flown to Los Angeles on April 23 and admitted to Daniel Freeman Memorial Hospital for a short stay. It would be many years before I came to terms with what my body had gone through. I recovered so quickly from what had killed my father that I couldn't believe it was a real heart attack. I was ready to catch up with my gig before they started thinking they didn't need me. After three or four low-income years, I didn't have time to be sick.

Back on My Feet

At the end of April I caught up with the gang in Lake Tahoe, where the comedian opening for our show was a young man named Jay Leno (who woulda thunk?). We were back in L.A. by May 10. I had some loose ends to catch up at home: neighborhood meeting, parent-teacher conference, NARAS board meeting, recording session for Plas Johnson, working on a record for Sonny—it was a rather busy month!

The renewed gig with Sonny was looking like it might fly. I was hopeful for both of us, but not convinced. Coming up in June was a gig in Cherry Hill, New Jersey; a *Tonight Show* appearance; and the *Mike Douglas Show* in Philadelphia. Those shows were hugely popular at the time, but they were just another gig to me, so I wasn't particularly excited. I didn't really want to face it, but this was the deal: it was just another plantation set-up. With only a few exceptions, the White artist (the plantation master) was in charge even when the more talented Black artists (the slaves) were running things and keeping the show going. For me it wasn't so much about being in the background, it was the inequity in pay and the lack of respect for my ability. I was walking onto more plantations than I cared to visit.

But the Cherry Hill show turned out to be special for me; an old friend of mine from my high-school band, Andrew Young, was in the audience, and we got to talk briefly. This was the same Andrew Young who worked as a foot soldier alongside Martin Luther King Jr. and later became mayor of Atlanta, a congressman, and ambassador to the United Nations during the Carter administration.

We kept things rolling through the summer, making some changes in Sonny's act as we went along. We did Dinah Shore's show, and Merv Griffin's. While in New York I got to spend time with some homeboys from back in the day—drummer Leo Morris (aka Idris Muhammad), saxophonist Clarence "Lukeman"

Harold and Harlis at the Los Angeles Civic Center;
PHOTO BY MARZIQUE BATTISTE

The big hit on Plas Johnson's album *The Blues,* "Parking Lot Blues," was composed on the spur of the moment. (THNOC)

Thomas, bassist George Davis, and drummer David Lee. I also dropped in on the folks at Atlantic to see Ahmet and/or Nesuhi Ertegun, but instead I had a talk with the office manager, Noreen Woods. And I got to raid their warehouse for free LPs for my jazz collection!

Recharging My Creative Batteries

I went back to L.A. for a few busy days with the family, mostly spending time with the kids and neighbors/friends. It was just Marzique and Harlis at home now. We went to the beach or to the park. I did some writing for my homeboy Plas Johnson, who had become the top tenor-sax studio musician in Hollywood. If producers couldn't get Plas, they got someone who sounded like him, and there were several who made their careers sounding like Plas. His recording credits are endless—Beach Boys to Sinatra, Sarah Vaughan to Dr. John. Plas's tenor sax is world-renowned as the musical voice of *The Pink Panther*, arranged and directed by Henry Mancini. I went in with Plas as arranger and coproducer for Concord Records to do some stuff that both of us needed for therapy. It wouldn't have mattered if we didn't even sell two dozen records. But then it did sell well! The famous jazz bassist Ray Brown composed the hit. We suspected that he wrote it on the spur of the moment, when Plas asked him in the studio for a tune. He had no music but started humming parts to the players until they got it together. One of the cats joked, "Man, you musta wrote this out in the parking lot!" "Parking Lot Blues" got the airplay for the album, entitled *The Blues.*

While working on the record I became completely engrossed in the life of Charlie Parker. I was reading Ross Russell's book *Bird Lives!: The High Life and Hard Times of Charlie (Yardbird) Parker.* It had a more meaningful relationship to me than had *Chasin' the Trane,* J. C. Thomas's biography of John

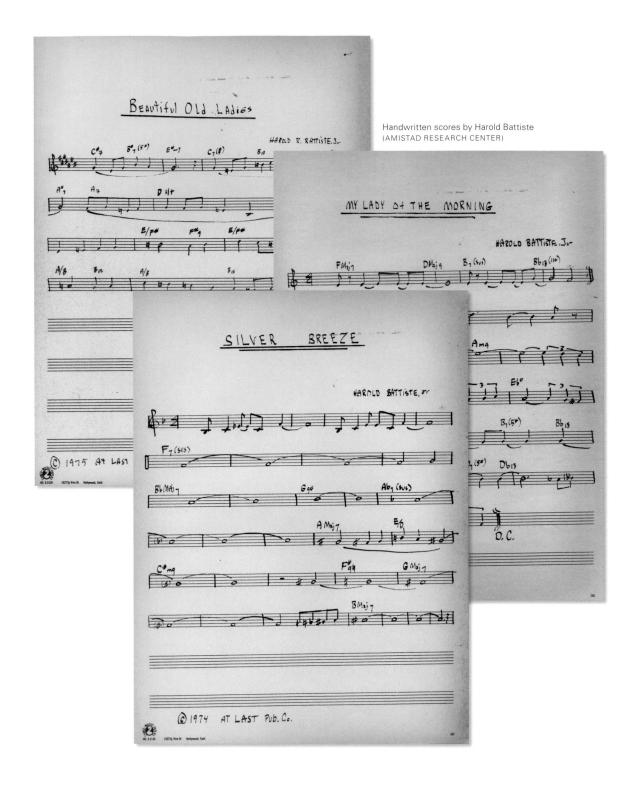

Handwritten scores by Harold Battiste
(AMISTAD RESEARCH CENTER)

Coltrane. Bird's life was almost my life; many of the major music and cultural signposts were similar. I started thinking about my own work and how I might improve. But I came along eleven years later, and that made a big difference. I really wanted to get back to playing jazz. I was inspired and got in a lot of practice on tenor and soprano sax, working on some of my compositions—"Marzique Dancing," "Lady of the Morning," "Beautiful Old Ladies," "Silver Breeze," "Soon We Will Be Together." I was getting the changes down fairly well and beginning to really hear the sound of the music.

Career Decision

When Sonny's tour was in Denver in November 1975, Sonny gave me the news that Cher and CBS had called him about the two of them doing another show together. We both had sort of expected that something like this would come about sooner or later. The television execs didn't want Sonny *or* Cher, they wanted Sonny *and* Cher. When Sonny said he wanted me to be the show's musical director, I was sort of caught off guard. Having turned that offer down for the *Sonny & Cher Comedy Hour* a few years back, I assumed my refusal still stood. Evidently, Sonny assumed that I would have realized my "mistake" and was now ready to "make it." I did not accept or refuse his offer that Sunday in Denver. I didn't want him to go into negotiations with my refusal on his mind: I worried that Cher—and certainly CBS—would fight for a big-name musical director and win.

On December 2 Denis called to tell me that everybody—Sonny, Cher, and CBS—had agreed and would be happy for me to be musical director of the show. The question in my mind at that moment—a question that is still unanswered—was, was I crazy for even considering refusing such an opportunity? Isn't this what every music writer wants? His name on the screen every week, lots of money every week, plus reruns, residuals, and side offers down the road? This was the second time opportunity had knocked; maybe it was time for me to answer.

Denis sensed my reluctance and urged me to take the gig. Sonny called to congratulate me. I told him of my doubt and he wouldn't hear it. He said that I must give it a shot—if I didn't like it, then quit. But I was most surprised at how Yette reacted: she was positively elated! It was as if she had been waiting for something big to happen, and this was it. That worried me: I interpreted her reaction to mean that she would be happier with me if I were somebody important. Nothing I had said or done in years had gotten this level of positive reception from her. I had thought that if anyone knew what I really wanted for myself as a musician and a person, she would have been the one, and she would know how I felt about doing this kind of show. We had discussed it at the time of the first offer, and I reiterated some of the problems this job could present. But she had answers. She would see that I had every convenience at my disposal. Anything I wanted—"Just take the gig!"

If I turned it down this time, would it mean that I would lose Denis and Sonny as potential employers, and as friends? Would they say, "Man, Harold just doesn't want to be successful"? Would I lose Yette and maybe even our children?

Harold on stage with Sonny and Cher, the *Sonny & Cher Show*, 1976 (THNOC)

chapter **10** seesaw

Finishing up each year might give the impression that the past year was the most important one yet. But I truly can't recall a year that has had more emotional and physical impact on me than 1975. It was the year of my going back to work: after four years trying to get my head together about family, marriage, and career (artistically and economically), I had decided to take the optimistic initiative and fling myself back into the commercial arena for one big effort to secure my family. I used the musical *To Be Fred* as a warm-up exercise to regain my writing confidence, then I made a commitment to Sonny to write music for him, to help him build an act.

After two and a half months of rehearsing, writing, and touring, I landed in the hospital with a mild heart attack. Within a month I was back on the gig, but I had thought long and hard about what I was trying to accomplish in my life and how I was going about it. It became clear to me that I must take a more direct route to realizing my personal artistic goals. All I had done since 1957 had been off on a tangent from the real Harold Battiste: the job with Specialty, then the Ric Records gig—even the AFO experiment with its twists, turns, successes, and failures—and certainly the Sonny & Cher music, which was completely the opposite of my musical feelings. After my illness, I began working on my old compositions and writing new ones, practicing my instrument and generally getting my heart back into Harold Battiste. However, I was still doing Sonny's thing because I had made the commitment.

Of course, there were some rewarding moments: the *Monkey Puzzle* LP, the *Compendium* LP during the AFO years, the *Good Times* score, the *African Genesis* project, the Angela Davis film score, even a couple of the Sonny & Cher records gave me some musical satisfaction. But for the most part I had little artistic pride in that work; however, I was proud, as a craftsman, that I was able to accomplish the goal intended for that music: to sell records and performers.

Passings

The deaths of a few of my peers reminded me of my own mortality. Cannonball Adderley died at age forty-six on August 8, 1975. We had visited each other about three weeks earlier. He was a stellar jazzman, my friend since college days. Alvin Batiste had been out in California, and Cannon was talking about getting his flute-playing together. His death had an effect on my head. Then, a few months later, my colleague Oliver Nelson died, which frightened me even more. He and I had worked together scoring an episode of *The Six Million Dollar Man*. Oliver was a brilliant writer and a respected jazz saxophonist. He had played with Cannonball, Johnny Hodges, and Stanley Turrentine. Oliver was my contemporary—forty-three—unhappy and frustrated, stressed out from all the arranging and production work. I began to wonder, *What's it all about? Why am I still doing somebody else's music? How much time do I have left for myself, or is it already too late?*

Just when I got it worked out in favor of doing my own music, Sonny threw the gig for musical director of the TV show in my lap. Everybody was happy for me. Friends, relations, professional acquaintances, all were saying, "What an opportunity!" In the meantime, the real Harold Battiste finished the year with an impossible decision to make.

Welcome to CBS

The Columbia Broadcasting System: the big eye at the corner of Beverly Boulevard and Fairfax. I had passed that corner a thousand times without paying any particular attention. Now I had a CBS photo ID badge and I'd be driving in those gates for work. I may even have an office and a secretary—naw! The music office, where I worked, was a trailer parked on the roof of a studio on a CBS lot. At first I thought it was a diss, but after a few weeks I realized I had enviable privacy up on the roof.

I had already met some of the team through Sonny and Denis. "Red" Mandel was the music contractor, whose job was to represent the musicians on behalf of the union, the American Federation of Musicians. I met with Red to discuss the personnel I wanted for the band. Politics and power plays started right away. The contractor was like the boss on the riverfront who stands over a mob of men trying to get a day's work. Studio musicians paid respect to contractors—they sucked up!—and that's no disrespect to musicians, just the way it was.

My rough spot with Red was pushing for some African-American players in the mix. I inherited the seventeen-piece band from Cher's show, which had one African American on sax, Ernie Watts. I submitted some names to Red and got two in: Oscar Brashear on trumpet and Robby Buchanan on piano. George Bohannon, a wonderful talent from Detroit, was my choice for trombone, but Red would not give up his man.

On Monday, January 12, 1976, at 9:30 a.m., I went to my first production meeting. I was nervous and excited but cool and curious. The curious part was necessary, because it allowed me to open up and ask questions about things I thought the others could help me with. The meeting was informal, with several conversations going on. The boss, Nick Vanoff, whom I'd met before only briefly, seemed like a friendly and accessible person. I had pretty much caught on to the routine by the end of this meeting and got right to my preparations. I had to check on some things at the musicians' union, pick up some manuscript paper at Roger Farris Music, and check with my friend Bill Coben, a lawyer. I had met Bill in the late '60s when I was at Pulsar. I wanted him to look over the contract from the *Sonny & Cher Show* and make sure that there weren't any problems. The day went well. I felt like I was going to like this gig.

Recording time was booked at Larrabee Studios for January 21, 1976, at 1:00 p.m. I asked Red when I would get something to start work on. I asked the associate producer, Al Lowenstein, and his secretary, Rita Rogers. They all said they didn't know and seemed reluctant to address the issue. I was worried because I wasn't sure that everything could be done in time. Everybody seemed to know that the whole thing was behind schedule, but they pretended to not be worried. Maybe they really weren't worried—they'd been through this before. But I have always feared falling behind in ways that might affect other workers. In a situation like this, I needed to know what was expected of me and when.

I met with the special musical material person, Earl Brown. I didn't really know what he did. He explained that his job was to create lyrics and music to fit skits with dance routines. After two or three weeks of seeing his work, I thought it was incredible. It was like a mini Off-Broadway musical!

The basic structure of a one-hour *Sonny & Cher Show* went like this:

Theme and opening song
Sonny & Cher banter
Reprise opener
Comedy skit 1 with dancers
Comedy skit 2 featuring guest star
Cher solo
Comedy skit 3
Guest star feature
Concert (big number with Sonny & Cher)
Closing theme

I quickly determined how I was going to line out my work. I sat with Denis Pregnolato to develop a list of songs from which Sonny and Cher could choose for each show. There would be at least three for each show: an opener (duet), a concert (duet), and a solo. We also set a scheduled time for Sonny and Cher to meet with me to rehearse and set their keys for each song. In the meantime, I had a lot of research to conduct. I needed to be in touch with the music popular with our expanded demographic—we had appeal with adults now, sort of.

I discovered the power of television when it was time to call the big publishing companies to get rights to songs. I was on the phone to Natalie Ellington at Jobete, Chuck Kaye at Almo, John and Eddie at Chappell, Lester Sill at Screen Gems, and so on. The moment they heard the words *musical director* or *television* or *prime time,* the vaults were open. *What do you need? When do you want it? Where shall we deliver it?*

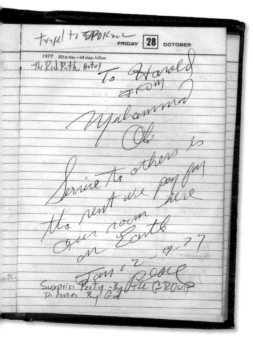

Daily Reminder (THNOC); Harold on the *Sonny & Cher Show,* 1976 (THNOC)

I spent the weekend of my first week on the job writing charts for the first show—the first of the three I promised Sonny I'd do before deciding to turn down the gig. But I was not as nervous about it as I had imagined I'd be, certainly not like when I stood in front of that orchestra at Paramount to lay down the score for Sonny's *Good Times* movie. I was less intimidated because I knew most of the cats, and the charts were a lot more simple.

By Monday morning I had written the first show's music and gotten it to the copyist to get the sheets done. There was a staff meeting at 10:00 a.m. to read through the next week's script, for the second show. As the weeks went by, I learned that all Monday afternoons and Tuesdays included some preparation for the next week's show, and even future shows. Wednesday was my big day in the studio, prerecording all the music for the upcoming show. That first Wednesday was a long day. We started at 1:00 p.m. and went until 8:30 or 9:00 p.m. Most of the problems were simply first-day adjustments: new cats in the band, a couple of new faces in the booth, new arrangers, and a new musical director—me!

The first show was to air on Sunday, February 1, 1976. On the Friday before air date, someone involved in postproduction discovered a serious glitch in the master tape. It had something to do with synchronization of vocals and music tracks. I was called in, but I had no idea what the problem could be—and besides, it was too late to get back in the studio with the musicians. Nick Vanoff and the engineers worked desperately to solve the problem before air time. They succeeded. The first *Sonny & Cher Show* aired on schedule, and we were off and running.

I was surprised and pleased when I got word that Nick was happy with my work. He was impressed with the way I arranged "The Beat Goes On" as the opening and closing theme for the show. When we recorded it at Larrabee, a couple of people in the booth were not comfortable with what they called the "groove change." In my thinking, people were going to hear this music twice every Sunday; it needed to have a quick lift to get their attention. Sonny, once again, got to wear his proud "I told you so" grin in front of the bosses. By this point I had already forgotten about our three-show deal; I was in it! Seems like Sonny had forgotten too.

A Variety of Artists

One of the pleasant perks of this gig was the variety of guest artists who would appear on the show. Jim Nabors, whom I had known only as a character on a sitcom, *Gomer Pyle, U.S.M.C.*, appeared on our fourth show not only as an actor doing comedy skits with Sonny & Cher but also as a singer; it sounded to me like singing was what he really wanted to do. Other notable guests included the Smothers Brothers, Diahann Carroll, Tony Randall, the Jackson Five, Bob Hope, Donny & Marie Osmond, Ed McMahon, Redd Foxx, Tom Jones, Bernadette Peters, Karen Valentine, Andy Griffith, Twiggy, Flip Wilson, Engelbert Humperdinck, Raymond Burr, Tina Turner, and Muhammad Ali, to name just a few.

Ali wrote in my 1977 Daily Reminder, on my birthday page! When Raymond Burr was in my office, I mentioned the nice scent of his cologne. The next day he brought me a bottle of Fahrenheit eau de toilette by Christian Dior!

I had to meet individually with guests who had or needed music. Usually they were prepared and/or they had their people to help. If there was a problem, my years in recording studios doing jazz, blues, gospel, rock, etc. had prepared me for these situations. The work was challenging and stimulating, which kept my mind and body motivated and activated. It was also very demanding—long hours leaving little time or energy for complaining.

All of it seemed like a perfect career situation. As I reflect on the various jobs I've had over the years and the people that came with those jobs, I realize that I felt more comfortable with this large team of professionals than I ever had before.

The Rebirth of AFO

During the summer of 1976, between the TV show's spring and fall seasons, another project I had been working on came to fruition. A few years back I had wanted to do something that would reconnect me to New Orleans and the music I originally brought with me to California—jazz. I had rescued the AFO master tapes from the IRS in the late 1960s. Among them were the jazz recordings from AFO's infancy—work by the American Jazz Quintet, the Ellis Marsalis Quartet, and the AFO Executives and Tami Lynn. The tapes wound up with the IRS because of our business with Juggy Murray. After "I Know" became a hit, Juggy made the IRS believe that AFO had received a payment of ninety-three thousand dollars, so naturally the feds wanted the taxes due from that check. Until we could get the situation resolved (i.e., prove we never received such an amount), the IRS put a lien on AFO's assets, and we didn't have access to the tapes. I had planned to try to settle and buy the tapes back, but I had to prove what the material was actually worth. I wound up paying five hundred dollars to get it all cleared up. I felt a strong urgency to preserve that music in some way, to keep it alive and give it another chance.

I was forty-three years old then, so I named the new label Opus 43 Records. It was not a real record company, just a name to put on the label. I met a young artist named Robert Rucker, who wanted to show me his artistic skills. He was big on creating album covers, which was huge at the time; many artists put a lot of effort into producing distinctive album covers as part of their body of work. Once again I would dig into my family's resources to develop an idea, one that had no real (read: *monetary*) value. And that's how *New Orleans Heritage Jazz: 1956–1966* saw the light. The four-album boxed set also included a book of bios and photos of the musicians with artwork by Rucker. That young cat also created the art for the *Hal-Mel* album cover.

I could afford to do only a thousand pressings, but I didn't know how to market, promote, distribute, and sell them anyway. I also didn't know how to price them, so since the year was 1976, I priced the set at $19.76. Ten years later I heard some collector in New York paid four hundred dollars for that set!

A New Generation

When I went to New Orleans to introduce the OPUS 43 box set, I attended a set at Tulane University, where Ellis Marsalis had a gig at a small student club. I heard that his boys might play with him. It was the first time I'd heard Wynton, and I was really excited about how he played. He was just sixteen years old, still developing.

The first thing he told me after I complimented him was that I needed to hear his brother Branford. He kept saying that's who I needed to hear, and it was clear that he looked up to his older brother. I don't think I got to hear Branford that day, but I talked to Ellis. He said that Wynton and Branford were playing in rock bands, but they were trying to get some jazz tunes together. I said, "Man, I sure would like to do something with them, take them into the studio." So I booked some time at Ultrasonic Studios, got some cats together, got Wynton and Branford, and we all did a tune called "Oneness" and another called "Summer/Spring."

It was a significant event in New Orleans jazz history. We had Herman Jackson on drums, Chris Severin on bass, and Ellis on piano and electric keyboard. Johnny Adams happened to be around the studio at that time, just hanging and feeling like getting in on the action. So Branford did "The Masquerade Is Over" with Johnny singing. We did one of Ellis's tunes, "Cry Again," with Tami Lynn, and I got in a soprano sax solo on that number.

I took the Ultrasonic tapes back out to L.A. with me and shared the music with some cats at ABC Records. But my reputation in the music world was with Sonny & Cher, so my credibility with jazz was minimal; those folks felt like I was out of my realm. I tried to shop it around to a couple of music execs, but nothing happened.

Not too long after that, Columbia Records said they wanted to do a project called *Fathers and Sons* featuring Ellis, Wynton, and Branford, and Von Freeman and his son, Chico. In 1982 the Marsalises recorded some of the same tunes from our Ultrasonic session for Columbia. I found out later that George Butler at Columbia was the cat who finally signed Wynton and Branford. That turned out to be his big thing: signing all the young jazz cats from New Orleans, like Kent Jordan. They treated those young men like oil in the ground, and they started digging wells around the city, mainly to keep any other companies from getting them.

George Butler wasn't really a jazz man, he was a music executive that was handling artists like Ferrante & Teicher, a piano duo in the pops/easy listening tradition. Butler wanted to snatch up talent before other labels got wind of them. I don't think he understood the New Orleans culture or jazz as a genre. It was a shame that he and Columbia never really did much with the talent they found. Butler and the label tried to turn Kent into another Hubert Laws (a jazz/R&B flutist)—they wanted him to play movie themes and such, but after about the third album he decided that wasn't what he wanted to do. Kent did some good work with Kevin Eubanks, who went on to become the *Tonight Show*'s bandleader. (Eubanks is a great guitarist—much too good for that show!)

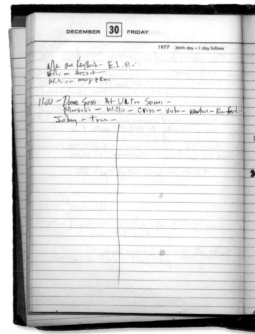

Daily Reminder (THNOC)

Cancellation!

The *Sonny & Cher Show* was cancelled. I found out at the beginning of 1977 after the fall season. Sonny & Cher began preparing to go on the road, capitalizing on momentum from the TV show. Sonny naturally assumed that I was on board too, and at the moment so did I. But I started thinking about the life/career-type things that had been on my mind back at the end of 1975. I called Denis Pregnolato and told him that I was not going to go on the road. Several proverbial straws—positive and negative—had been piling up, until I finally felt compelled to free myself of the burden.

Among the straws that led to my decision was a conversation between Sonny, Cher, and myself during a rehearsal at Sonny's house. The discussion originated when I said I felt a need to drop out of the rat race. My feeling was shared by Cher—who, by that time, was tired of being a star. She was really longing to have a regular life again. She often wanted to just go to the beach or to a movie, but she couldn't because she would be mobbed by people wanting to touch her, take a picture, get an autograph. There were times when she had to rent an entire theater so that she and her friends could see a film without being disturbed.

But not Sonny. He insisted that to drop out of this would be to drop out of life. Sonny believed that the capitalist system was the best order, that the pursuit of happiness was parallel to the pursuit of money; capturing that elusive freedom was the same as possessing money. He believed that money buys freedom and that's the only kind of freedom there is, that the only reason anyone did anything was for money. Sonny was always the pragmatic one. Cher and I seemed to be idealists; we were liberals, and Sonny was conservative—a real Republican. Sonny was always trying to get us to see what he considered "real."

We never came to an agreement, but it was eye-opening to me to find out that their feelings were so drastically at odds. I had suspected as much all along, but I didn't know how deep the differences were and how closely aligned I was with Cher. It was funny: despite Cher and I being in agreement about escaping the rat race and how we wanted to pursue our careers, I never saw her as a grown woman. I still saw her as a teenager who got catapulted into this thing.

After our conversation I went over to Jane's to hear the tape she had made of the music for *To Be Fred*. Before I left, she played a track that she had made of the song "Movie Star." The song really impressed me. My interest was so intense that I went right home and immediately made a transfer to reel-to-reel and overdubbed my soprano sax—I didn't want to lose the feeling. I wanted to spend my time working on music I cared about, and not working for Sonny & Cher.

I was tired of the lackadaisical approach Sonny & Cher had toward rehearsals. And their musical limitations bothered me. For some time I had been growing increasingly impatient with the songs they were doing. This impatience may have been heightened by the fact that we had just finished thirty-three TV shows, each one requiring music for them to perform. I just felt that they had done all the stuff they could do.

I was also unimpressed with the proficiency of the musicians Jerry Ridgeway had hired as the rhythm section for the tour. All the fellows may have been quite adequate for their level of experience, but I was impatient with the fact that they were so immature. It just seemed like I'd been dealing with third- and fourth-rate musicians in all the Sonny & Cher road bands. After having such tremendous musicians in the TV band, I wasn't ready to go back to that. Plus, the overwhelming load of work put on Jerry rendered him inefficient, thereby leaving some responsibilities to spill over to me—responsibilities I did not want to contend with.

All these straws were about to break this camel's bad back. But when I called Denis, he wouldn't take no for an answer. He set up a meeting for the following morning for Sonny and me to talk over my reasons for quitting. I told Sonny that my decision to leave was ultimately based on the fact that their musical direction was different from where I wanted to go. I didn't think I should forfeit any more of my life to become more deeply entrenched in perpetuating their music.

Sonny refused to accept that as reason for leaving a prestigious and "financially remunerative" position. We talked for three hours, partially as colleagues, but I think even more as friends, two men whose experiences had been somewhat similar. Having gone through marital problems himself, he felt that, as a longtime friend from way back when, he could give me some advice. In his opinion, it was not just the music. Part of the blame, he figured, should go to my private life—happiness in my family and whatever social life I had. He insisted that I took work too seriously and that I didn't have enough fun; and that, in part, was due to the fact that I was "uptight" about my situation at home. He even suggested that I take a vacation with another woman: "Go to Hawaii or somewhere, and take someone else with you, like Janie [McNealy]." Now where did that come from? Even though I wasn't expecting that, I think there was a deep and sincere effort to get at whatever was really disturbing me.

This wasn't the first time I'd been told that I must not be satisfied at home. Yette had expressed the same idea. Maybe she overstated her case and made me rebel. Yette had insisted over the years that I was not satisfied with her. I did not want to accept that as fact, partly due to my deep convictions about the sanctity of a family, which I accepted as a rule for living. I was afraid of separation and divorce. I had always had a sincere love for Yette, but I think she recognized that my feelings for her had changed—from romantic feelings to feelings of devotion, a family type of love. She recognized that I didn't have that surge of romantic inspiration for her anymore, nor she for me. Hearing it from Sonny, though, I had to admit that Yette had been right all this time. I had been using whatever argumentative reasoning ability I had to convince her that she was wrong. That always frustrated Yette, because her gut told her a truth that I denied.

Sonny's persuasive and pragmatic arguments made me conclude that I was, in fact, making an irrational and emotional decision, blaming all of my frustrations on the music. I left Sonny's house with the thought that I'd go on the road with them for two weeks, get the music straightened out, and help prepare someone to take my place. It was about one in the afternoon when I left. I stopped by Denis's office to talk to him about my plans and expectations. "Well, man," he said, "just tell the cats what you want, and if they don't understand it, tell them to see me."

I went on to the so-called rehearsal, which was supposed to start at one. I arrived forty-five minutes late, and three of the guys were there, ready to rehearse, but I still felt no urge to start even when the fourth guy showed up. While we were all sitting around, Jerry called and asked me about the rehearsal fee. Evidently, Denis or Sonny had mentioned to him that I was complaining about the way he was handling it. I told him what I needed in an abrasive and abrupt way, which I found offensive in other people—and didn't expect of myself. He asked me what else I wanted. I told him I needed an assistant, and of course he wanted to know what for. I became completely indignant. The guys asked me if I wanted to rehearse. I was frightened by my harsh response.

Here I was back in a situation where I had already decided I did not want to be, and I was beginning to act irrationally. I asked myself, *What kind of person am I? Why can't I say no and stick to it? I don't want to be here!* So I got my briefcase and walked out.

Unraveling

At the start of 1977 I had admitted to myself that I wasn't happy, wasn't having fun, wasn't experiencing the personal enjoyment, the freedom from tension that I should have been. I didn't want to go home. I just wanted to go away—from Sonny and Cher and Denis and Yette. I didn't feel that way about the kids; I didn't want to be away from them, but I didn't really think about how they felt.

I wanted to go by Jane's. I thought about something Sonny had said: "You probably feel a lot happier with Jane, in her presence, because you have a lot in common with her." Sonny's words could have come out of Yette's mouth. I wondered, *Am I in love with Jane? Is this what they call love? Are my feelings about her something other than the love and respect I have for her music? Does it show?* Maybe it showed to Yette and Sonny and other people, so maybe I did feel more for her than I was aware. I thought I should go see her and find out. I headed to her house, but she was not home, which was probably for the best because I was crazy right then. I didn't know what I was going to do next. My feelings were all jumbled up: What was right, what was wrong? Was there any right? I didn't know anything! I just didn't want to face anything, so I drove around awhile. Smoked some pot and got high. Didn't help much. I had to make some decisions. I thought I'd go home and get some clothes and leave for a while. Hopefully nobody would be there.

I began to feel sorry for myself—that all anybody wanted from me was what I could provide for them. Sonny had persuaded me to go on the tour not because I was a friend he wanted to help make a wise and rational decision but because he needed me to do what he wanted. Jane and Tami and everybody else, including Yette, wanted me either because I could do something for them or because I was a part of the Sonny & Cher thing. Nobody wanted me just for me. If I could just split the scene, leave 'em all—I really needed to find out who cared about me.

When I got home, Yette was there. I told her I had to leave. I didn't feel like talking about why or what. I couldn't say where I was going because I didn't know. I didn't know when or if I'd be back. She took it calmly, sensing that I was quite disturbed. I took a couple of things and left, then drove around some more, still not knowing where I was going. I had a vague notion that I would probably just get a hotel room for the night. I thought about going to Falling Springs, a place up in the San Gabriel Mountains I had been before with family and friends. I knew I would be able to relax there, but I wasn't sure I could get a cabin. I thought I wanted to be away from everybody, but then I began to feel angry, and I wanted to be with people. I called Sharon, a friend who I knew from CBS, to see if she was at home because I wanted to talk. She wasn't there. I considered talking to Jane but thought better of it.

As I drove back toward Hollywood on Beverly Boulevard, Sharon and another friend from work, Bernadette, happened to be coming out of the CBS lot. I waved and asked about their plans for the evening. Sharon said to call her at home in about an hour. I decided that in the meantime I would find a place to stay at the beach, then invite her to go to the Sea Lion, a restaurant by the beach where we'd been together before. I went out to the beach but couldn't find a place to stay, so I came back into town. I called Sharon and Bernadette just as they were about to go to their hangout and convinced them to join me at the Sea Lion. I didn't mention the crisis I was in—we just hung out and talked.

It was good to be with friends, people who looked up to me. Sharon and Bernadette were young Black women, assistants at CBS (though they didn't work directly with me) who were excited because it was a rarity to see a Black man in the position I was in. When I got back to the hotel I thought, *Well, I got through this evening, but it's still early.* It was too late to play my horn so I tried TV and reading—I had bought three magazines: *Psychology Today, Penthouse,* and *Hustler.* But all the while I knew I had to stop and do some thinking, try to work some things out. That's why I'd left home, after all.

I started to make a recording of my thoughts, but I didn't really know what I was thinking yet. I tried to write a few things down—no good. I began to think more about Jane. Why did I hate to use the word *love* in relation to her? Why did I continue to say *I respect her music* and *I admire her talent?* I'd say any kind of complimentary thing, but I would not, could not, bring myself to say I loved her.

I had an urge to call her and see if I could just let her know that something was going on with me and that somehow she figured into it. But it was one thirty in the morning, and it would not be right to intrude on her at that hour with my irrational thoughts. Even if I did, what could she do about it? I kept thinking until I managed to get to sleep. I woke at six thirty disoriented. *Where am I? Why am I here?* I began to collect my thoughts. I'd just taken two major steps: walking away from Sonny & Cher and leaving home.

I thought more about Jane. She was the black sheep in a wealthy family (she was heir to the Wells Fargo fortune—accumulated over several generations, going back to the Pony Express days). Her parents had expected her to go into the family business, but she was artistic and she really wanted to do Broadway shows. I'd met her parents back in '68 when we recorded a few of her songs. After they heard her music wrapped up in the arrangement that I'd put down, I was somebody in their eyes. We developed quite a friendship. Like a lot of rich White folks, they wanted to know you, know your family and all that stuff. They wanted to be close, but they didn't know how to act. In Jane's world there wasn't much interaction with Black folks, and there was a fear of saying the wrong thing.

At about eight o'clock I got Jane on the phone and said that I had great respect for her music, that our connection was clearly based in art and music. I told her that there was also a possibility that I might be in love with her. It was very difficult for me to say that, particularly not knowing if it was really so. It was so difficult for me to look rejection in the face; saying these things opened up the possibility of my being completely turned away. But I felt that if I was going to get anything out of this dilemma, I had to do something, right or wrong, and face the consequences.

Jane's response was gentle and understanding, almost as though she had anticipated it. We talked about it for some time. We met for breakfast and talked about the situation some more. We decided that there may have been something between us but that we didn't have to come to grips with it right then. We decided to maintain the status quo and to see what happened. I felt relieved.

I decided that I needed to stay away from home for at least a week, not just a couple of days as I'd originally planned. I didn't want Sonny or Denis to know how to reach me. Since they would not accept my *no* for an answer, maybe I could drive them to say no to themselves. I didn't have enough clothes to last a week, so I went back home to get some more. I think Yette recognized that I was feeling better when she saw me. I told her and Andrea that I was going to stay away a little longer. I did not tell her about meeting with Jane. I had to re-evaluate my personal thing with the family. I had to see whether or not my previous beliefs and philosophies about family still held up. I had to admit that many of my expectations were imposed by my upbringing and beliefs about manhood. I thought that if the family was completely organized and operating in an efficient manner, then I would be more free to pursue the music that was dear to me.

Jazz represented spontaneity and freedom of thought. The free-spirit part of me that wanted to play jazz was at war with the part of me that wanted to follow the "rules" of marriage and family—a deep part of my makeup. I suppressed or postponed my dreams, and as a result I made undue impositions on my family, extracting the proverbial pound of flesh as revenge. Would it have been better for everyone if I had pursued the life of a jazz musician and not felt so guilty and afraid about financial consequences?

I had to admit that Yette and Andrea supported me; I had their approval to pursue whatever I wanted. Andrea seemed not to understand why I would continue to do something I didn't want to do. I had stubbornly denied that I had options. I had told myself that I could not exercise that freedom because I had to pay the house note. They didn't realize what I believed: that if my family went bad, it was me that was going bad. If we became financially impoverished, it was on Harold Battiste, not any other member of the family. I had a great fear of that stigma. I operated on the basis that my self-esteem depended upon how well I took care of my family first, and only then on how well I performed in my chosen career. So I never took a real chance on my music for fear that if I went totally after the music I would not be able to take care financially.

After talking with my family, I decided to seek further advice from our close friends and neighbors of fifteen years, Bill and Elaine James, mainly because I felt I should let them know what was happening in our home. They'd see me gone and be curious. I also knew that they were both genuinely concerned about us, as we were about them. So Yette and I went over and had a long talk. They wanted to help me figure out whether I could pursue what I wanted and still remain true to my commitment as a husband and father in the home.

I was almost fifty and there I was again, asking the question, "What am I going to do now?" Nothing had changed: I was not doing what I wanted to do, and it was taking me further and further away from my family. I could almost hear my younger daughter say in her innocence, "Do whatever you want." What I wanted, whatever it was, was buried somewhere all those years back when the career choices I made were based on what I considered my responsibility as a husband and father. I thought about trying something new, something that came closer to my youthful aspirations toward jazz—as a performer, composer, and arranger. But at age forty-seven? "Do whatever you want," at that point, was more like "Do whatever you can."

Then, at the end of January 1977, Yette let me know that she was ready to leave, split, "separate." This information hit me hard and deep—I didn't know how to handle it. How long had this been in her thoughts? Or maybe (I hoped) this was just a momentary flash that would pass. It was ironic: I had a twenty-one-year-old son that didn't want to leave (Bunny) and a forty-one-year-old wife that didn't want to stay. But I was about to get the chance to get away from my troubles at home. I had a grand opportunity to go on the road with someone other than Sonny & Cher, and maybe expand my musical horizons a bit.

A Much-Needed Break

I met Marilyn McCoo and Billy Davis when they appeared as special guests on the *Sonny & Cher Show* in 1976. The two of them were wonderful, warm, and professional—just good people. A few weeks after their appearance, they asked if I would serve as musical director on their tour. Word must have gotten around the industry that Sonny & Cher's show was ending, and they probably figured I'd be available. I was really excited: Marilyn and Billy were highly respected performers, both as a husband-and-wife singing entity and in their work with the chart-topping group the Fifth Dimension ("Up, Up and Away," "Aquarius/Let the Sunshine In," "Stoned Soul Picnic," "One Less Bell to Answer"). I needed to make some money now that the Sonny & Cher train was reaching the station, probably for the last time. I truly looked forward to working with Marilyn and Billy for several reasons: mainly because they were successful Black entertainers, their musical abilities were at a higher level than what I'd been working with, and I envisioned that the whole experience would be something different for me. Billy and Marilyn were nice, spiritual, peaceful people—Marilyn was into meditation, prayer, and yoga—and their vibe was truly welcoming.

I toured with them for most of 1977. Working with them was so easy, it felt like a vacation. It was not just Billy and Marilyn—although they were the main ingredient—but the whole scene: the band, the manager, Marilyn's personal assistant, the roadies. It was so different from the environment I had been in for so long. Race did play heavily in my feelings. I was never really aware of being uncomfortable in my previous scene until I happened into one like this, where so many familiar things started calling me home.

Even my departure from their employ was easy. Gail Deadrick, their extremely talented longtime pianist, was curious about directing shows and asked me a lot of questions during the tour. I had never known a female to be in a musical director's position for a recognized show, but I approached Marilyn and Billy and asked if Gail could direct one night. They agreed, and Gail took the baton for a show in Las Vegas and did a fantastic job. She was elated and truly wanted the opportunity to continue directing the rest of the tour, so I was willing to concede. I stepped away after directing a show in the Blue Room at the Fairmont Hotel in New Orleans. I was back home, and it seemed like a good point in time to regroup—again.

The Beat Goes On . . .

The concept that gave birth to All for One Records seemed even more meaningful and valuable now, as we neared the start of a new decade, as it had been back in 1961. After AFO left the city in 1963, no other record company produced contemporary jazz in New Orleans: during the late 1960s, '70s, and '80s, very few if any up-and-coming players were recorded locally. I began thinking about how much New Orleans had continued to remain in my life. People I knew from home—acquaintances, professional colleagues, personal friends—contacted me from time to time, for a variety of reasons. Some wanted to let me know that they were out in California and others wanted to see what professional connections I could help them make. I decided to try to start a nonprofit organization (with the same ignorance I had years ago with AFO!) for New Orleans musicians—a sort of clearinghouse for information and a way to uplift my cultural compadres.

National Association of New Orleans Musicians/ Dedication–Mission

NANOM is a non-profit service and educational organization dedicated to recognizing, perpetuating and documenting the heritage of New Orleans music and the people who make the music.

NANOM was formed as a result of the many inquiries and requests we received over the years for information, literature, biographies, recordings, etc. about New Orleans music and musicians. We recognize that this music and the people who create it occupy a unique place in American cultural history and that America's gift to the world of art is rooted therein. We therefore dedicate the work of NANOM to supporting this music through various forms of educational and financial aid.

Projects and Programs
NANOM has undertaken several ambitious activities, each of which is designed to fulfill the goals to which we are committed.
1. NETWORK: Forming and maintaining a communications link among members on a national and international scale for the exchange of vital and valuable information.
2. ARCHIVES: Conducting interviews, collecting biographies, pictures, recordings, published articles and other memorabilia for the benefit of members and the public at large.
3. SAFE LANDING: Providing information for job contacts in major cities, career counseling and financial aid to relocating musicians whenever possible.
4. EDUCATION: Coordinating lectures, workshops, seminars and performances between members and various schools and organizations including K through 12th grade and college.
5. SCHOLARSHIPS: To deserving students of New Orleans music.

Keepin' the Music (and the musicians) Alive!

When I learned that a lawyer to do the paperwork would cost about five hundred dollars, I enlisted the help of my daughter Andrea instead. We studied up and got it together ourselves. Innocence, ignorance, naïveté—whatever—my approach to this project was some of all of that. Following the instructions on how to set up a nonprofit was the easy part for Andrea and me. We got familiar with downtown, the business district, the courts, and various public offices. And we got a legal 501(c)3 and a California State Charter for the National Association of New Orleans Musicians. But I never thought about how or where nonprofits got money. There seemed to be a pattern in my career: I'd overlook or forget about the money aspect. I did know that donations to nonprofits were tax deductible, but how to get people to make donations had not occurred to me.

Setting up NANOM focused my attention on the importance of New Orleans as the "cradle of jazz" and the fundamental spirit of Afro-centric culture in America. My awareness of these ideas had been growing over the years: I had felt their spiritual influence even before I realized why I responded the way I did to certain incidents at the beginning of my career. I had been influenced by a few books—some literature and history on the subject—and by cats like Jimmy X (who'd had such an impact on me back at the Dew Drop Inn) and Umar Sharif (the trumpet master formerly known as Emery Thompson). And the experiences I had teaching in Louisiana—the incidents at Carver High in DeRidder in '53, and the way they got rid of me in New Orleans in '56—that stuff changed something deep inside me. So deep I didn't see it myself. I had become a "quiet militant."

Back in the early '70s I had started to think, on many levels and from many angles, about the social and economic problems that Black people face. Since I had already pointed myself in the direction of a social activist, I thought I would try to start something. I sent a letter to a bunch of artists, asking them to help me compile a record of New Orleans musicians.

July 7, 1971

Gentlemen,

I would like each of you to whom this letter is given to help us in a project which I strongly feel will be . . . IS of superlative importance to all of us.

We, The New Orleans Musicians of our generation, are quite unique in that we are the only musicians who bridge the past and the future. For example, we have played gigs with men like Paul Barbarin, Willie Humphrey, etc. and we have extended these roots to such diverse scenes as Dizzy Gillespie, Ahmad Jamal, Yusef Lateef - New Orleans Symphony, Hair, Sonny & Cher, Frank Sinatra, Count Basie, etc.

The old cats who gave us our roots are dying. And the new cats in N.O. can't absorb the full heritage because too many of us are not there or have quit playing or caring.

I wish to begin an organized effort to collect our generation's experiences for the Preservation of our Past for Posterity as a legacy to the future musicians of New Orleans.

What you must do:

If you will make a chart like the one enclosed it will be convenient for you to put in as many names and/or "nicknames" as you can think of. Of course, each of you will put many of the same names on your list, but that's all right because each of you will remember some names that the others of us have forgotten! Don't assume that someone else will remember certain obvious names. If you do not know under which instrument to place a name like George Davis (sax, bass, guitar, arranger) then put the name under whichever category you want.

Before August 1, 1971, send your list to me. Don't forget your own name and include your address & phone number so that the communication between us remains open.

Love & respect, Harold Battiste

I was hoping that the responses from various musicians would give me a framework to shape a vision, then jump-start some action. But other than one great and thorough response from drummer Charles

"Honeyboy" Otis, who was known for staying in touch and keeping up with cats, the response was zero. I did not feel encouraged to pursue the idea any further.

Still, at age fifty and without a job I tried to go the nonprofit route again. That Andrea and I were able to figure out how to get the state of California to grant us a 501(c)3 status for our association pushed me to think we could figure out how to accomplish our goals: networking and supporting musicians. I had no doubt about the need for the association—just as I had felt in 1959 about AFO Records. But I was able to put only about two years of optimism and work toward its mission. There was a lot I wanted to do in terms of scholarships for young cats, music education, and music archives, but I couldn't organize things sufficiently or raise enough money. Again, as with AFO, I ultimately had to put NANOM on the back burner.

Other aspects of my life, such as my family and a paying job, were waiting for a shot. Yette was busy doing an internship in geriatrics, and I would drive her to the nursing home where she was working with the residents. While she did her thing, I would get on the piano and entertain whoever was willing to listen. It was good practice and a little creative time, but I wasn't getting paid.

It was nearly the mid-'80s, and I'd been hittin' and missin' since the late '70s. In the absence of a "real job" on which to focus my efforts, I was open and vulnerable to a variety of temptations. I spent seven years—from 1980 to 1987—as minister of music at Harvest Tabernacle Church. I had met the pastor, Reverend Donald Cook, in the late '60s, before his call to the ministry, when he and his sister Ruth were seeking a recording deal for their versatile vocal group. Melvin Lastie and I produced them when we were at Pulsar, but Pulsar never released the records. Ten years later I ran into Cook, visited his church, and became his minister of music.

And I got involved with a smooth jazz group through Victor Sirker, a marvelous New Orleans guitarist who did wonders with all the latest technology of the day. He could be a smooth jazz band all by

Harold Battiste's New Orleans Natives; *left to right:* Harold, Lenny McDaniel, Ike Williams, Henry Butler, Tami Lynn, John Goines, Leo Nocentelli, and Jerry Jumonville, ca. 1984 (THNOC)

himself, but we put a group around him, called it NOVIA, and got a few gigs at the Rapa House in L.A. Then, Bill Bentley, a writer at the *Los Angeles Times,* wanted to produce a series of New Orleans concerts in Hollywood. He approached New Orleans drummer Earl Palmer to put a band together. Earl told him, "Get Harold—if you can." I knew immediately that I needed to line up a group of New Orleans homeboys. No point in searching through L.A.'s finest—there were enough cats out here to have choices. The New Orleans Natives included John "Gumbo" Goines on drums, Lenny McDaniel on bass, Leo Nocentelli on guitar, Henry Butler on piano, Jerry Jumonville on tenor sax, myself on alto sax, Ike "Diz" Williams on trumpet, with vocals by Tami Lynn.

The shows, held at Club Lingerie on Sunset Boulevard in Hollywood, made headlines and history. Week after week people waited until midnight to get in to see the lineup of stars Bentley booked from the Big Easy. The New Orleans Natives, which had been assembled for this series only, got so much press that we received calls for appearances all around Southern California. I couldn't fully enjoy this touch of success, though, because a frightening thing was happening to my family.

Marriage Storm Brewing

Yette was continuing her studies at California State University, Dominguez Hills. The school was quite a distance from our house. We had only one car, so the commute was a little inconvenient for us unless I drove, which I did once in a while. So in order to be closer to the school, Yette got an apartment down there in 1983 or 1984. I discovered that this cat Joe Mills was sort of sponsoring her apartment so he would have somewhere to stay when he came to Los Angeles. I wasn't sure if he was paying for everything or if they shared expenses. He was an old boyfriend, someone that she had been seeing before we got married. I remembered one time back in New Orleans when she and Joe were on the porch of her house on Toledano Street when I walked up. She told me she was with him just to say goodbye before he left to join the army, but I was suspicious.

They had gotten back in touch with one another sometime in the '70s, when he was living in Sacramento. He had come to our house and everything, and I had welcomed him, being the kind of cat that I am. I was never suspicious or anything, so maybe he thought that I was oblivious—and maybe I was just dumb. I knew there had been a lot of phone calls between them because I had the phone bills. Yette was in school and wasn't earning enough money to afford an apartment, and Joe had been hanging around, so it didn't take much to put two and two together. When I realized that Joe was sort of supporting her, I was frightened.

Yette had often been burdened thinking that I was with some other woman; her suspicions had always caused problems in our relationship. But all she would have had to do was come with me on tour sometimes or meet me at a few of the concert dates and she would have seen better, she would have known better. My family was not a "show business" family; that is to say that there seemed to be a lack of interest in the social aspect of that world. We didn't socialize with "stars" but with neighbors and friends. We often had social gatherings at our home with free-for-all, high-spirited conversations on predetermined subjects that I selected. I always liked to document things on tape because it's like taking pictures. Once or twice I recorded our informal conversations and gave everybody tapes. Usually these events turned into parties—eating, drinking, smoking cigarettes and pot, listening to music, and sometimes even a little dancing.

Even though we didn't socialize with showbiz folks, Yette had met Sonny back during our Specialty Records days, and later I'm sure she met Cher, and I had many other friends and associates with whom there was a brief social exchange. But Yette never seemed too comfortable with them. I spent much of my family social time with people not in showbiz. But maybe if she'd joined me more in that world, she would not have been so intimidated.

A couple of times Yette had told me that she wanted to be by herself and had gone up to Monterey or someplace like that. She had made a few new friends at college, and I wondered if all these new experiences were influencing her feelings to be more independent. I started adding up all of the behaviors. Again, Yette was letting me know through her actions that she was ready to leave. She never said it in specific terms, but I got the message. I didn't want to think that she was having an affair; I had to have evidence. I'd rather say that she didn't instead of saying that she did. I know that sounds naïve, but that's just my way of thinking. I didn't want to look for trouble; what would be the point? I think that I was really afraid of what I might do—I might kill that nigger. Whatever way it might go, it wouldn't be something good. It would wind up that I would be hurt or she would be hurt—somebody would get hurt—physically as well as emotionally. So rather than face that, I let it be and let it work itself out.

Back to School

With Yette back in school, I had been thinking about teaching, lecture tours, or something else to do with education for myself. In the early '80s I applied at the school board for high-school substitute work to get a feel for it—it had been years since I'd been in the classroom. I got a few assignments as a short-term substitute (for one or two days). At Crenshaw High I engaged the students in conversations about current events I thought might be of interest to them. During one of the conversations, a student brought up the subject of the school's curriculum. Many of them, mostly boys, thought they were wasting time. I listened and learned more from them than they learned from me. These young men told me they could do bigger and better things—earning money by fixing cars, doing manual labor, etc.—rather than sitting in a classroom all day. The curriculum was flawed; it didn't have their best interests in mind. The practical intelligence these young men possessed was not being recognized or addressed.

During an assignment at Dorsey High, I discovered that the music program was badly neglected. I fired off a letter to the principal and superintendent stressing the importance of music in schools, especially in the Black community:

> . . . At the risk of sounding like a throw-back to the 60's, Blacks are still without identity. In the absence of basic ethnic identifying symbols, i.e. sir names, religion, native land, etc. (symbols taken for granted by other ethnic groups), Blacks are continually searching for ways to know themselves. The society has provided many negative ways for Blacks to identify and many, if not most of them have been accepted as valid by Blacks. But there has always been an underlying positive hope that persisted in the MUSIC! Throughout the most depressing and de-humanizing times in our brief history, the MUSIC was the tie that bonded, the salve that healed and the food that filled our soul!! MUSIC, then, became and remains a way of Expressing an Identity . . .

Then, in 1982, Dr. Stanley Coben, emeritus professor of history at the University of California at Los Angeles (and brother of Bill Coben, my trusted friend and sometime lawyer), invited me to present a lecture on the Harlem Renaissance. This invitation resulted in presentations at UC Santa Barbara; Cal State, Dominguez Hills; and others. In July 1983 violinist Charles Veal asked me to get involved in starting a jazz studies program at Los Angeles Trade Technical College. Although Trade Tech did not follow through, I was able to use the curriculum I'd created when Ellis Marsalis inquired a few years later, in 1988, about my possible interest in developing a jazz studies program in New Orleans.

COLLEGE/UNIVERSITY LEVEL CURRICULUM: AMERICAN MUSIC: GENERAL OUTLINE

I. The Art
    A. Appreciations:
        1. Cultivating 'Big ears': Basic techniques of identifying the elements of music, instruments, voices and how they work together
        2. Survey of the 'Hot 100': Study of current musics, music critics, the public and you

    B.   Histrosophies:
       1.   Whose Story? His Story: History of American music in the oral tradition by those who were there
       2.   State of the artist: Studies in the ways cultures view and use art and artists
    C.   Theories:
       1.   All the standard courses (musicianship, harmonies, etc.)
       2.   New theories and techniques for American Music

II.   The Professions
    A.   Performing (concert, stage, studio)
    B.   Writing (composition, arranging, orchestrating, copying)
    C.   Teaching (institutional, professional, private, media)
    D.   Management (personal, financial, career)
    E.   Misc. (commercial uses of music and satellite/spin-off professions)

III.   The Business
    A.   Promotions (concerts, festivals, etc.)
    B.   Publishing/Manufacturing
    C.   Productions (stage, screen, audio, video)
    D.   Educating (the business of schools)

IV.   The Community Service
    A.   Performing ensembles (community resources)
    B.   Outreach to community institutions and organizations

Prepared by: H. R. Battiste, Director, N.A.N.O.M, January 1982

In 1984 I got a call from Joe Thayer, dean of the Colburn School of Performing Arts. I was not familiar with him or the school, but he knew Wynton Marsalis, whom he had met at a summer music camp on the East Coast. While he was in Los Angeles, Wynton had visited Joe at the school. Though it was focused on classical piano, Colburn had recently experienced an influx of students interested in jazz, and there was a trend at the time toward including this recently recognized American art form in music-school curricula. Joe wanted Wynton's help identifying a professor to start a program, and had suggested his father, Ellis. Wynton is said to have asked, "Don't y'all know Harold Battiste? He's already out here!"

Getting things started at Colburn brought me back to DeRidder in 1952, when I had to start a music program from scratch. The Colburn students were not beginners, but the jazz concepts were intimidating to some of them. After five or six weeks, I noticed students from the classical classes bunched up around our door, checking us out. I invited them in with their instruments and tried to show them how to learn the jazz way—by improvisation—but they always backed off. It terrified them that we were playing without music sheets!

The program attracted several highly talented students with church-music backgrounds. I recall Myron McKinley and Eric Reed, both outstanding pianists who went on to play professionally in the pop and jazz fields. Reed played piano with the Wynton Marsalis ensemble, recording several early CDs with him before launching his solo career.

It was an adventure teaching at Colburn. I was doing what I wanted to do: melding classical constructs with jazz as an art form and setting a new criteria for music excellence. I had an opportunity to show my students how to play by ear, to help them be more creative and familiarize themselves with their particular instrument.

Breaking Apart

Family Man was the only job or position that I had held consistently—for thirty-one years. All my other work was supportive of and subordinate to that. My children carried my life in their lives. Yette was already spending most of her time at her apartment close to college. I thought the family needed time together— quality, open, honest time with each other, both one-on-one and as a group. We held a family meeting at

Wynton Marsalis (*left*) teaching Eric Reed (*center*) and Myron McKinley at the Colburn School in L.A., ca. 1984 (THNOC)

the house on Bowcroft on Saturday, December 11, 1984, and promised to meet every week. But I feared that the promise of a weekly meeting might be jeopardized. That first meeting was accomplished only after I had delicately proposed it, and I had to leave all the details and decisions to the children. Bunny was already twenty-nine and considered himself the "elder statesman" of his sisters and brother, Andrea was twenty-five, Marzique was twenty-one, and Harlis was twenty. Adults, yes, but I guess I still saw them as little kids. And yes, they were physically different, but in my mind I couldn't make the shift to place them in adulthood.

Although some important issues were brought out, I still saw so much more we needed to spell out and address; there wasn't a clear consensus on anything. Our family meetings when the kids were younger wound up being a discussion about chores and the division of labor—at least from their standpoint. I wanted to talk about us being better people and how to improve the family unit. But they were just young people still shaping themselves; my mistake was thinking that they could think on a broader scale that approached my level and experience.

In May 1985 Yette moved to her apartment on a full-time basis. She gathered whatever she needed to live but didn't strip out the house or anything. It was a clear statement of departure from the household and the marriage. Our family was not doing well, and neither was I. I even contemplated killing myself. I recorded myself on audiotape on July 19, 1985, considering the possibility.

Scenario for Suicide

Scenario . . . for . . . just laying down . . . and as I lay down, I recognize that laying on one's back is a passive gesture or symbol. Is it the position of defeat or surrender? Recognize that often I lie down because I feel helpless . . . and that gives a feeling of being tired. The law states that ". . . a body in motion tends to . . . etc."

Suddenly, in the midst of my confusion about what to do with myself . . . how to face . . . [long pause] realities, whatEVER they are; and to choose . . . what it is I want, and, what do I want to pay for it? The feeling going through what seems to be . . . a very, very low point [long pause].

Various signs . . . little things continue to remind me of the overwhelming task ahead if I am to survive. And if I am to survive, what am I to survive? And for what purpose? A cycle which feeds itself has new input: the scenario for . . . suicide.

It has become very reasonable in my mind now, to select suicide as an alternative way to live. It's like deciding that you've "seen the movie, now it's time to go" . . . no point sittin' around in the theatre watching the same thing over . . . might as well go home . . . go out . . . get out of here . . . see what's out there. Maybe the sun is still shining out there . . . there may be time to go somewhere else. This life is over. . . .

Then I talk about it and go over it in my head . . . talk to myself about it, try to write about it, record it . . . so I can listen to myself talk about it and see if I can frighten myself out of it. But then I lay down . . . and that's not the gesture of . . . "fighting my way out" . . .

Even though Yette had moved out, our conflicts continued—if we couldn't fight in person, we fought on the phone. I was also in regular conflict with the kids. Bunny and I had a terrible fight in which he said some hard things: "You're crazy and panicked like an old man"; "You ran Mama away . . . she didn't want to leave"; "You should cool it and let me take care of everything"; "You don't know how to work with Black people"; "You're not as Black as you think." I wrote his words down so that when I had forgotten more positive words from Bunny, I'd still remember those (maybe). I had often been in that position: when a family member remembered the one negative word from me and forgot the ten positive.

Then I was hurt by Marzique when she wouldn't accept a gift from me. 'Zique was in the Air Force and was going to be stationed in Spain for a tour of duty. I wanted her to take my father's ring with her to Spain, so she'd have a token, but she said it was too "heavy"—too deep. Yette and Andrea agreed it was too risky; she might lose it. I felt cheated.

BluesDecemberBluesDecemberBluesDecember

The aggregate of losses I suffered in 1985—emotional, psychological, physical, and financial—were the greatest in my life so far. I was not able to make any long-range commitments to anything. I had no clear perception that I could survive this far and at times had no desire to continue. I continued to have conflicts with Yette, conflicts with the kids. Then, on November 17, 1985, I was confronted once again with my own mortality. It started when I fell over a bench in the backyard. Although I was able to minimize the impact, I still sustained damage to my knees and legs. When I went to bed five hours later, I felt acute pain in my left ribcage. Was I having another heart attack? I didn't think my children would know how to care for me, and I feared they didn't want to know.

DAILY REMINDER / 12-85

12-11 Somewhere, in my deep belief, God has work for me. I have seen myself declining in much of what was good in my life. Even as I saw that decline, the deep belief kept me looking to the future, knowing that at some point, things would change to incline.

12-12 The car is sick, the house is ailing, my body is breaking down, my mind is confused, my family is splintered—the writing is where I dump my downs. So, only reading the writings gives an unbalanced picture of me. The music is where I dump my ups.

12-18 All day running from aloneness. Yesterday, for a moment, I felt like crying. I needed a place and a time to cry. I would like a shoulder . . . no, a bosom. When I lost my parents in 1957, I suppressed the grief. I was afraid to cry. It seemed like if I started, I would never be able to stop. So I never cried. That's how I feel now.

12-9 When rewards of living seem not worth the effort it takes to stay alive, then one is on the way to death—either by self-neglect, self-punishment or direct self-destruction. I know by my behavior that I am seeking a way to die without long-suffering or to live without this daily pain. Suffering is relative—subjective. I define my own suffering as having no one to care for me and no one for me to care for.

12-26 Christmas Blues
If I git thu Wensday
I think I got it made
Yeah . . . if I make it thu Wensday
I think I be okay,
But I work up this Thursday mawnin
And things seem worse than yesterday.

Split, Patch, Split

Three days into 1986, I contacted Yette about throwing things away. We had to begin work on disconnecting our lives. The physical things we shared over the years were a constant, unrelenting reminder of the hard issues of separation. After a release of anger and frustration by Yette, I offered to take her out to dinner. We talked till 5:00 a.m., still trying to unravel what went wrong. We had many similar struggles over the next few months, in person and on the phone.

On January 6 our neighbor died suddenly. I talked with Andrea about the urgent need for the family to learn about how and what to do as far as handling family business, dealing with a will and such. We needed to continue talking about the business of family—our rights and responsibilities—who does what, who gets what and why. Harlis and I in particular were having trouble. I thought his understanding of the father-son relationship was dysfunctional. "Honor thy father" had no clear meaning for him. He said that he saw me as a unique intellectual who asked hard questions—that it was too much "mental work" for people to talk to me. He said he wondered what the "average" father said to his sons. He said that he had found himself not talking when the views of others were limited—that he was learning how to deal with holding back his mind or disguising his intellect. It concerned me that Harlis felt that he couldn't be like an ordinary person or connect with his peers.

I wanted to make a public effort to reinvigorate my marriage, and on May 6, 1986, I created a poem/invitation to be shared with neighbors and friends if Yette would have agreed to such an event. Unfortunately, it was something that I only wished could have happened.

All of our friends, from all the facets of our lives, are invited to a
Second Time Around Celebration

We want to thank each and all of you for your love and
support through our 'tough' times. All of you have shown
the highest qualities of friendship . . .
and some have gone beyond words!

So, come . . . Let us say thanks
Come and break bread with us . . .
Sing songs and talk, talk . . .

We will need you now more than ever!

The Battistes

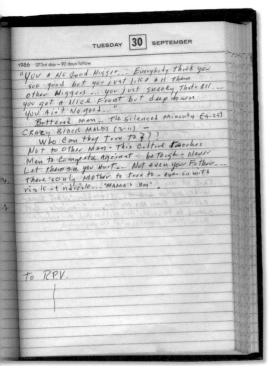

Yette and I continued to struggle. I felt that we were in a situation that could be better understood if the word *love* were replaced by the word *need*. Yette was in and out of the house, getting things, in and out of my life. And I was fighting with Andrea. I couldn't tolerate the feeling of isolation in my home. She expressly did not want to talk to me, except about superficial things. I reached the end of my rope one night when Yette's cousin showed up with a duffle bag, drunk, looking for a place to stay. I could not tolerate another reminder of the position I was in: all looking *for* help, none looking *to* help.

DAILY REMINDER / 7-28-86

For several mornings now, I've been trying to talk to Andrea. The wall gets thicker. I left her a note. She was gone when I got back. The note said: "I keep trying to say I love you."

On the last day of September 1986, Yette and I had a terrible fight. The next day I called her for help—deep, intimate help, the kind that can only come from agape love. I was struggling for my sanity; the awareness of aloneness—not loneliness but the knowledge that I was alone—was torturing me. Once again, I did not get help. We were both trapped by our early childhood programming regarding gender roles and expectations. My behavior resembled that of my father, and my expectations of wife/mother resembled what I experienced from my mother. Similarly, Yette's behavior seemed to resemble her mother's, and her expectations resembled what she experienced with her stepfather.

Yette traced my childhood and how I related to my parents. Her view was that because I never experienced hard times, I was "paying for it now." She said she felt like she and the kids had been "just slaves" to me. She thought of our business as not ours but mine, and therefore to work for it meant working for nothing, which equaled slavery. But, if she believed that, how could she treat our assets as ours? If she really perceived our relationship as master/slave or employer/employee rather than as partners, then her attitude and behavior would be different.

I sought help from people who were long-time, mutual, close friends of our family, people who wanted to help us. But they spoke to me through their view of me as presented by Yette, which they seemed to accept as truth. It was clear that an assassination was taking place: I was being killed, softly and slowly.

Blackwell Tribute

In April 1987 I was offered a chance to get away. Rob Gibson, a concert promoter, proposed doing a tribute to Ed Blackwell in Atlanta; Gibson was a huge fan of Blackwell and admired his music. The gig would be held near the end of the year. I participated in the event as the leader of the original American Jazz Quintet, which had made its debut recording in Cosimo Matassa's studio in New Orleans in 1956. Gibson knew that we were the first group Ed had played with, and he was determined to bring us all together again. At rehearsal Ellis stood at his piano and recalled those early days when we were together at Dillard in 1952: "Man, you know, if it hadn't been for this music, I don't think I would have [graduated] . . ."

Now, after thirty years, the five of us would come together again. We played together for three days and it was wonderful. Richard Payne (bass) and Alvin Batiste (clarinet) came in from New Orleans and Baton Rouge, respectively. Ellis Marsalis (piano) was brought in from Richmond, Virginia, where he was coordinator of the jazz studies program at Virginia Commonwealth University. The fierce Earl Turbinton

The last photo of all the members of the original American Jazz Quintet together; *left to right:* Ellis Marsalis Jr., Harold Battiste, Richard Payne, Alvin Batiste, and Ed Blackwell (THNOC)

was our special guest on alto sax. Earl brought the excitement of the generation of New Orleans jazz players that followed us. Of course, Alvin's performance on clarinet was stellar.

It was a two-night affair, and since the AJQ had been the first stop in Blackwell's brilliant career, we opened the tribute. Our performance was recorded and released as *From Bad to Badder* on the Black Saint label out of Italy. And the gig gave birth to the idea for the *Silverbook,* a compilation of music transcripts and information on the AFO composers. I knew that it was up to me to catalog the work we had created over the years: I was the only one that had sheet music for most of our tunes. I'm so glad that I followed my first mind and didn't allow myself to let go of the *Silverbook* concept.

Divorce Letter

On April 21, 1987, I went to New Orleans for Jazz Fest. For the last few years I'd been renewing my spiritual and personal connections with the city. My Daily Reminder book is filled with familiar names on April 22: Lorraine Farr, Pat Jolly, Tom Dent, Roger Dickerson, Dooky Chase, Lolis Elie, James Borders, Kalamu ya Salaam, Warren Bell Jr. I was feeling bonds there that had faded from my life since I'd been living in Los Angeles. Forward to Sunday, April 26: Yette came to town for the funeral of her stepfather, Mr. Clarence. In an attempt to help us talk through our domestic problems, our oldest and dearest friends, Alvin and Edith, arranged a summit with Yette and me at a hotel on the West Bank (across the river from the French Quarter). It was just the four of us in the room, and me and Yette had a nice conversation. It was a good time. I thought that we had come to an amicable reconciliation and had agreed to work toward a solution. The next day, I took Yette to the airport. I thought that we were going to stay together.

I arrived home in Los Angeles on Tuesday, May 5, at about 5:00 p.m. Among the mail awaiting me was a letter and papers from Yette's attorney. A divorce suit had been filed on April 13!

I felt like I'd been brought into a battle I never wanted. I could not even acknowledge that there was a battle. When I tried to psych myself into a combat mentality, deep inside me I could not do it; I'd rather not fight. I didn't know how to switch from the life commitment I'd had. Even though I could fashion a rational argument for saving myself, I couldn't sustain the spirit for struggling against my wife for that salvation. It was a losing battle for me either way. "A house divided" truly describes my predicament. I chose to just not fight.

Rather than call her lawyer, I called Yette first to tell her of my feelings about the situation. I told her I'd rather she have all the assets. I saw no benefit for me in dividing our meager material things. We argued. There was too much fear, anxiety, anger, etc. for us to talk.

I had called to surrender, but she would not accept it. It seemed like she needed to keep the battle going to make me suffer. No, that's not it—she needed to feel justified in her actions toward me. She needed me to be the man she was programmed to expect husbands to be.

1988 July 8

My Dearest Alviette:

As I continue to resist the destiny of my life, it becomes absolutely clear to me that I cannot escape that destiny . . . that the responsibility for that destiny is mine, like it or not. As I have become clearer in 'seeing' that destiny I realize that the work has in fact been being done while my conflict has been the contradictory, almost schizophrenic choice between going with the flow of my destiny or, to resist that flow to be accepted by the people I love. I know you understand what I'm saying: that it has always been a tug of war between (1) my love for you, my children, my family, my friends & neighbors; and (2) the destiny that I could always feel lurking in my subconscious (and conscious) mind. There was fear that following the path toward that destiny would alienate me from all the people I love and need. But the alienation had been happening anyway in spite of my effort to avoid it. And as I have been following the command of 1984 to 'write it down' (12-12-84), and I realized that I had been doing that but the directive was saying, 'organize it . . . put it into a form that it can be usable by someone . . . so that it might be recognizable as something of value. Ever since I received the command to do that, the pressure to follow that destiny has mounted . . . to the point that I'm obsessed with its fulfillment. Even though now I struggle to stay alive in order to fulfill it, there had been the ultimate effort to resist the destiny by contemplating leaving this life . . . by developing a scenario for suicide (7-19-85). But the command to fulfill was stronger than the effort to abort.

I am painfully aware of how your personal feelings about me may be. I am painfully aware of your need to fulfill your destiny as prescribed for you before you became a part of me. I have often thought about what it was that you wanted to 'be' . . . how, as a child, did you 'see' yourself in the future . . . what got put on 'hold' when you decided to become a part of my life . . . what unfinished business was there? In that painful recognition I realize that my love for you makes me want that destiny to be fulfilled. I also realize, however, that your destiny with me is molded and sealed in the years we have spent together. Your life has been transformed from whatever it was as you took on the task of becoming Mrs. Battiste. You became Mrs. Battiste and you still are . . . you will always be. Neither the abstract dictums of laws nor the concrete application of those laws can change the reality of our years together.

I am, at this point, in full awareness of the work that needs to be done. And as I search desperately to find help, I am back to basics. The people who have shared my life are a part of that destiny, and you, Alviette, are the principal person. Without your support and contribution the struggle to do the work is overwhelming. I cannot replace you. Your position in my life (and destiny) is not one that can be filled by another . . . no matter their qualifications. No one can match your years of 'on the job' experience. No one can become MRS

HAROLD R. BATTISTE, JR.

Matthew 12:26

Ellis Marsalis Jr. and Harold performing with David Pulphus in the atrium of the Bultman Funeral Home, St. Charles Avenue, New Orleans, ca. 1994 (THNOC)

epilogue

The judge gave the furniture to me and the house on Bowcroft to Alviette. The notice to vacate gave me until 5:00 p.m. on Saturday, November 12, 1988. I was determined not to leave, and I had made signs to prove it: OVER MY DEAD BODY. It's hard to believe now that I was ready to end it all right there. But I was rescued by Brenda Myers and Calvin Goines. Brenda took my stuff and Calvin took me, and we were out with two hours to spare. That day seems like a part of another life. Or maybe, since that day, *this* seems like another life: on that day I had to face a new life, a life after Bowcroft Street.

"Jim Dandy to the Rescue!" If you remember that Ruth Brown hit, you're old as me. That's how I felt when my two Jim Dandys saved me. I don't know if they planned earlier that week to be on stand-by, but Calvin and Brenda showed up right on time with the objective of getting me to leave before the eviction deadline. Calvin is a strong, fast-talking negotiator, and he talked me down from being a stupid ass who wanted to confront law officers. He offered his living-room sofa as a place for me to "think about this crazy bullshit!" I had planned my end, but I had to succumb to their better idea for a new beginning. A New Orleans native, Calvin had been a friend of my family for twenty years or more. He, his wife, Evelyn, and their kids had vacationed with us, and we enjoyed lively discussions of social issues, music, science, medicine, politics, and race. He had graduated from Xavier University in New Orleans as a pre-med major, and he was the first Black student to crack the color line at UCLA's dental school. He went on to mentor several Black students through the program. He had gone through a divorce from Evelyn, so I trusted that he knew what I was going through.

I had known Brenda for only a few years, so she was not as familiar with my family as Calvin was. She was a mathematician, a divorced single mom whose teenage son was a student at the Colburn School, where I taught. I got to know her and some of her friends, and she got to know some of mine, including Calvin. I guess our common bond was marriage troubles.

Calvin lived in a small, one-bedroom house. He liked to cook, and that suited me fine. Sleeping on Calvin's living-room couch, I really began to understand my new life. After twenty years in a house with three bedrooms, two and a half baths, living room, dining room, kitchen, family room, office, and two-car garage—a real home!—well, Calvin's cooking didn't cut it *that* much. After a few months' camping at his

Left, Harold at the New Orleans Jazz & Heritage Festival with Harry Connick Sr. and Jr., 1978; *right,* with James Booker at Jazz Fest, 1978 (THNOC)

pad, I began to realize (or rationalize) that my old life was over. I had crossed over to the other side: I had become the divorced, unmarried, estranged man without a family or a home.

Blues Unfinished . . . Not the End

In the midst of all this upheaval, some light shone. Since attending Jazz Fest several times in the last few years, I'd been having thoughts of developing a professional jazz school in New Orleans like the ones flourishing in Los Angeles. New Orleans natives like Alvin Batiste, Edward "Kidd" Jordan, Ellis Marsalis, and many more were great educators already. Chancellor Gregory O'Brien of the University of New Orleans was already talking to Ellis about starting a jazz studies program at UNO. I met with Ellis and Dr. Charles Blancq, professor of music at UNO, in San Diego. I don't recall all the details of the meeting, but I remember that everything was agreeable; we needed each other. If I accepted their offer, I would start at UNO in the fall 1989 semester.

Could I, at fifty-eight years old, start all over? My parents died in1957, at ages fifty-five and fifty-seven. Given my genes, I had accepted that my life would not last much longer than theirs. I had a job offer that could become a long-term position. Yet I hesitated. But the call home won out.

Despite all the uncertainty I had about the move, things went much better than I anticipated. Whenever I visited New Orleans, I usually stayed at my cousin Raymond's house on Baronne Street, three blocks from where I was born. But when I arrived they were loaded with folks, so I was sent to his daughter, Renee's, house. I decided to go to a hotel instead and took a room at the Fontainebleau Hotel at Carrollton and Tulane avenues. It turned out that there was a reunion for Gilbert Academy and Dillard University taking place there that weekend. It was purely an accident that I wound up attending the reunion. None of my classmates knew that I was coming to town. I was happy to connect with old friends, but I was having such a difficult time that it was hard to fully participate. My main concern was finding a place to live.

I ran into the flutist Kent Jordan (Kidd Jordan's son), and he told me about the apartment complex where he lived, Parc Du Lac in New Orleans East. New Orleans East? This was my first really *new* experience since coming home. I had to learn that there was a whole newly developed area of the city. Parc du Lac was built long after I left New Orleans. New Orleans East didn't even exist when I lived here before. Back then, the only reason to go that far east was to hang out at Lincoln Beach, a recreation spot on Lake Pontchartrain for "colored" folks. Beyond that, past the Industrial Canal going east, was nothing but Highway 90 running through the swamp to Slidell.

I decided to rent an apartment in Parc du Lac. It was one of several apartment complexes in New Orleans East that, along with a big shopping mall (Lake Forest Plaza), a hospital (Pendleton Methodist), and some schools, created a suburban annex to the city. By the time my furniture arrived from California, I had secured a nice two-bedroom place on the third floor, and I had a storage unit to house extra stuff from my past life. I had no trouble finding my way around this new New Orleans. I enjoyed driving the new streets and discovering all the areas that had once been swamp.

Professor Battiste

In general, my past experiences with schools were never all that I had hoped for, particularly from the administrative realm. When I was negotiating with UNO, Stanley Coben had advised me not to put too much emphasis on salary but to make sure that I was put on a "tenure track." He did not explain what that meant; I thought I'd just have to figure it out. I was having lunch one day and two other Black professors came up to me and told me that they had found out I had tenure. They said that they were happy for me, but I was still pretty clueless. I had a lot to figure out about the structure of the university system.

I was at UNO because Ellis invited me. Ellis held the UNO Coca-Cola Endowed Chair in Jazz Studies. And I knew that Dr. Jeff Cox was chair of the music department. But I didn't know who my boss was. Shirley Cronin, secretary for the music department, was the warm, southern voice I'd been hearing over the phone from the beginning of my negotiations with UNO. I knew how she looked before I saw her; I felt comfortable with her. She was important in helping me learn what I needed to know: that the department chair reported to the dean of the college, who reported to the next level, straight up to the chancellor. Ellis, because he held an endowed chair, reported directly to the top. Thank God for Ellis. His influence helped me in so many ways; I could bypass most of the hierarchy and go through his direct line to the administration. My ignorance of how a university works set me up to trip a whole bunch of mines in the field.

I got the feeling that the music department was not unanimous in the decision to introduce the students to jazz. I felt as though the jazz studies program was perceived by some other members of the music faculty to be harmful to the reputation of the department. But there we were in New Orleans, with all the many jazz resources that originated in the city. In my mind, a jazz education program based in New Orleans was like a perfect storm—all of the right elements were here and had been here for a very long time. This is music's epicenter, a cultural ground zero—I could really get carried away. Yet the controversy became an issue that merited a few faculty meetings with the department chair. It was decided that we would have two divisions, classical and jazz, with some rules and regulations to manage the situation until some curriculum issues could be worked out.

I was already thinking about how I could operate in this new arena. I wanted to do the things I believed would educate students *and* help the university. My experiences at Colburn had given me the hands-on and heart-in opportunities to test my thoughts and theories about jazz in an academic environment. And the curriculum I had developed back in L.A. for Trade Tech was ready to go. I wanted to employ new approaches that resembled the way the original jazz masters had learned. Though there had not been any formal research done on the ways that they had learned, it was the same way that I had learned. I respected the method of the masters because it had worked for me. I focused on ear use—not ear training. Ear training involves learning to read music from sheets and transfer that knowledge through sight down to the fingers in order to play the assigned notes. Ear use involves playing notes and chords that are pleasing to the ears—with the optimum word being *playing,* which is associated with fun. This was the theory I wanted to incorporate into an academic setting.

AFO All Over Again

It was 1991—thirty years since six enterprising young musicians formed AFO, the record company that, under my leadership, made the first recordings of New Orleans's modern jazz musicians. I believed that now more than ever a record company with a commitment to and concern for music and musicians was needed in New Orleans.

I sought the advice and guidance of Kalamu ya Salaam, who I'd met during one of my visits to Jazz Fest in the 1980s (he and Bill Rouselle, his partner at Bright Moments Inc., were producing the festival

program). I had known of Salaam from the three-album set he produced for Rounder Records featuring several New Orleans artists; in the liner notes, Salaam had credited AFO for some of the inspiration for this work. I felt that he understood my mission.

We agreed that AFO should launch its return with a remastered CD of AFO's major modern jazz release back in the day, *Monkey Puzzle* (1963), which featured Ellis on piano, Nat Perrilliat on sax, and James Black on drums. The album had already been remastered before I left Los Angeles, but we had to do a few things to convert to the CD format. Salaam developed the package—the cover photo, liner notes, and information about the project and its musicians. *Monkey Puzzle* was rereleased in 1991. AFO hosted a special release party at the Sandbar, a now-defunct lounge on UNO's campus. The CD is still considered a top-notch work by jazz aficionados around the world, even though it never sold a whole lot of copies.

Soon after, I was approached by John Broven of Ace Records in England. I had met John back in 1971 when I toured with Tami Lynn in Britain. He was very familiar with the AFO catalog, as he was with most of the New Orleans music culture. He had authored *Walking to New Orleans: The Story of New Orleans R&B* (1974), published in later editions as *Rhythm & Blues in New Orleans*, which chronicles the music scene from the 1940s through the '70s. He wanted to lease some of the AFO masters so Ace could produce and distribute the music in the United Kingdom.

The lease agreement between AFO and Ace resulted in three CDs of AFO masters: *Gumbo Stew, More Gumbo Stew,* and *Still Spicy Gumbo Stew.* So, after thirty years, many of the previously unreleased productions were finally available. That there was still interest in these masters was encouraging and inspired me to look deeper into the history of my career.

Academic Ropes

I continued to develop my ideas about teaching. I structured an upper-level course for a few select students, focused on studio work. I assigned a couple of textbooks—*Sound Advice: The Musician's Guide to the Recording Studio* by Wayne Wadhams and *Multi-Track Recording for Musicians* by Brent Hurtig—and three hours a week of individual studio work and observation. I wanted the students to learn the same way all top studio engineers learned: watch, work, ask. I wanted to give students opportunities to experiment with recording.

In order to establish some guidelines and priorities regarding the direction I intended for this course, I had several meetings with Ellis and Philip Coulter, the dean of the College of Liberal Arts. It seemed to me that there was some hesitation about recording and publishing due to possible conflicts with the state's flagship university, Louisiana State University in Baton Rouge. UNO tended to walk a fine line regarding its place in the LSU system, and this scenario required some particular tip-toeing. But I wanted (with Ellis fully on board) to have the first graduate of our music program perform and produce a CD. It was important to us that our students have a definitive work to go along with that UNO diploma.

I had to convince the department and the college that the course was not intended to produce sound engineers. They needed to understand that although the students were musicians first, the recording studio would be a key part of their future working environment. I began to feel that my attempt to institute this approach might be somewhat premature; my ignorance of the financial and political aspects of university policies and procedures had led me toward unrealistic expectations.

Despite all the controversy, our first graduate from the UNO jazz studies program, David Morgan, completed production of his own CD, titled *Comment.* It was arranged, produced, and performed by Morgan with fellow students Gray Mayfield on alto sax, Brice Winston on tenor sax, William Sperandei on trumpet, Brian Blade on drums, Geoff Clapp on drums, and Neal Caine on bass. The reborn AFO Records helped us reach this critical goal: it handled the publishing and distribution of Morgan's CD. The album was well received in music circles.

Touching Base

"Breaking Up Is Hard to Do!" It seemed like that Neil Sedaka song had described my life since August 1989. Since my return to New Orleans, I'd had to satisfy my need for communication with my family with telephone calls and letters. I had seen my kids in 1990 during a quick visit back to Los Angeles over Christmas break. But attempts for more visits—especially visits in New Orleans—were hit and miss.

> *August 26, 1991*
>
> *Dear Children,*
>
> *When I re-read my note to y'all, it did read as though I wanted ALL of you to come visit me together. Although that would be nice, what I meant was that I would like any ONE, or TWO, THREE OR ALL of you, in any combination, to spend some time with me here.*
>
> *And Andrea, thank you for responding to my note. I do believe you love me and miss me as I do you. In my excitedness to hear from you . . . and trying to hear your voice as I read your words . . . cherishing each of them, I was 'in-tune' with whatever you were saying: 'no bullshitting around . . .', 'straight forward . . .'—yeah!*
>
> *When I started to write this note I began feeling my estrangement and isolation from all of you, and also my fear that maybe my need for you to visit is only MY need. A hard part of the 'straight-forward' reality is that I have needs that can only be met by those who are the flesh of my flesh and blood of my blood.*
>
> *No one else has answered me yet. Have y'all talked? Should I call? If any one of you wants to call, I'll pay the charges.*
>
> *Dad*

An unexpected part of being a newly estranged husband/father was my feeling that people saw me differently—close friends I'd known since the 1950s. I began to think and rationalize that society looks at unmarried men of a certain age—fifty plus—with questions on their minds. Maybe they're not comfortable inviting such men to gatherings of couples? Most of my closest friends were couples that married back in the '50s and '60s. No one ever snubbed me or did anything in an overt way, but I still felt left out.

King and Queen Reunion

In November 1992, as I stood in line at the Galleria movie complex on the opening day of *Malcolm X*, I was approached by a tall, handsome lady who looked somewhat familiar. She asked my name, and, when I replied, a glowing, toothy smile came to her face.

"I'm Berweda!" she said.

I was stunned! Berweda Hatch from F. P. Ricard Elementary? She and I had won a contest to be the school's Mardi Gras king and queen. What an exceptional chance meeting! She was back in New Orleans after a teaching career in Chicago; she had retired and returned to take care of her aging mother, who had since died.

Berweda and I kept in touch and found that we had a lot in common; we enjoyed similar social and intellectual activities. We gradually—*very* gradually—began to discover each other as a couple through social, political, and cultural outings. We were also enjoying the fact that we had known each other as children; it was comforting and brought us closer together. I felt comfortable with her and more comfortable around others when I was with her. As we began to be seen together by family, friends, and acquaintances, they began to view us as a pair. One morning in 1993 I sat in Berweda's Uptown home and thought about things: present and future, friends and relatives, Uptown and New Orleans East, single and couple. A pleasant surprise turned into a passionate commitment, creating a crescendo of feelings that continue to bewilder me.

Discussions about marriage could not get beyond a reasoned analysis of my past. I wanted no part of involving myself in any way with the legal system. My experiences in Los Angeles were major disappointments—not just my divorce but also my attempts to develop real estate and dealing with the careers of King Floyd and Dr. John. There had to be another way that Berweda and I could be together as a couple. We decided that the way would be in the form of a traditional "jump the broom" ceremony of our forefathers.

For guidance we picked up the book *Jumping the Broom: The African-American Wedding Planner* by Harriette Cole at the Community Book Center and had a meeting with attorney Greer Goff to cover the legal stuff, mostly for Berweda's sake. We talked and talked for hours: at the Lakefront, over dinner at Bennachin, a West African restaurant. There was still so much for us to discover about each other and I sensed that we both felt the urgency to get closer. But at the same time, I was feeling antsy. I just didn't want to get married at that point in my life. I didn't want to be tied legally, but if it satisfied Berweda, I would go ahead and jump the broom.

For several weeks we went about the preparations for the big celebration, to take place at Berweda's beautiful home on the first day of Kwanzaa, December 26, 1995. We met at the house of a friend named Merigold to plan our attire, and Berweda invited Jacob Carruthers, who had been her professor when she studied at one of the Afrocentric schools in Chicago, to conduct our Umoja (unity) ceremony. He and his wife, Ifé, were happy to visit us in New Orleans. Our celebration was a huge success and brought together a vast array of friends and well-wishers: friends as old as Mrs. Williams, our third-grade teacher, and as new as several of my students from UNO. My two sons, H. Raymond and Harlis, honored me and Berweda by blessing our union with original poems:

Companionship

Is truly a human trait and need.
If it is accompanied with
Mutual respect,
Patience, understanding, compassion and
Love,
It will last to the end of time.

To have a loving companion in life
Is truly
A gift of life.

Cherish one another . . .
Take care of one another . . .
Congratulations!!

H. Raymond "Bunny" Battiste

Two Queens

My father left his village at early dawn
to go build and share his life with a
Beautiful African Queen.
They loved and built a family.
That work is done.

He returns at dusk to find
that he has been blessed with another
Beautiful African Queen
and now they can share lives and experiences
ripened by days in the sun.

Thank you, Harlis

A part of my old self followed me into this relationship. I needed to feel that I, as a man, had made a contribution to our living space, which was Berweda's home. The house had a third floor that was closed off and being used as a storage attic. I drew up plans to develop it into an office/bedroom apartment with a small kitchen, bath, and other amenities. I consulted with Berweda and got the OK to go ahead with the changes. She knew some wonderful craftsmen who had renovated the house when she took it over after her mother died.

Harold and Berweda Hatch
on the day they "jumped the
broom," 1995 (THNOC)

Young Lions' Endorsement

The jazz program at UNO was growing; in fact, jazz was enjoying a new acceptance in the academic world in general. I believe that the arrival of Wynton Marsalis on the music scene was a significant factor in the renewed focus on the genre—especially since he had conquered the classical giant before turning his skills to jazz. And since he was a New Orleans native, attention was turned to the birthplace of jazz and its new crop of creative, unique musicians, including Wynton's older brother Branford, Harry Connick Jr., Terence Blanchard, Donald Harrison, Nicholas Payton—the list goes on. Students from all over sought out our jazz program after being told by the young Marsalis men, "Man, you got to go down there and study with my dad 'n' them!" The students would get involved in the community and the culture; someone should have warned them that they might not be able to escape! I had already been feeling the pull of the environment, and it was saying to me: "This is where you belong . . . this is your home." I began thinking of New Orleans itself as a university and the people (musicians included) as the faculty.

New Orleans jazz musicians were also teaching the world. Ellis and Dr. Blancq, who was teaching jazz history, had taken a student group on a European tour in the summer of 1992. The tour yielded a live recording of the group as they performed at the Rome Jazz Festival and at Jazzclub Unterfahrt in Munich, Germany, where Wynton made a surprise appearance. It was released by AFO as *The UNO Jazz Band in Europe, 1992.*

While in Innsbruck, Austria, Dr. Blancq made the acquaintance of Henner Kroeper, a producer of jazz events in Europe. Kroeper was interested in doing a jazz workshop for local students, led by the UNO program. Between Dr. Blancq, Kroeper, and Ellis, they worked out the details and approached me

Harold teaching in Innsbruck, Austria, ca. 1995 (THNOC)

to conduct the workshop. For two glorious summers (1995 and 1996) I took groups of students from our program to Europe to gain the experience of learning by teaching. Kroeper selected sites in Innsbruck and in Lanciano, Italy. And I was able to bring Berweda, my new bride; even though I wanted to go, I needed a travel companion.

Love Changes

Life always has twists and turns. The *Gambit* weekly newspaper put Berweda and me on the cover of their Valentine's Day issue, on February 6, 1996. But by early 1997 some uncomfortable situations were coming up between Berweda and me. She often talked about men who earned six-figure salaries, and I questioned why that was important. I realized that Berweda's years in Chicago were quite different from mine in Los Angeles. She was a much more active person in her Chicago environment—sort of a social butterfly. She had been divorced for a long time when we ran into each other again after all those years. She had done a lot of traveling—to Africa and beyond—and she had a lot of material things, fur coats and the like. She even tried to get me to wear a fur coat, which was definitely not my style! I also knew that she, along with most people, had followed

my professional life through the media and associated me with Sonny & Cher. It was obvious that she thought I was a wealthy man.

At her request, I provided a credit card. The card did not have unlimited credit, which disturbed her. It became clear that she was a material girl who thrived on things that represent the appearance of wealth and/or class. I realized that I needed to rethink my life . . . again!

September 15, 1997

Dear Friends:

Berweda and I are separating.
I have experienced much joy and happiness in this brief relationship and I have enjoyed the joy it seems to have brought to my friends. I thank you for that support.
I have failed in many ways, however, to meet Berweda's expectations and have therefore caused her to become unhappy.
I deeply regret having to make this announcement, but my personal sense of honor demands that I inform those friends whom I feel I have also failed or disappointed.

Harold R. Battiste, Jr.

Life Goes On . . .

I was on my own again, and I needed to find a place to live. I told Lolis Elie, a high-school classmate of mine, about my search for a house or apartment to buy or rent. He didn't hesitate with a response: "You tried Park Esplanade? My daughter lives there and she thinks it's pretty nice."

The Park Esplanade is a midrise building on Bayou St. John overlooking the grand entrance to New Orleans City Park. I had never even thought to look in that area, because all of that was off limits to Blacks when I left New Orleans in 1963. It was hard to let go of that feeling of not belonging—it was so intense. I remembered taking my young family for a Sunday evening automobile ride back when Bunny was about twelve years old. As we passed City Park, where "colored" people weren't allowed, Bunny asked from the back seat, "Who made us colored?" I had no answer. Alviette quickly responded, "God." After a moment of thought, Bunny said, "Somebody ought to whip God!"

I took the first apartment the manager showed me when I came to check out the place: a two-bedroom apartment on the first floor. It seemed a bit small, but I reminded myself that it would be just me.

To stay busy, I plunged into my work. Of course, each of my projects had a complete life of its own and needed personnel I could not afford. Maintaining and managing all these projects became my whole life, with little time or space for much else. In addition to teaching at UNO and running AFO, At Last, and Marzique Music, I was leading a band of young jazz musicians called the Next Generation. This was the first full band that evolved out of our UNO music program. The Next Generation included Glenn Patscha on piano, Geoff Clapp on drums, Roland Guerin on bass, Nicholas Payton on trumpet, John Ellis on tenor sax, Brice Winston on tenor sax, and Derek Douget on alto sax. A stellar group, if I may say so myself.

I was also working on the *Silverbook*, the workbook I'd started in the late 1980s. Publication became more of a possibility when I started teaching at UNO. It had been used in several workshops by students, who encouraged and inspired me to complete the project. I finally put it out as *The Silverbook: Modern Jazz Masters of New Orleans (Millennium Edition)*.

Left, The *Silverbook; right,* friend Darlene Jones prepares Harold to receive an honorary doctorate of humane letters from Dillard University, 2008. (THNOC)

Turning Over the Reins

Time kept passing. A new century came upon us. The UNO faculty was undergoing changes. Victor Goines, our woodwind and saxophone instructor, took a position with Wynton Marsalis's Jazz at Lincoln Center Orchestra in New York. He was replaced by a brilliant musician from Chicago, Ed Petersen. Steve Masakowski, a New Orleans guitarist, also joined the faculty. And Ellis retired. A gala tribute concert at UNO's Lakefront Arena, called *Satchmo to Marsalis* and featuring Branford, Wynton, Delfeayo, and Jason Marsalis, along with Harry Connick Jr., was attended by throngs of happy jazz lovers and supporters. I had mixed feelings about Ellis's retirement. I was not prepared to be alone at UNO.

Filling the Coca-Cola chair became the department's urgent mission. Ellis talked with us about the various concerns that should be considered when looking for a replacement. As I anticipated, several friends and associates had placed me (in their minds) as his successor. I had to make a concerted effort to quell their arguments for me to go after that position. When the dust settled, we selected New Orleans–grown and –educated Terence Blanchard. Terence met and exceeded everything we were looking for to take the reins of this program and bring it up to where it belonged. Terence has, with the support of renowned director/producer Spike Lee, carved out a position among the great film composers in America, and the Coca-Cola chair at UNO is now filled by Steve Masakowski.

Katrina

I'd been hearing about Hurricane Katrina for a week. The same thing had happened before Hurricane Ivan in 2004, and I'd gotten myself together and run (flown) to Houston. The storm didn't hit New Orleans that time, but I had a nice time with the family of Jesse McBride, one of my students at UNO.

The Park Esplanade had been designated as a shelter by the city, so I thought I'd ride out Katrina at home. Bunny was living in New Orleans and came by on Sunday to check in with me about my plan. He

Harold with Terence
Blanchard, ca. 2000
(THNOC)

thought that we should get out, but I convinced him to stay. We went to get food and stuff to hunker down for the storm, but everything was closed. There wasn't any traffic on the street. I flip-flopped right then and there and headed for the highway—didn't even go back to the apartment for anything. I had been told that there was a place in Monroe, in north Louisiana, where I could stay if I needed to.

Me and Bunny headed north on I-55 toward Jackson, Mississippi. I stopped to call and check in with the folks in Monroe. They already had a full house, so they directed me to Brookhaven, Mississippi. We arrived in town at midnight with the address of a Mrs. Lena Pope, a cousin of my friend Dr. G. Jeannette Hodge. Mrs. Pope welcomed us—two strange men—into her home at that ungodly hour. I was surprised but grateful.

On Monday morning we watched the tragedy begin to unfold on TV, which was full of news about Katrina and New Orleans. Bunny was concerned about his car, which he had left parked in my building's lot. Jeannette (aka Mama G) joined us at Lena Pope's home and we all began to realize the fullness of this terrible situation. We soon realized that we would not be able to return to New Orleans any time soon.

Bunny got an invitation and a plane ticket to Houston to meet a friend from his old job in New Orleans; when he left I was without driving help. I spent about two beautiful weeks in Brookhaven, then figured out a plan: I still could not return to New Orleans, but I could drive to Baton Rouge, leave my car with my cousin George, then fly out to Los Angeles.

I was greeted in L.A. by Harlis, my youngest son, with whom I was to stay temporarily. I had started to develop a Walmart/Target wardrobe in Brookhaven, but I didn't have much; as soon as I contacted a few old Los Angeles friends, they offered me clothes and cash. It looked like I would be out there for awhile, according to the news about New Orleans. I made arrangements with Alviette to move back into the house. I don't have words to express the feelings and emotions that filled my spirit for the short time I was able to live on Bowcroft Street again. I was in that house with my daughters, Marzique and Andrea, and with Alviette. I had been gone for fifteen years. I actually found myself thanking Katrina!

I've been back in New Orleans since August 2008. I am still here, but I am tired! By coming home again, I got to meet Harold Raymond Battiste Jr. He got lost in Los Angeles; New Orleans found him.

ARRANGEMENTS & PRODUCTIONS
by Harold Battiste Jr.
(alphabetical by artist)

ARTIST(S)	TITLE	LABEL	YEAR
Ace, Buddy	Oh Why	Specialty	1959
	Someone	Specialty	1959
Adams, Johnny	Closer to You	RIC	1960
	You Can Make It If You Try	RIC	1959
Adderley Brothers	Adderley Brothers in New Orleans	Milestone	1962
AFO Executives	A Compendium	AFO	1963
AFO Executives & Tami Lynn	A Compendium	AFO	1992
American Jazz Quintet	In the Beginning	AFO	1991
Alexander, J.W.	Raw Turnips & Hot Sauce	Thrush	1966
Arrangement	Go to Black	Pulsar	1970
	Prophet Lady	Pulsar	1969
Aubrey Twins, The	Love Without End Amen	Epic	1968
	What Is Love	Epic	1968
Battiste, Harold	AFO Executives & Tami Lynn	OPUS 43	1973
	Next Generation	AFO	1996
	Original American Jazz Quintet	OPUS 43	1973
	These Are the Things I Love	Cinderella	1962
	This Is How We Do It in New Orleans	Uptown	1964
	This Is Truth	Uptown	1964
Bazzle, Germaine	Standing Ovation	AFO	1991
Blackwell, Ed	Boogie Live...1958	AFO	1958
Bo, Eddie	Bless You Darling	RIC	1961
	I Got to Know	RIC	19561
	It Must Be Love	RIC	1961
	Tee Na Na Na Na Nay	At Last	1962
	Twinkle Toes	At Last	1962
	What a Fool I've Been	RIC	1959
Bradford, Alex	Too Close to Heaven	Specialty	1958
Byrne, Jerry	I Can't Say No	Specialty	1958
	Carry On	Specialty	1958
	Honey Baby	Specialty	1958
	Lights Out	Specialty	1957
	My Little Girl	Specialty	1958
	It's Raining	Specialty	1958
	Why Did I Ever Say Goodbye to You?	Specialty	1958
	You Know I Love You So	Specialty	1958
Cake, The	A Slice of Cake	Decca	1968
	Baby That's Me	Decca	1967
	Fire Fly	Decca	1967
	Have You Heard the News	Decca	1967
	Pit 280	Decca	1967
	Rainbow World	Decca	1967
	The Cake	Decca	1968

ARTIST(S)	TITLE	LABEL	YEAR
Caronados, The	Lying	RIC	1961
	My Elise	RIC	1959
Carr, Linda	Jackie, Bobby, Sonny, Billy	SAR	1964
	Sweet Talk	SAR	1964
Carr, Wynona	I'm Mad at You	Specialty	1958
	If I Pray	Specialty	1957
Ceasar & Cleo	String Fever	Vault	1964
	The Letter	Vault	1964
Cher	Alfie	Imperial	1966
	All I Really Want to Do (single)	Imperial	1965
	All I Really Want to Do	Imperial	1965
	Backstage	Imperial	1967
	Bang Bang	Imperial	1966
	Behind the Green Door	International	1967
	Cher	Imperial	1966
	Cher	United Artists	1970
	Cher	United Artists	1972
	Cher's Golden Greats	Imperial	1967
	Elusive Butterfly	Imperial	1966
	I'm Gonna Love You	Imperial	1966
	Mama—Homeward Bound	International	1967
	Our Day Will Come	Imperial	1967
	Song Called Children	Imperial	1968
	Take Me for a Little While	Imperial	1968
	With Love	Imperial	1966
	You Better Sit Down Kids	Imperial	1966
Chico & Cha Cha	Every Day's a Holiday	Scorpi	1967
	Hollywood	Scorpi	1967
Common Cold	Come Down	ATCO	1967
	Dream World	ATCO	1967
Cooke, Sam	Forever	Specialty	1957
	Good Times	RCA	1964
	Happy in Love	Specialty	1957
	I Don't Want to Cry	Specialty	1958
	I Need You Now	Specialty	1959
	I'll Come Running Back to You	Specialty	1957
	Tennessee Waltz	RCA	1964
	That's All I Need to Know	Specialty	1958
	You Send Me	Specialty/ Keen/RCA	1957
Crozier, Rhoyia	Poverty Struk (Pt. 1 & 2)	OPUS 43	1973
Crystals, The	In the Deep	Specialty	1959
	Love You So	Specialty	1958
DeShannon, Jackie	Splendor in the Grass	Imperial	1968
	The Weight	Imperial	1968
Dorsey, Lee	Do Re Mi	Fury/Roulette	1961
	Lottie Mo	Valiant	1959
	Lover of Love	Valiant	1959
	Ya Ya	Fury/Roulette	1961

ARRANGEMENTS & PRODUCTIONS

ARTIST(S)	TITLE	LABEL	YEAR
Dr. John	Babylon	ATCO	1968
	Dr. John's Gumbo	ATCO	1972
	Gris-Gris	ATCO	1967
	I Walk on Guilded Splinters (single)	ATCO	1967
	I Walk on Guilded Splinters	ATCO	1968
	Iko Iko	ATCO	1972
	Jump Sturdy	ATCO	1967
	Mama Roux	ATCO	1967
Dunn, Joyce	Turn Away from Darkness	Mercury	1969
	You're Givin' Me the Push I Need	Mercury	1969
Executives, The	Falling in Love	Derby	1965
	Happy Chatter	Derby	1965
Farrell, Ernie	The Scream	Colpix	1965
Fiends, The	Quetzal Quake	Dan D.	1964
	Thank You, Thing	Dan D.	1964
Five Knights	Miracle	Specialty	195
	Yo Te Amo	Specialty	1958
George, Barbara	I Know	AFO	1962
	I Know (single)	AFO	1961
	Love (Is Just a Chance You Take)	AFO	1961
Goines, Victor	Genesis	AFO	1992
Gospel Harmonettes	He's Calling Me	Specialty	1958
Grady, Don	Don't Let It Happen	Challenge	1966
	Out	Challenge	1966
Hal-Mel	Alone Together	OPUS 43	1970
Henderson, T.B.	Blue Stone	Pulsar	1968
Henderson, T. Wood	The Price of Love	Pulsar	1969
Hill, Jessie	Free and Easy	Pulsar	1969
	Mardi Gras	Pulsar	1969
Issacher	Can This Be Love	Fidelity	1960
	Whole Lot of Love	Fidelity	1958
Johnson, Plas	Buck Dance	AFO	1963
	Grease Patrol L.A. '55	Carell Music	1985
	Lift Off	AFO	1963
	Positively	Concord Jazz	1982
	The Blues	Concord	1979
Jones, Joe	Here's What You Gotta Do	Roulette	1960
	One Big Mouth	Roulette	1960
	You Talk Too Much	RIC/Roulette	1960
	You Talk Too Much (single)	RIC/Roulette	1959

ARTIST(S)	TITLE	LABEL	YEAR
King Floyd	A Man in Love	Pulsar	1968
	Groov-A-Lin	Pulsar	1969
	Heartaches	Pulsar	1969
	This Is Our Last Night Together	Pulsar	1969
	Times Have Changed	Pulsar	1969
	Together We Can Do Anything	Pulsar	1969
	You Got the Love I Need	Pulsar	1969
Lane, Daymon	Lovin' Man	Del Con	1966
	The Battle Hymn	Del Con	1966
Lastie, Mel	That Old Time Religion	AFO	1993
	The Pastor's Journey	Pulsar	1969
Little Joey w/Little Tootsie	Comin' Down the Chimney	Fidelity	1958
Little Richard	Dance What You Wanna	Vee Jay	1965
	Without Love	Vee Jay	1965
Lopez, Rosie	I'll Never Grow Tired	Pulsar	1969
	Too Hot to Hold	Pulsar	1969
Lynn, Tami	Baby	AFO	1963
	Old Man River	Nine Hundred	1963
	Where Can I Go	AFO	1963
	You Don't Know	Nine Hundred	1963
Magnificent Malochi	As Time Goes By	Brunswick	1966
	Your Daddy's Come Home	Brunswick	1966
Manuel, Phillip	A Time for Love	AFO	1992
Marsalis, Ellis	Ellis Marsalis Quartet	OPUS 43	1973
	Monkey Puzzle	AFO	1963
	The Classic Ellis Marsalis	AFO	1991
	Yesterdays, Part 1	AFO	1963
	Yesterdays, Part 2	AFO	1963
Monitors, The	Closer to Heaven	Specialty	1958
	Rock 'N' Roll Fever	Specialty	1957
Morgan, David	Comment	AFO	1992
	Hands of Time	AFO/Turnipse	1996
Neville, Art	Cha Dooky Doo	Specialty	1958
	Arabian Love Call	Specialty	1958
	That Old Time Rock & Roll	Specialty	1958
	What's Going On	Specialty	1958
	Zing Zing	Specialty	1958
Nookie Boy (Oliver Morgan)	I Got a Feeling for You Baby	AFO	1962
	I'll Make a Bet	AFO	1961
O'Jays, The	Lipstick Traces	Imperial	1965
	Think It Over, Baby	Imperial	1964
Paige, Joey	Cause I'm in Love with You	Tollie	1964
	Yeah Yeah Yeah	Tollie	1964
Payne, Curtis	Fool That I Am	Fidelity	1959
	Never Let Me Go	Fidelity	1957

ARTIST(S)	TITLE	LABEL	YEAR	ARTIST(S)	TITLE	LABEL	YEAR
Prince La La	Don't You Know Little Girl	AFO	1961	Standells, The	B. J. Quetzal	Vee Jay	1965
	You Put the Hurt on Me	AFO	1961		Big Boss Man	Vee Jay	1965
Raymond, Shirley	What a Wedding Day	At Last	1962		The Boy Next Door	Vee Jay	1965
	You Gonna Miss Me	At Last	1962		Don't Say Goodbye	Vee Jay	1965
Rebennack, Mac	One Naughty Flat	AFO	1962	Stevens, Geoffrey	Do That Again	York	1966
Rhodes, Glory	Old Laces	ATCO	1967		Grape Jelly Love	York	1966
	She's a Big Girl Now	ATCO	1967	Stokes, Simon T.	Big City Blues	HRB	1967
Robinson, Al	Give Her Up	Pulsar	1969		Truth Is Stranger than Fiction	HRB	1967
	Shine On	Pulsar	1969	Stone, John	Be Sure	Specialty	1959
	Soulful Woman	Pulsar	1969		Mirror Mirror	Specialty	1958
Rubini, Michel	Moonlight Mood	ATCO	1966	Talbert, Wayne	Dues to Pay	Pulsar	1968
	Summer Song	ATCO	1968		Lord Have Mercy			
Rushes, Ami	Look Up at the Bottom	20th Century	1968		on My Funky Soul	Pulsar	1969
	Sweet Talkin' Candyman	20th Century	1968	Taylor, Johnny	Oh How I Love You	SAR	1964
Shine	Empty Talk	Pulsar	1969		Run but You Can't Hide	SAR	1965
	Sho 'Bout to Drive Me	Pulsar	1969	Tee, Willie			
Sims Twins, The	A Losing Battle	Omen	1964	(Wilson Turbinton)	All for One	AFO	1962
	I Go-Fer You	Omen	1964		Always Accused	AFO	1962
Smith, Carrie	One Hundred Years	Hot Line	1967		Anticipation	United Artists	1973
	Trouble	Hot Line	1967		Foolish Girl	Cinderella	1962
Sonny	Georgia & John Quetzal	ATCO	1965		I Found Out	AFO	1963
	I Told My Girl to Go Away	ATCO	1967		Why Lie	AFO	1962
	I Would Marry You Today	ATCO	1969	UNO Jazz Band	In Europe 1992	AFO	1993
	Laugh at Me	ATCO	1965	Valentine,			
	Misty Roses	ATCO	1967	Patience	Lost and Lookin'	SAR	1964
	The Revolution Kind	ATCO	1965		Woman in a Man's World	SAR	1965
	Tony	ATCO	1966	Valentinos, The	It's All Over Now	SAR	1964
Sonny & Cher	Baby Don't Go	Reprise	1964		Tired of Living in the Country	SAR	1964
	Circus	ATCO	1968	Various Artists			
	Good Combination	ATCO	1968	(AFO artists)	Gumbo	OPUS 43	1973
	Good Times	ATCO	1966		Gumbo Stew	AFO/ACE	1991
	Have I Stayed Too Long	ATCO	1966		More Gumbo Stew	AFO/ACE	1992
	I Got You Babe	ATCO	1965		Still Spicy Gumbo Stew	AFO/ACE	1993
	I Look for You	ATCO	1965	Ware, Delores	Falling in Love	Lloyd & Logan	1959
	In Case You're in Love	ATCO	1966	Williams, Larry	Bad Boy	Specialty	1959
	Just You	ATCO	1965		The Dummy	Specialty	1958
	Little Man	ATCO	1966		Give Me Love	Specialty	1958
	Living for You	ATCO	1966		Here's Larry Williams	Specialty	1958
	Look at Us	ATCO	1965		Hoochie Koo	Specialty	1959
	Love Don't Come	ATCO	1966		I Can't Stop Loving You	Specialty	1959
	Sing C'Est La Vie	ATCO	1965		I Was a Fool	Specialty	1958
	The Beat Goes On	ATCO	1967		Little School Girl	Specialty	1958
	The Best of Sonny & Cher	ATCO	1967		Peaches and Cream	Specialty	1958
	The Wondrous World of				She Said Yeah	Specialty	1959
	Sonny & Cher	ATCO	1965		Steal a Little Kiss	Specialty	1959
	Walkin' the Quetzal	Reprise	1964		Teardrops	Specialty	1958
	What Now My Love	ATCO	1965		Ting-A-Ling	Specialty	1958
	You and Me	ATCO	1968				
	You Got to Have a						
	Thing of Your Own	ATCO	1968				

COMPOSITIONS

by Harold Battiste Jr.

TITLE	YEAR	TITLE	YEAR
All Alone (lyrics by Tami Lynn)	(1964) S3*	Nevermore	(1954) S1*
Alviette Is Her Name	(1982) S2*	Novia	(1976) S3*
Arabian Love Call	(1958)	On a Lark (incomplete)	(1998)
Barefoot Lady (lyrics by Mac Rebennack)	(1968)	Ohadi	(1956) S1*
Beautiful Old Ladies	(1975) S2*	One Daze	(1964) S2*
Belle Ami	(1958)	One Tiger to a Hill	(1971
Carrie Mae	(1959) S1*	Opus 43	(1982) S3*
Child Playing	(1973) S3*	Quartette	(1950)
Circle Cycle	(1964) S2*	Relax	(1970) S1*
Croker Courtbouillon	(1967) S1*	Relaxing	(1980) S3*
Danse Ka Linda Ba Doom	(1967)	Scream, The	(1965)
Dat Da Dah	(1965)	Silver Breeze	(1979) S3*
Ecology Walk	(1970)	Sompum Sorta Fonky	(1975) S3*
Experiment in Two Eras	(1951)	Song for Andrea	(1964) S2*
Faith	(1957)	Song for Cannon	(1964) S1*
Falling in Love	(1957) S3*	Song for Dance (sleep)	(1964) S3*
Free My Brother [movie theme]	(1971)	Song for Yette	(1964) S2*
God Made Everything Good	(1971)	Soon We Will Be Together	(1964) S2*
Gumbo	(1965)	Soul in the Hole [movie theme]	(1964)
Harlis Laughing	(1980) S2*	Stephanie	(1956) S1*
Harold's Church	(1962) S3*	Thank You Lord	(1984)
He Is Mine (lyrics by Tami Lynn)	(1964)	This Is How We Do It in New Orleans	(1964)
Hey Flo	(1958)	This Is Love	(1951) S1*
Honey Baby	(1958)	To Brownie	(1956) S1*
Hopscotch	(1958)	Two Daze	(1955)
I Guess	(1962)	Whole Lot of Love	(1960)
I'm Gonna Stop Loving You	(1970)	Why Oh Why	(1958)
If You Think You Can	(1963)	WYLD	(1962)
J. B. Jazz	(1962) S3*	You're Gonna Miss Me	(1958)
Just Want to Say Thank You Lord	(1981)		
Leaving	(1998)		
Let Our Peoples Go [movie theme]	(1971)	* music sheets can be found in *Silverbooks 1, 2, 3*	
Lizzie	(1957)		
Love Moods Suite	(1982)		
Love Ye One Another	(1984)		
Madrid	(1954) S3*		
Malibu	(1983) S3*		
Marzique Dancing	(1973) S2*		
Me 'n' Willie Tee	(1982) S2*		
Mikima Mikima	(1971)		
Minor Theme	(1964) S2*		
Minuette in F-unk	(1964) S3*		
My Heart Is Sad and Blue	(1957)		
My Lady of the Morning	(1974) S2*		
My Little Girl	(1957)		
My Song	(1964) S3*		

AWARDS

Gold Records

"You Send Me," Sam Cooke, 1958

"You Talk Too Much," Joe Jones, 1960

"I Know," Barbara George, 1962

"Ya Ya," Lee Dorsey, 1962

"All I Really Want," Cher, 1965

"I Got You Babe," Sonny & Cher, 1965

Look at Us, Sonny & Cher, 1965

"Bang Bang," Cher, 1966

"The Beat Goes On," Sonny & Cher, 1966

"Sit Down Kids," Cher, 1966

Citations

Humanitarian Services Award, Cerebral Palsy Association, 1966

Certificate of Appreciation (MVP Concept), NARAS, 1973

Eye on Music Winner's Circle, 1991

Jazztown Award, Louisiana Jazz Federation, 1992

Cultural Arts Award, Black Arts National Diaspora (BAND), 1992

Beaux Arts Award, Contemporary Arts Center, 1993

Certificate of Recognition, Alpha Kappa Alpha Sorority, 1993

Lifetime Achievement, Louisiana Governor's Award, 1995

Harold Battiste Day, New Orleans, 1996, 1998, 2000, 2006

Certificate of Merit, city of New Orleans, 1996, 2000

Phi Kappa Phi Honor Society, 1996

Arts Award, Amistad Research Center, 1996

Certificate of Appreciation from New Orleans Mayor Marc Morial, 1997, 1998

AFO Exhibit Recognition, New Orleans City Council, 1998

Certificate of Recognition, Meritorious Service, American Federation of Musicians, 1998

Jazz Legend, New Orleans Jazz & Heritage Festival, 1998

Mayor's Arts Awards, New Orleans, 1998

Certificate of Appreciation, Louisiana State Museum, 1998

Role Model Award, Young Leadership Council, 1998

Trailblazer Award for AFO, National Black Music Hall of Fame, 1998

Tipitina's Walk of Fame, Eighth Floor Foundation, 1998

Sidney Bechet Award for Innovation in New Orleans Music, New Orleans International Music Colloquium, 1999

IAJE Award for Outstanding Service, International Association of Jazz Educators, 2000

Arts in Education, Arthur Ashe School, New Orleans, 2000

Certificate of Appreciation, International Association of Jazz Educators, 2000

Pathfinder Award—AFO Legacy, Contemporary Arts Center, 2001

Heartbeat Award—Keeping the Music Alive, OffBeat magazine, 2002

Recognition from the Street Art Council, 2002

Big Easy Award—Lifetime Achievement, Gambit, 2004

Scroll of Honor for Outstanding Achievement, Omega Psi Phi, 2004

Proclamation—Outstanding Musician, New Orleans City Council, 2005

Outstanding Musical Achievement, Ladies in Red, 2005

Certificate of Proclamation for Lifetime Achievement, state of Louisiana, 2005

AFO MUSICIANS

PETER "CHUCK" BADIE, an acoustic and electric bassist in the New Orleans tradition (two-beat funk), learned his rhythms as a child attending innumerable parades. His father performed with the Olympia and the Eureka brass bands. Badie attended the Grunewald School of Music, a haven for up-and-coming musicians. He began performing at New Orleans's famed Dew Drop Inn, where he met Roy Brown ("Good Rockin' Tonight"), with whom he toured for two years. He went on to play with Paul Gayten, Dave Bartholomew, Lionel Hampton, Sam Cooke, Hank Crawford, and the American Jazz Quintet; and he was tapped by Allen Toussaint to play in the studio with Ernie K-Doe, Jessie Hill, Chris Kenner, Lee Dorsey, and Barbara George.

ALVIN BATISTE, a modern-jazz clarinetist and jazz educator, performed as a guest soloist with the New Orleans Philharmonic while still a student at Booker T. Washington High School. Years later the philharmonic debuted one of Batiste's compositions. He chaired the jazz studies program at Southern University in Baton Rouge for over thirty years. His students included Henry Butler, Branford Marsalis, and Donald Harrison Jr. Batiste served as artist-in-residence for the New Orleans public school system and was head of the jazz program at the New Orleans Center for the Creative Arts (NOCCA). The National Endowment for the Arts commissioned him to compose a concerto for African instruments and orchestra. Batiste performed with the Ray Charles Orchestra, Larry Darnell, Joe Jones, Smiley Lewis, Joe Robichaux, Guitar Slim, George Williams, the American Jazz Quintet, and the Jazztronauts. Alvin Batiste died on May 6, 2007, just a day before a scheduled performance at the New Orleans Jazz & Heritage Festival.

WARREN BELL SR., alto saxophonist, started his career with the original Dooky Chase band after graduating from Xavier Prep. He was a member of the group that included trumpeter Teddy Riley, trumpeter Tony Moret, trombonist Benny Powell, Arnold Benjamin, Harry Sweetwyne, and trumpeter "Big Fat" Emery. Bell went on to play tenor sax with Dave Bartholomew's band. He also performed with a group at the Caravan and at the renowned Mason's on Claiborne Avenue. Bell curtailed his music career to support his family and worked for a chain of local food stores. Warren Bell Sr. died on November 6, 2006.

JAMES BLACK, a master drummer and composer, was well versed in the deep groove of the second-line rhythm. His difficult and somewhat quirky compositions employ odd meters, nonstandard forms, and unusual phrase lengths. He played trumpet and piano at Joseph S. Clark High School (studying under respected teacher and band leader Yvonne Busch) and played piano with June Spears and the Rocketeers. He was soon playing sessions as a drummer with Fats Domino. Though he received a scholarship to study music at Southern University in Baton Rouge, he withdrew about six months before graduation to play with Ellis Marsalis at the Playboy Club in New Orleans. Black contributed compositions to Nat and Cannonball Adderley's *In the Bag* and wrote four of the seven cuts for Marsalis's *Monkey Puzzle*, including the landmark 5/4 piece *Magnolia Triangle*. He went on to perform with Joe Jones and the Dixie Cups. In New York he performed with Lionel Hampton, Horace Silver, and Yusef Lateef; he returned to New Orleans in the 1970s to lead his own group. James Black died on August 30, 1988.

EDWARD "BOOGIE" BLACKWELL was a principal influence among New Orleans drummers in the 1950s. He was a member of the American Jazz Quintet and recorded and toured extensively with Ornette Coleman, Sonny Rollins, John Coltrane, Randy Weston, and others. Edward Blackwell died on October 8, 1992.

JOHN BOUDREAUX, a drummer from New Roads, LA, shuttled back and forth between that town and New Orleans most of his life. He started his career with the Hawkettes (pre–Art Neville), Clarence "Frogman" Henry, Melvin Lastie's band, Dr. John's band, and others around New Orleans. Boudreaux was the studio drummer for Ernie K-Doe's "Mother-In-Law," Chris Kenner's "Land of 1,000 Dances," Lee Dorsey's "Ya-Ya," and Jessie Hill's "Ooh Poo Pah Doo."

MELVIN LASTIE, trumpeter and cornetist, performed on many classic New Orleans R&B recordings of the 1950s and '60s. The professional jazz band he organized in his senior year at Booker T. Washington High School featured pianist Antoine "Fats" Domino. His exuberant trumpet solo on Barbara George's hit "I Know" made him a musical pacesetter. He spent several years as a studio musician for Atlantic Records in New York, playing on many of Aretha Franklin's recordings. Lastie returned to New Orleans to run his father's concession business and play a regular gig at the Show Bar on Bourbon Street. He opened his own nightclub—the High Hat—in 1957; it took up an entire block and featured three bars. He went on to arrange music and play for Willie Bobo and produce several artists with Harold Battiste. Melvin Lastie died on December 4, 1972.

TAMI LYNN (real name: Gloria Brown; nickname: Toledo Slim) is a New Orleans vocalist known for her distinctive renditions of spirituals, often joining traveling gospel groups such as the Clara Ward Singers. She could be heard for years every Sunday on the Dr. Daddy-O (Vernon Winslow) Gospel Show on WMRY Radio in New Orleans. Lynn began singing R&B as a teenager at the Joy Tavern with Alvin Tyler. She toured with AFO artists and performed at the famed Birdland in New York, opening for John Coltrane. She worked with King Floyd and Dr. John, with whom she toured one last time before retiring.

ELLIS MARSALIS JR., known for his trained ear and deft touch, is a highly respected jazz pianist and music educator. Marsalis attended the Xavier School of Music, where he played saxophone, and graduated from Dillard University, where he became a pianist. After a stint in Los Angeles, he returned to New Orleans to assist with the family business and then joined the Marines. Marsalis was stationed in California and served as the pianist for an armed-forces band with a weekly television show. He returned to New Orleans and formed a trio to play at the new Playboy Club in the French Quarter. Marsalis was tapped by renowned trumpeter Al Hirt to tour and play at his French Quarter club. Marsalis started his teaching career at NOCCA and moved on to the University of New Orleans, where he was chair of the jazz studies program; he also taught at Virginia Commonwealth University. He is the father of saxophonist Branford, award-winning trumpeter Wynton, trombonist Delfeayo, and drummer Jason Marsalis.

RICHARD PAYNE, a trumpeter and bassist (who also played French horn, bassoon, and violin), was classically trained at various high schools in New Orleans, including Booker T. Washington, Xavier Prep (under Clyde Kerr Sr.), and McDonogh No. 35, where he was introduced to jazz. He often drifted back and forth between jazz and classical music. Payne was a founding member of the American Jazz Quintet. He became a teacher in the New Orleans public school system and continued in the classical tradition, performing with symphonies in New Orleans, Baton Rouge, Lake Charles, and Alexandria, LA, and in Jackson, MS. Richard Payne died on May 17, 2000, in New Orleans.

NATHANIEL PERRILLIAT, an alto and baritone saxophonist, studied at Joseph S. Clark High School under Yvonne Busch. He began his career performing with Professor Longhair and other New Orleans musicians in the mid-1950s, his style reminiscent of Illinois Jacquet, Coleman Hawkins, and Lester Young. Perrilliat joined forces with Ellis Marsalis in 1955 and performed in his original quartet and in his band at the Playboy Club in New Orleans. He later toured with R&B saxophonist Junior Parker and blues singer Joe Tex. Perrilliat played on nearly all of Allen Toussaint's studio dates at Minit Records in the early 1960s and then joined Fats Domino's band. Nat Perrilliat died on January 26, 1971, in Sacramento.

ALVIN "RED" TYLER was a revered New Orleans tenor and baritone saxophonist. He got a late start in music, performing after he completed his military service in 1947. He attended the Grunewald School of Music with Peter Badie. Tyler performed in Clyde Kerr Sr.'s big band and moved on to Dave Bartholomew's ensemble, with some of New Orleans's finest musicians. He also worked as a studio musician with independent labels. His warm New Orleans tone graced recordings by Ray Charles, Fats Domino, and Huey "Piano" Smith, and Little Richard, with whom he toured extensively. In 1967 Tyler wanted a steady paycheck and the freedom to pick his own gigs, so he became a liquor salesman by day and a jazz musician by night. In the 1980s he performed regularly with Clyde Kerr Jr., Germaine Bazzle, David Torkanowsky, James Singleton, and Johnny Vidacovich. Alvin Tyler died on April 3, 1998.

ACKNOWLEDGMENTS

DURING THE LATE 1990s—the end of a century!—I received several unexpected awards that resulted in more exposure for me. I began to look over some of my earlier writings and saw them as more relevant than before. Kalamu ya Salaam had a writers' workshop that met regularly (the NOMMO Literary Society), and they allowed me to visit. I brought some of my work for the group to edit. They suggested that I should think about doing a biography. That seed was planted and pushed its way through to the front of the line.

The thought of writing a book had been in the back of my mind for years. During the mid-1980s I gathered many of the thoughts I had written in my Daily Reminders over the years and started to organize them. After about two years, I had created four "books," which I called Scriptures. This was the material that I had brought to the workshop. I was excited at the thought of doing a biography, but I thought that Kalamu or someone in the workshop would do the writing.

Kalamu assigned two writers to the project—Cassandra Lane and Karen Celestan—but time kept passing and I didn't understand what was happening. Cassandra and Karen taped a series of interviews covering my childhood and youth, school and college, but the whole thing seemed to take a long time to get off the ground, especially since both women had careers and lives. Cassandra was a reporter for the *Times Picayune* and Karen worked in public relations for Festival Productions, producers of the New Orleans Jazz & Heritage Festival. Things took so long, I decided this book was going to have to be an autobiography.

Cassandra (known to friends as Sand) was born in DeRidder, Louisiana, which is where I had my first teaching assignment coming out of college. Meeting her brought back some wonderful memories. One evening Sand and Karen came by to inform me that some adjustments relating to the project needed to be made. Sand, who had recently married photographer Ric Francis, was moving to Los Angeles. She was planning to return to college and work on a master's degree in creative writing. I was sad, but I understood. It wasn't long before I missed her laughing spirit in my life.

Work on the book was painfully slow. I was still teaching at UNO, so Karen and I would get together some evenings, Saturdays, or Sundays after church to discuss what should be included and what should be tossed out. We'd make a little more progress in the summertime when both of us would be on hiatus from work.

Man, we struggled a lot! Karen would ask some personal questions and push me to talk about what I felt regarding certain aspects of my life. Sometimes I'd get irritated, and sometimes she would get irritated. Feelings!—all of this talk about deep stuff that I either never thought about or didn't want to think about. For example, choosing words to express what I felt during the time of the divorce was impossible. I didn't have them. I tried, but nothing felt right. I did hear melodies, but no words.

Karen would ask one of those probing questions; I'd say, "I don't know"; and she'd move on to something else; then, before I knew it, she'd be asking the same question again but in a different way. A couple of times when she pushed a bit harder and I pushed back equally hard, she'd playfully threaten to pluck me on top of my head or hit me with a baseball bat; then we'd both laugh.

One of the difficult research challenges for me in revisiting these parts of my life was the Sonny & Cher tours. I had thought that the William Morris Agency would have archives with this kind of stuff, but apparently they don't. I'm sure there must be some devoted, die-hard fans who have held on to that kind of material, but I wasn't able to find it. I did find some of my address and appointment books from the '60s, however, and was able to put together what must have been our first tours.

Typing was always such a struggle for me. My thoughts would run out ahead of my fingers. I'd also have to stop and do research or look for certain pictures to jog my memory. Sometimes I'd forget to eat or take my medicine, and that was critical because my health wasn't good. I had suffered a stroke in 1993 and later had surgery on my neck to open clogged arteries. I'd also try to get a little exercise, work on other projects, and have a bit of a social life.

But Karen stuck with the project, helping me to shape chapters, forcing me to backtrack and fill in holes in the story; she kept asking the hard questions. She also kept looking for agents and publishers. An agent in New York expressed strong interest and "signed" us, but after two or three years with no action, we decided to sever the relationship. We kept working with the belief that some entity would pick up the book. Karen continued to canvass writers, agents, and publishers. One day, we realized that we had been working on my memoirs for ten years!

There was also a group of friends who were vital and loyal workers, who frequently met for breakfast at Robin's Restaurant on Canal Street. They were Janice Brown and Darlene Jones, who were originally students of mine at UNO and were always available for support. Jesse McBride from Texas, a graduate of UNO's jazz studies program, has taken up permanent residence in New Orleans and continues to take care of me like family. He and his mother, Jessica, are the guardians of my sanity. There was Ana Robinson, Dianne Mack, and Souzan Alavi, who also were very supportive to my efforts in completing this project. Drs. Les Theard and Keith Ferdinand, my two jazz-loving physicians, took extraordinary care of my body, while John "the Dobanian" took care of my mind. I would like to also thank Joy "the Poet" Wilson and her daughter, Nadira "the Princess," who helped initiate my first website and balanced the beautiful side of my life.

I would like to especially thank my New Orleans kinfolk, Albert and Lark Fall, Raymond Lewis and his daughter, Renee, for always being there for me. I would also like to thank her son, Langston, for making me a very proud *parran* (godfather). There have been many friends along the way, however, I'd like to pinpoint some who have been exceptional. They are the late Alvin and Edith Batiste, who were best man and maid of honor at mine and Yette's wedding and our best friends for many years. Also Bill and Elaine James, our next-door neighbors in Los Angeles, and Bill and Linda Coben, who provided me with a beautiful Malibu escape. Bill was a warm person and an exceptional attorney. I must thank Ellis Marsalis for instigating my initial Los Angeles "escape," and his wife, Dolores, for supporting the two of us over these last thirty years. And to Calvin Goines and Brenda Myers, Kysha Brown-Robinson, and Ric Francis, I offer my gratitude.

In my spiritual life I include Jimmy X, who introduced me to Elijah Mohammad, leader of the Nation of Islam; pastor of the Harvest Tabernacle Church in Los Angeles, Rev. Dr. Donald Cook and his wife,

Deborah; and my New Orleans pastor, Rev. Dr. Dwight Webster of the Christian Unity Baptist Church and his wife, Trudell. While Hurricane Katrina brought much disruption to my life and countless other lives, it also brought many good friends, including Dr. G. Jeannette Hodge, Mrs. Lena Pope, and George and Essey Cooper, who gave me refuge in the wake of the storm. Kalamu ya Salaam has also been a blessing to my life in New Orleans; I am eternally thankful.

So many others helped bring this book to life: the energetic and creative art director, Alison Cody; editor Sarah Doerries, director of publications Jessica Dorman, reader Toy Harmon, and manuscripts curator Mark Cave at The Historic New Orleans Collection, where many of my papers are archived; Brenda Square and the Amistad Research Center; Bruce Raeburn and the Hogan Jazz Archive; and Mike Campbell at Dillard University.

There were countless musicians, singers, and people in the business along the way, but I would like to acknowledge Robert "Bob" Ogden, Sam Cooke, Art Rupe, Larry McKinley, Sonny and Cher, Plas Johnson, Mike Post; Tami Lynn, Henry Butler, Leo Nocentelli, John Goines, Ike Williams, and Jerry Jumonville (the original New Orleans Natives); Cosimo Matassa; Alvin Batiste, Edward Blackwell, Richard Payne, and Ellis Marsalis (the original American Jazz Quintet); Melvin Lastie, John Boudreaux, Peter "Chuck" Badie, Alvin "Red" Tyler, and Roy Montrell (the original AFO Executives). If I have forgotten anyone, charge it to my head . . . not my HEART!

—*Harold Battiste Jr.*

WHAT A JOURNEY! I've learned so much about Harold (and some things that I didn't want to know), yet watching him get HIStory down on paper has been an incredible experience. I'm honored that he has trusted me enough to be involved in the production of his memoirs.

Special thanks to Carol Haynes for her patient and "eagle" editing eye.

Also, Gregory "Blodie" Davis, Cassandra Lane, Ben Sandmel, Mrs. Thelma Amedee, Marzique Battiste, Harlis Battiste, Germaine Bazzle, Reginald Toussaint, Asante Salaam, Lynn Pitts, Dodie Simmons, Jennifer Turner, Vera Warren-Williams, Jesse McBride, Jarvis DeBerry, Steve Morrison, Alex Rawls, and Jane McNealy.

In my writing life, I must thank those who guided me and became my dedicated support system: Randy Bates (University of New Orleans), Fred Leebron, Dr. Michael Kobre, Dr. Margot Singer and Naeem Murr (Queens University of Charlotte), and my Queenies (aka MoFAers): Dartinia Hull, Angele Davenport, Beth Johnson, Angela Chatman, Jim Walke, Jack King, Rita Juster, Sam Wilson, David Locke, Susan Bray, Michelle Williams, Kelly Simmons, Hobie Anthony, and Steven Patton, M.D.

Love and thanks to my daughter, Nikki Lee, my parents, Amy and George Celestan, my brother, Gregory Celestan, my sister-in-law, Joanne Tremont Celestan, my niece Bryce Taylor Celestan, my aunts, Minerva "Tootsie" Simmons, Doretha Willis, and Emily Sylva (cake!), my uncles, Melvin Victor and Albert Victor Jr., my cousins (too numerous to mention by name), and Ronald Motley, who all gave me their unwavering support.

I'm also grateful for all of the love and protection sent from the spiritual realm—Evelyn "Mother" Victor, Ida Rene Williams, Bertrice Richard, Alma Celestan, Emily Rose, and Albert Victor Sr.

—*Karen Celestan*

SUGGESTED READING

Berry, Jason, Jonathan Foose, and Tad Jones. *Up From The Cradle of Jazz: New Orleans Music Since World War II.*

Bono, Sonny. *And The Beat Goes On.*

Broven, John. *Walking to New Orleans: The Story of New Orleans Rhythm & Blues.*

Dr. John (Mac Rebennack), with Jack Rummel. *Under a Hoodoo Moon: The Life of the Night Tripper.*

Gillett, Charlie. *Making Tracks: Atlantic Records and the Growth of a Multi-Billion Dollar Industry.*

Guralnick, Peter. *Dream Boogie: The Triumph of Sam Cooke.*

Hannusch, Jeff. *The Soul of New Orleans: A Legacy of Rhythm and Blues.*

Kelley, Norman, ed. *R&B (Rhythm & Business): The Political Economy of Black Music.*

Litweiler, John. *Ornette Coleman: A Harmolodic Life.*

Ritz, David. *The Brothers Neville.*

Scherman, Tony. *Backbeat: Earl Palmer's Story.*

Suhor, Charles. *Jazz in New Orleans: The Postwar Years Through 1970.*

Ward, Brian. *Just My Soul Responding: Rhythm and Blues, Black Consciousness, and Race Relations.*

Wolff, Daniel, et al. *You Send Me: The Life and Times of Sam Cooke.*

INDEX

Note: Italicized page numbers indicate photographs or illustrations.

HAROLD R. BATTISTE JR. is a retired composer, arranger, musician, and music professor. He was a producer, conductor, and musical director for studio, stage, motion pictures, and television with credits in jazz, classical, blues, and pop. Battiste has been awarded ten gold records from ASCAP. He has helped to shape the careers of many artists, including Sam Cooke, Sonny & Cher, Cannonball Adderley, Dr. John, the O'Jays, Billy Davis and Marilyn McCoo, and Ornette Coleman. He assisted in creating the respected jazz studies program at the University of New Orleans with renowned pianist and music professor Ellis Marsalis. Battiste is a graduate of Dillard University with a bachelor of arts in music. In 2008 he was awarded an honorary doctorate of humane letters from Dillard University. He lives in New Orleans.

KAREN CELESTAN handles community relations and policy in government affairs for Tulane University. She was senior director of university communications for Dillard University, publications and media coordinator for Festival Productions, Inc. (which produces the New Orleans Jazz & Heritage Festival and other events), and a copy editor for the New Orleans *Times-Picayune* and *Louisiana Weekly*. Her work has appeared in a number of publications, including the *Times-Picayune, Gambit, Louisiana Weekly,* and several literary magazines and poetry collections. Celestan is a graduate of the University of New Orleans with a bachelor of arts in communications and English, and Queens University of Charlotte, North Carolina, with a master of fine arts in creative writing. She lives in New Orleans.

The publication of this book was made possible through the generosity of the Laussat Society of The Historic New Orleans Collection and the New Orleans Jazz & Heritage Festival and Foundation, Inc.

Special thanks to
The Amistad Research Center
Concord Music Group, Inc.
Dillard University Will W. Alexander Archives and Special Collections
The Hogan Jazz Archive, Tulane University
Louisiana Division/City Archives, New Orleans Public Library

The Williams Research Center of The Historic New Orleans Collection is home to the Harold Battiste Papers, a collection of manuscripts, photographs, and music-industry memorabilia. All images in this book credited to THNOC are from the Harold Battiste Papers, The Historic New Orleans Collection, 2008.0225, gift of Mr. Harold R. Battiste Jr.